CW01425692

The Family Face

THE FAMILY FACE

Geoffrey Dicker

The Pentland Press
Edinburgh – Cambridge – Durham – USA

First published in 1998 by
The Pentland Press Ltd
1 Hutton Close
South Church
Bishop Auckland
Durham

ISBN 1-85821-596-x

Typeset in Goudy 11/14
by Carnegie Publishing, Carnegie House, Chatsworth Road, Lancaster, LA1 4SL
Printed and bound in Great Britain by
Bookcraft (Bath) Ltd., Midsomer Norton, Somerset

Heredity

I am the family face,
Flesh perishes, I live on,
Projecting trait and trace,
Through time to times anon.
And leaping from place to place
Over oblivion.

The years-heired feature that can
In curve and voice and eye
Despise the human span
Of durance – that is I.
The eternal thing in man,
That heeds no call to die.

                              Thomas Hardy

Contents

Illustrations

Introduction and Acknowledgements

It is customary for an author to write some preliminary words by way of acknowledgement or appreciation for the assistance which he or she has received in writing a book of this sort. For me, this does not follow the usual pattern; my deepest gratitude is due to my great-aunt Ella, who was intensely interested in "the family", and who died some 66 years ago. Ella wrote a fascinating book, which I have included as Chapter Two, and which describes in detail the way of life of some of our ancestors in the eighteenth and nineteenth centuries. In addition she preserved for posterity a number of letters and other documents, and what she described as the 'family treasures', many of which have now been handed to me. As the only surviving Hamilton Dicker of my generation, at least in England, it has fallen to me to bring the family records up to date.

For several generations the family has been using Armorial Bearings which, on enquiry, seem to have been unauthorised, but Garter Principal King of Arms has been most helpful in enabling me to rectify the situation and arranging for a Grant to be issued, so that the regular family Arms can be reproduced as part of this book.

George Dicker, formerly Treasurer/Bursar of Canberra University, whose relationship to me was never established, nevertheless carried out a great deal of research in Australia before he died in 1994.

I must also express my thanks to many, both inside and outside the family, who have advised and assisted me in my researches. These include my cousins Stuart Morrison and June Griffiths, Richard Childs (Sussex County Archivist), Nigel Argent (Ardingly College Archivist), Julian Jeffs QC, Mrs Mary Sweetman and Macdonald Hennell at Five Ash Down, Buxted, Glenson Jones in Kanata, Ontario, Florence Hamilton-Dicker in Toronto, Peter

Sturgeon in Vienna, the Soldier Career Management Agency of the Australian Army, Dr Pam Oliver, and Pentland Press, who have been most helpful with advice and guidance. I have greatly appreciated the encouragement and support of my wife Josephine (aka Fifi), who has put up with me for 56 years, and may have to do so for a bit longer.

Geoffrey Dicker
September 1998

NON MIHI SED CHRISTO

	Age
John Dicker of Buxted b.1498 d.1565	67
William Dicker of Buxted b.1530 d. *c.*1590	60
William Dicker of Buxted b.1557 d.1616 m. Jone	59
John Dicker of Buxted b.1598 m. Margaret Bennett	
Thomas Dicker of Buxted b.1641 d.1702 m. Alice Dray	61
John Dicker of Buxted b.1676 d.1730 m. Elizabeth	54
Thomas Dicker of Buxted b.1723 d.1789 m. Mary Pike	66
Thomas Dicker of Lewes, banker, b.1754 d.1822 m. Rebecca Davis	68
Thomas Dicker of Lewes, banker, b.1785 d.1868 m. Martha Hamilton	83
Hamilton Eustace Dicker b.1829 d.1868 m. Catherine Sarah Cornwell	39
Seymour Fane Hamilton Dicker b.1865 d.1938 m. Ethel Margaret Buckeridge	73
Arthur Seymour Hamilton Dicker b.1892 d.1974 m. Margaret Katherine Walley	82
Geoffrey Seymour Hamilton Dicker b. 20.7.1920 m. Josephine Helen Penman	
Christopher Hamilton Dicker b.2.2.1950 m. Deborah Gail Nicholson	
Mark Seymour Hamilton Dicker b.4.11.1979	

The Stallibrass, Cornwell and Hamilton Connections (incomplete, as prepared by Ella Dicker)

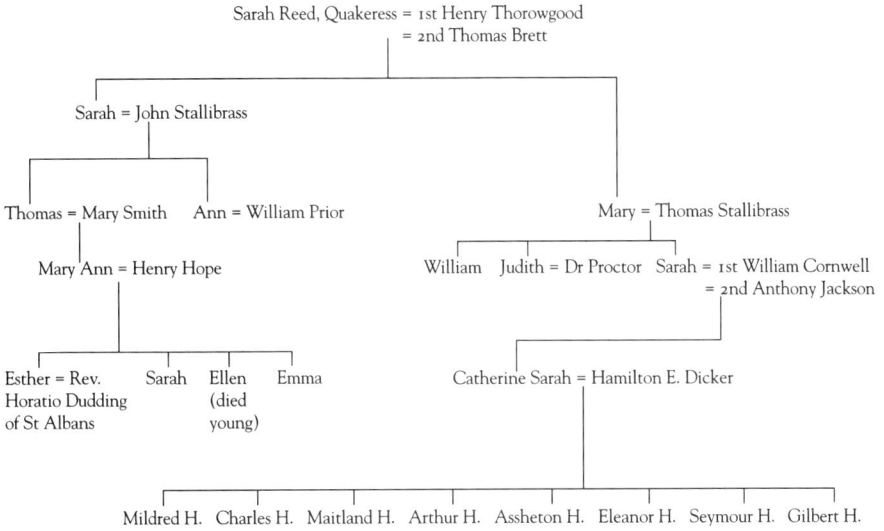

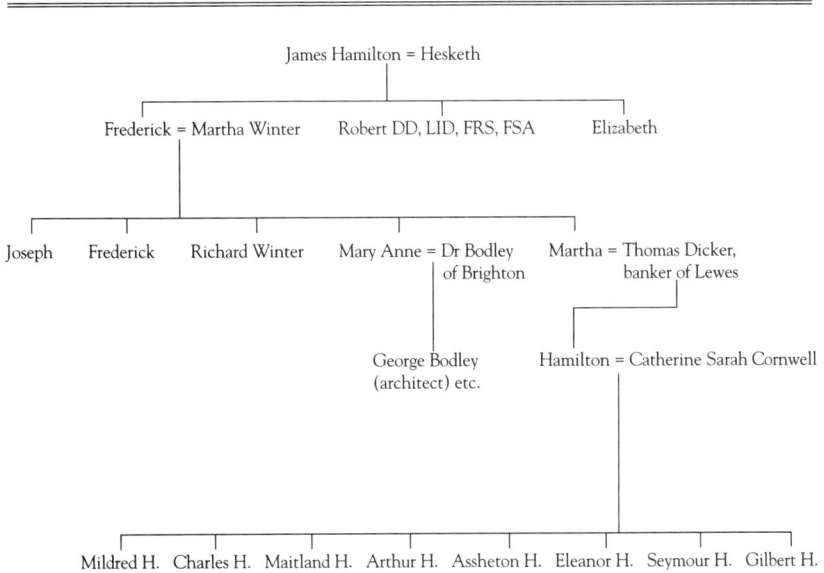

Sarah Reed, Quakeress = 1st Henry Thorowgood
= 2nd Thomas Brett

Sarah = John Stallibrass

Thomas = Mary Smith   Ann = William Prior

Mary = Thomas Stallibrass

Mary Ann = Henry Hope

William   Judith = Dr Proctor   Sarah = 1st William Cornwell
= 2nd Anthony Jackson

Esther = Rev.   Sarah   Ellen   Emma
Horatio Dudding   (died
of St Albans   young)

Catherine Sarah = Hamilton E. Dicker

Mildred H.   Charles H.   Maitland H.   Arthur H.   Assheton H.   Eleanor H.   Seymour H.   Gilbert H.

James Hamilton = Hesketh

Frederick = Martha Winter   Robert DD, LID, FRS, FSA   Elizabeth

Joseph   Frederick   Richard Winter   Mary Anne = Dr Bodley   Martha = Thomas Dicker,
of Brighton   banker of Lewes

George Bodley   Hamilton = Catherine Sarah Cornwell
(architect) etc.

Mildred H.   Charles H.   Maitland H.   Arthur H.   Assheton H.   Eleanor H.   Seymour H.   Gilbert H.

Descendants of Thomas and Rebecca Dicker

Thomas Dicker m. Rebecca Davis
b.1754 b.1756
d.1822 d.1838

John m. Ann Galley
b.1783
d.1821
(four)

Thomas m. Martha Hamilton
b.1785 b.1790
d.1868 d.1875

Joseph m. Mary Reyner
b.1787
d.1861
(eight)

Ebenezer m. Lucy
b.1789
d.1817

Elizabeth m Robert Fletcher
b.1791
(three)

Mary m.(1) Samuel Salter
m.(2)William Rees
b.1793

Rebecca m. Rev.William Davies
b.1797
(six)

Margaret m. Thomas Edward Crallen
b.1818
Sophia
(six)

Louisa m.Rev. Richard Henry Killick
b.1819
Martha
b.1819
(thirteen)

Harriet m. Rev. John Pockleton Power
b.1821
Rebecca

Thomas m.Margaret Frederick Yale Hamlin
b.1823
(ten)

Winifriede m. George Engleheart
b.1826
(three)

Eustace m. Catherine Sarah Cornwell
Hamilton
b.1829 b.1829
d.1868 d.1903

Emily m. Rev. Winter Melville Lauriston Lee
b.1831
d.1918

Josephine m. B.Skeate
b.1833
(five)

Mildred Hamilton
b.1853
d.1939
(six)

Charles William Hamilton
b.1855
d.1912

m. Mary Margaret Swan

Maitland m. Hettie Crallen
Hamilton
b.1857
d.1913

Arthur Wrey Hamilton
b.1859
d.1860

Asshteton m. Helen Alice Dunn
George Hamilton
b.1860
d.1949

Eleanor Hamilton
b.1862
d.1932

Seymour m. Ethel Fane Margaret Hamilton Buckeridge
b.1865 b.1869
d.1938 d.1950

Gilbert m. Elizabeth Hamilton Jane
b.1867 Taylor
d.1952 (Bessie)

Charles Christine m.(1)Edward Molyneux Waldo m.(2)William Dickie Sturgeon
George Hamilton
Hamilton b.1897
b.1896 d.1962
d.1977

Katherine m.Rev.Geof- Ernest m. Florence Mildred m. Eric Broomfield Biden
Hamilton frey Justus George James Ethel
b.1903 Richard Hamilton Hamilton
d.1989 Stott b.1906 b.1891
d.1969 d.1961

Rev John Hamilton
b.1901
d.1988

Arthur m. Margaret Gilbert m.Eleanor Nancy Violet m.Alexander
Seymour Kathleen Charles Chapman Hamilton Ella David
Hamilton Walley Hamilton b.1895 Hamilton Morrison
b.1892 b.1895 b.1894 d.1992 b.1897
d.1974 d.1971 d.1974 d.1988

Richard m. Milly Maitland Hamilton
b.1900
d.1965

Dorothy Catherine Hamilton
b.1902
d.1964

Family tree chart (rotated). Names, birth/death dates, and marriages:

Michael

David Hamilton b.1936 d.1995 m.Marina Avery — Carol Daughn b.1948 — John Hamilton b.1950 m.(1)KGlynn Survivall m.(2)Greig Mitchell — Sally Ann Hamilton b.1950 m.Thomas Budani — Selwyn Hamilton b.1957 m.Janice de Vries b.1959

Peter Asheton Hamilton b.1916 m.Inés Maria Clara Forte d.1985 m.(1)Dorothy Fillinghame m.(2)Mary Mair m.(3)Marion Dugan — Edward Hamilton b.1918

6 children 5 grandchildren

Tiha Florence Glynn b.1970 — Christian David b.1973 — Nicolina Samuel Florence b.1977 — Gabriella Christine b.1985 — Monique Anna b.1986 — Michael Alan b.1988 — Wendy Shane b.1990 — Michele b.1970 m.Geoffery Campbell

Sharon Eleanor Hamilton b.1941 d. m.James Malcolm Foster — Peter b.1919 d.1941 — Paul m.Pauline Grace b.1922 Marcelli — Margaret Anne Hamilton b.1918 m.John Carisbrooke Murison — Geoffrey Seymour Hamilton b.1920 m.Josephine — Susan Helen Hamilton Penman b.1925 d.1998 m.William Apsey — June Hamilton b.1919 m. Walter John Griffiths — Eleanor — John Stuart b.1925 m.(1)Eileen Maude McGrane m.(2)Carole June Equeall

Jane Helen b.1951 m.Peter Regan — Judith Clare b.1953 m.Jon Harman — Helen Celia b.1965 m.Jeremy Bird

Terry Paul b.1945 m.Mary Bush — Beverley Ann b.1948 m.Gary Richard Trevithick — Mary Anne b.1947 m.Noel June Ward Edward Goulding — Robert Charles Carisbrooke b.1951

Sara Elizabeth Hamilton b.1947 d.1955 — Christopher Hamilton b.1950 m.Deborah Gail Nicholson — Elizabeth Anne b.1957 m.(1)Craig Manion m.(2)William Brown

William James b.1948 d.1994 — Peter Francis b.1950 m.Brenda m.David m.Arthur — Judith b.1941 — Eleanor Anne b.1946 — Mary John Garland Kittle — Penelope Bath — Philippa Peta b.1951 m.Stuart John Holland

Paul b.1979 — Becky b.1981 — Jason b.1988 — Holly b.1990

Michael Charles b.1978 — Nicholas John b.1981 — Selina Louise Hamilton b.1977 — Mark Seymour Hamilton b.1979 — Joseph William b.1988 — Sarah Elizabeth b.1990 — Sophie Phillips b.1993 — Graham Peter Hamilton b.1979 — Matthew John b.1973 — Patrick Alexander Walter b.1976 — Richard b.1969 — Roger Leonard b.1974 — Samantha Clare b.1973 — Tecwyn Ormund b.1984 — Emma Keeley b.1979 — Sarah b.1980 — Katherine b.1985 — Julia b.1983

Daniel b.1984 — Charlotte Abbi b.1989

Fiona b.1961 — Jennifer b.1963 — Jonathan b.1968 m.Adam Richards m.Sarah King

Eleanor Olivia b.1996

Descendants of Seymour Fane Hamilton Dicker and Ethel Margaret Dicker

Seymour Fane Hamilton Dicker b.31.7.1865 d.20.6.38 m.10.9.80 Ethel Margaret Buckeridge b.1869 d.23.11.50

Mildred Ethel Hamilton Dicker
b.1891 d.13.8.61
m.Eric B.Biden
b.1892 d.1970

Arthur Seymour Hamilton Dicker
b.2.9.1892 d.25.4.74
m.4.2.18 Margaret Kathleen Walley b.17.4.1895 d.14.6.71

Gilbert Charles Hamilton Dicker
b.1894 d.21.5.74
m.Eleanor Chapman
d.13.5.74

Nancy Hamilton Dicker
b.11.9.1895 d.13.2.92

Violet Ella Hamilton Dicker
b.27.6.1897 d.7.2.88
m.4.5.23 Alexander David Morrison b.18.3.94 d.30.3.72

Richard Maitland Hamilton Dicker ("Bobs") b.1900 d.26.12.65
m. Milly

Dorothy Catherine Hamilton Dicker
b.29.12.02
d.23.6.64

Peter Biden
b.1.7.19 b.19.4.22
d.1941 m.9.10.43
Pauline Grace Marcelli
b.2.3.19

Paul Biden

Margaret Anne Hamilton Dicker
b.4.11.18
m.24.7.45
John Charles Carisbrooke Murison b.1914
d.27.12.86

Geoffrey Seymour Hamilton Dicker
b.20.7.20
m.11.4.42
Josephine Helen Penman b.14.2.20

Susan Alice Hamilton Dicker
b.20.8.25 d.5.5.98
m.6.7.46 William John Apsey b.25.11.19

John Stuart Morrison
b.3.1.25

June Dicker
b.25.7.19 m.1939 Walter John Frederick Griffiths d.28.8.91

Ray Elodee Parsons m.(2) 8.8.73 Carole June
b.20.5.42   Equeall b.7.6.41

John Stuart Morrison
m.(1) 20.8.49 Eileen
Maude McCrane b.18.8.24

Terry Paul Biden
b.28.4.45 b.27.2.48
m.Mary m.31.5.68 Gary
Bush Richard
b.17.5.53 Trevithick
b.15.4.45

Beverley Ann Biden

Mary Anne Mercy Murison Murison
b.7.3.47 b.20.10.51
m.1988 m.6.7.74
Noel June Ward
Edward b.8.5.53
Goulding
b.25.12.30
d.1993

Robert Charles Carisbrooke Murison

Sara Elizabeth Hamilton Dicker
b.19.5.47 m.14.7.73
d.23.6.55 Deborah Gail
Nicholson
b.5.4.54

Christopher Hamilton Dicker
b.2.2.50

Elizabeth Anne Hamilton Dicker
b.5.11.57 m.(1)
26.2.77 Craig
Manion b.6.1.55
(div.1979) m.(2)
6.6.87 William Brown
b.22.3.47 (div.1991)

William James Hamilton Apsey
b.3.4.50
m.8.5.76
Brenda Mary Garland
(div.)

Peter Francis Hamilton Apsey
b.5.6.48
d.3.1.94

Judith Eleanor Griffiths
b.1941
m.1969 David
John Kittle
d.1986

Pemelope Anne Griffiths
b.1946
m.24.7.93
Arthur Bath

Phillippa Peta Griffiths
b.1951
m.1970 Stuart Holland
(div.1983)

Jane Helen Morrison
b.21.6.51
m.Peter Regan

Judith Clare Morrison
b.20.2.53
m.Jon Harman

Helen Celia Morrison
b.8.10.65
m.Jeremy Bird

Wendy Biden
b.11.11.76

Shane Michele Michael Nicholas
Trevithick Ann Charles John
b.28.11.68.' Murison Murison
          Trevithick b.21.7.78 b.26.5.81
          b.18.9.70
          m.16.1.93
          Geoffery
          Campbell
          b.24.6.62

Selina Louise Hamilton Brown
b.5.4.77

Mark Seymour William Dicker Brown b.21.3.88
b.4.11.79

Joseph William Elizabeth Brown Brown b.21.8.90

Sarah Sophie Phillips Brown b.22.9.93

Graham Peter Hamilton Kittle Apsey
b.29.8.79

Matthew Patrick Richard Roger
John Alexander Walter Leonard Clare
Kittle Griffiths Griffiths Griffiths
b.20.11.73 b.15.12.76 b.28.8.69 b.15.7.74

Samantha Teewyn Ormund
Griffiths
b.5.3.73

Erima Keeley Griffiths
b.14.10.84

Sarah Katherine Julia Regan Regan Regan
b.16.4.79 b.11.11.80 b.19.2.83

Paul Becky Harman Harman
b.19.11.79 b.6.10.81

Jason Holly Bird Bird
b.18.8.88 b.25.5.90

Eleanor Olivia Apsey
b.5.7.96

xviii

Chapter I

Early Dickers

My mother once told me, with some shame, that one of my ancestors came over with William the Conqueror in the eleventh century. He was a member of the King's Court, and one day in fun he pulled the King's nose. For this he was banished from the Court, and given the land, later known as Dicker, in what became Sussex. But I have never seen this story substantiated in any of the family records. I don't think my mother would have made it up, but I am sure that someone did!

Among the numerous sources to which the origin of surnames can be traced, one of the most ancient is the adoption of the name of a particular locality, town, or district, where a family once settled. In this class of surnames the family of 'Dicker' belongs. 'The Dicker' was the name of an extensive plain comprising several Lordships in the southern Division of the Rape of Pevensey, in Sussex. In 1230, Gilbert de Aquila, the representative of a great Norman family, and founder of the Priory of Michelham, gave certain rights in these lands, then called 'Le Dykera', to the Priory, and later frequent mention of them appears in public records. One of these rights was the privilege of felling timber for the use of the Priory. A sight of the land now might give the impression that the licence was of no value, but there is evidence to show that the area at that time, over 700 years ago, was covered with woodlands, and they are known to have continued in this state for over 400 years. Indeed, such was its abundance of timber, that in the Act of Henry VIII, 1543, for restraining the consumption of timber by the ironworks, this place, with some others, was exempted from the operation of the statute. However, Norden, in a work published in 1607, mentions 'The Dyker' among 'the famous woods in the Weald' that had been 'devoured by the forges and furnaces for the making of iron'. After that, the whole area lay neglected and desolate for a long period, and it was not until the early part of the nineteenth century that it became developed.

The Rev. T. W. Horsfield (*The History and Antiquities of Lewes*, 1827) wrote:

The Dicker common (inclosed by Act of Parliament in 1813), lies principally in the Parish of Chiddingly. Previously to the inclosure, it was, comparatively, a barren heath; the hand of cultivation has, however, drawn out its riches, and it is now equal to the best corn land in the district. The farms are in general small, few exceeding 300, and many under 50 acres. The surface of the parish is pleasantly undulated with hill and dale, and from Pick Hill is a rich and extensive project. There are evident vestiges of iron-works at the Stream, which were formerly carried on to a considerable extent; but owing to the scarcity of fuel, in common with many other founderies in Sussex, this has long been disused.

The precise date when the name 'Le Dyker' was assumed by the family is not known, but during the reigns of Henry III and Edward I (i.e. some time between 1216 and 1307) Geoffrey le Dykere was proprietor of certain lands in the Rape of Pevensey, and in 1344 Philip Dikere was one of the Barons of the Cinque Ports (Hastings). He was also one of the Commissioners for levying the 'Fifteenths', a tax raised for the support of the wars against France. Another member of the family, Hugh Dyker, became Sheriff of London in 1438.

Some time in the fifteenth century Nicholas Dyker, of the same family, lived at Rotherfield Pypard in Berkshire. He had a son Joseph Dicker, and a daughter Anne, who married Sir James Darrell of Calehill, Kent. Sir James attended Henry VIII in his campaign against France in 1512, was knighted at Tournay, and died in 1525. His widow Anne died in 1562, and was buried with him at Little Chart, Kent where their monument, representing Sir James in complete armour, and his lady in the costume of the times (both in the attitude of devotion) remained in good preservation until 1944, when the church at Little Chart was destroyed by a flying bomb, and sadly the monument of Sir James and Anne was destroyed.

A branch of the family lived for several generations at Buxted, about ten miles north of Dicker, (which now consists of Upper Dicker and Lower Dicker). The first that we can trace in a direct line was John Dicker of Buxted, who was born towards the end of the reign of Henry VII, in 1498, and died in 1565. He was a witness to the will of his neighbour Edward Penkhurst, of Buxted, gentleman, dated 9 October 1558. John had three sons, Richard, William and Thomas, and a daughter Myldred. William, born about 1530, continued the line at Buxted. We do not know exactly when he died, but his will was dated 1590, and he directed that his body should be buried in the church or churchyard of Buxted. He had two sons and two daughters, and his elder son William succeeded him at Buxted, dying in 1616. This second William was succeeded at Buxted by his eldest son John, born in 1598. He married Margaret Bennett, and he was senior churchwarden of Buxted in 1637. Thomas Dicker, of Buxted, third son of John and Margaret Dicker, was born in 1641. He married Alice, daughter of Mr John Dray, and died in 1702. John Dicker, son of Thomas and Alice, also lived in Buxted. He was born in 1676, married Elizabeth (surname unknown) and had an only son, Thomas who was born in October 1723.

This, the first of three successive Thomas Dickers, lived at Buxted throughout his life. Apparently he did not inherit much of the comparative wealth of some of his immediate forefathers, and this affected his social standing in the area. In 1751 he married Mary, the daughter of a Mr Pike of Ashford, Kent, who was 'his aid and solace in the journey of life, and his fellow helper in every virtuous path'. They had nine children, of whom all but two died in infancy. We have a description of this Thomas:

In person he was rather above the middle stature, of a well-formed muscular frame, which in his youth enabled him to oustrip all competitors in feats of agility, as well as in most of the old English exercises. His dark lustrous eyes also, and open expressive countenance, were the index of those higher qualities of intelligence and benevolence for which he was no less distinguished.

The small estate that he inherited from his father, though it provided him with a house, was too small to be a source of dependence, but it was said that he was not without other means, perhaps in themselves of more value. He had energy, strength, diligence and prudence by which he secured a competence and contentment; and among the healthy rural scenes and occupations in which his days were passed he experienced a degree of tranquillity and true enjoyment of life, which those with larger possessions often fail to secure. His general excellence of character was such that he earned the esteem of the local society, but it was not until the age of fifty, in 1773, encouraged by his son, that he became deeply religious. This changed his whole life. At that time there was apparently, within a convenient distance of Buxted, no minister of the Anglican Church, or of any other

"Calm on the bosom of thy God,
Fair Spirit! rest thee now!
E'en while with ours thy footsteps trod,
His Seal was on thy brow."

Thomas Dicker (1723–1789)

Five Ash Down Chapel, Buxted. Opened 1784

denomination, who taught the doctrines which he wished to follow, so he decided to have services in his own house. He realized that this might cause umbrage in some quarters, but he determined to go ahead with his plans. The ministers who took part in these services at Thomas Dicker's house were chiefly those who went to preach at the Countess of Huntingdon's seat at Oat Hall, Wivelsfield, a few miles from Buxted. Lady Huntingdon, a friend and follower of John Wesley, was a prominent Methodist, who, with George Whitefield, another follower of Wesley, became leader of 'The Countess of Huntingdon's Connection'.

As expected, at first this practice caused some concern among his neighbours, but gradually the number of people attending these services increased, so that after about ten years the Dicker accommodation was too small, and Thomas gave a piece of ground adjoining his house for the building of a chapel, which was opened in the spring of 1784. This chapel was registered under the Toleration Act, as 'a place of worship for Protestant Dissenters', although the question between Church and Dissent had nothing to do with the movement which had been started by Thomas. Wesley himself, although technically a Dissenter, was determined to remain loyal to the Church of England. Thomas Dicker had no feeling of hostility towards the Church, but he wanted to supply what none of the pulpits in the immediate neighbourhood at that time afforded. The movement adopted a simple form of worship to the Nonconformists, which was thought to be very similar to that in which the primitive Christians conducted their religious assemblies. During the next few years Thomas was gratified to see the success of the cause which he had instituted, but on 9 June 1789 he died, in his sixty-sixth year. On the evening before returning home, he told his wife that he felt as if his days were numbered, and that he must soon rest from his labours. He died a few hours later, and was buried at Buxted on 13 June 1789, leaving his widow Mary to survive him by eight years.

The chapel at Buxted is still there, and flourishing, services being held each Sunday, together with a Tuesday Bible Club and other activities. Two hundred years ago the village of Buxted was centred on Buxted Park, and the old Parish Church of St Margaret. Now the larger part of the village is a mile or so to the east of the Park, while the chapel is at the extreme west end of Buxted, known as Five Ash Down. The monthly newsletter of the chapel states:

> Our village Chapel is an Independent one
> (that is, not controlled by any outside
> organisation or denomination), which
> was founded over 200 years ago.
>
> The Chapel's Articles of Faith are the
> same main ones which the Church of
> England has held since the Reformation.

Thus, the aims for which the chapel was founded over two hundred years ago have been maintained. Each year a Chapel Anniversary Service is held. How gratified Thomas Dicker would have been to see the success of his vision. Perhaps he does.

The eldest son of Thomas and Mary was also Thomas Dicker, born on 22nd February 1754. This Thomas inherited his father's religious convictions, and indeed it was his inspiration which caused the religious conversion in his parents in 1773. Again we have a description:

He had fine and regular features, a beautiful complexion, with expressive

Thomas Dicker
(*1754–1822*)

black eyes, and ringlets of rich auburn hair. His engaging appearance
caused him to be greatly admired and caressed in his childhood, and
he soon became a favourite, not only with his immediate neighbours,
but with others in the vicinity whose rank made the notice he received
from them to be more observed. From these, however, he does not
appear to have derived any subsequent more substantial benefit.

As a child, although he had very little religious instruction (he was nearly
twenty when his father got so involved in religion), he often had serious
thoughts about death. Once, when there was a great storm in the area,
preceded by darkness which caused the birds to roost, thinking it to be
night, many supposed that the end of the world had come. The terror he
saw in others increased his own fears, and he became greatly alarmed as to

what might happen to him, if this was to be the day of judgment. After the storm had died away, he resolved to be more holy and dutiful than he had ever been; yet he childishly prepared a place of security among the rocks and caves near his home, where he imagined that no storm could reach him.

During his childhood Thomas went regularly with his parents to the parish church in Buxted Park but he was not taught to have any idea of religion other than what consisted of outward appearance, and a strict attention to moral duties. He was made to say such pieces of the ritual as the Catechism and Creed, but all in a spirit of lifeless formality. Later, when preparing for confirmation, which took place in Lewes, he said that he had no thought of the solemn responsibility that he was about to take on himself in that service; and the day was made by him and his friends as much a day of hilarity and amusement as if that had been its only object.

At an early age he displayed great aptitude for learning, and after his mother's first lessons he was sent to a schoolmistress living in the adjoining parish of Maresfield. Later he went to the Grammar School at Uckfield. After leaving school he was sent for a time to a Mr Burgess, a builder in Buxted, with a view to his being articled as an apprentice, although this occupation does not seem to have been his first choice. A little incident will indicate his prevailing inclination at that time. Among the various things he was engaged in during his new employment, he once attended Mr Burgess to assist in making some alterations in Mr Medley's Library at Buxted Park; but while the workmen were busily pursuing their labours, he was so excited by the literary treasures around him, and so absorbed in examining and reading some particular books he had found, that he was almost useless in the object for which he had come. His employment with Mr Burgess only continued for a few months, and then he occupied himself with his father in agricultural and pastoral affairs. For a time he considered the possibility of entering a university, having regard to his love of learning, but then he thought of going into the Church, or at least being actively associated with it. He attended a number of meetings of various denominations, and he was eventually baptized by a Mr Booker, who was the Pastor of the Baptist Church in nearby Wivelsfield. Having failed to get employment with a firm of bankers in London, he obtained a clerkship in a house in the woollen trade at London Bridge. During this time he continued to study religious subjects, and was often disturbed by what he read and heard. Here is a letter written to Thomas by his mother in 1773:

My Dear Son, – I hope this will find you resting on Christ, the sure foundation. The Lord increase your faith, and enable you to live upon His word! You know there never were any that trusted in Him and were confounded. I have thought much of you since I saw you, and often remembered you in my prayers. May He that heareth prayer 'fulfil all our petitions', and 'turn darkness into light before you!' He has promised for our encouragement, that we shall not be tempted beyond what we are able to bear.

I should not have written just now, but that Mr Pierce has desired me to inform you, he intends to be at Blackfriars next Thursday morning to hear Mr Romaine, it being the festival of the Ascension. He hopes to have the opportunity of receiving the sacrament on that occasion; and it is his particular request that you will meet him there, if possible.

Commending you to God, and praying Him to bless you with all spiritual blessings in Christ Jesus,

I remain, your affectionate mother,

Mary Dicker

We have copies of many letters written to and from Thomas. Here is a letter from Thomas to his parents in the following year:

London, May 23rd 1774

Dear and Honoured Father and Mother,

I received your kind letter today, which I read with pleasure and thankfulness. I feel your mercies as mine, and must join my praises with yours to the Giver of all. Oh, that our time, health, strength, and all that we have, may be devoted to God and His cause!

I rejoice to learn that the service you have established, or, as the apostle says, 'the church in your house', is going on so well, not only in the encouraging attendance, but in the blessed effects produced. The 'word preached' is only valuable as it is received by faith, and confirmed by 'signs following;' for signs follow faith now as well as in the days of the apostles: not, indeed, the casting out of devils, speaking with new tongues, or healing bodily diseases, but signs that equally show the work to be of God:- casting out evil habits, speaking the new language of the regenerate mind, and making the spiritually 'halt and withered' to 'rise and walk' in the way of God's commandments.

I hope that these Divine testimonies will continue to follow the preaching of the truth among you and that many more will have to declare 'how great things God hath done for them;' especially that the Holy Spirit will make the word a word of life and power in your own experience, and cause you daily to grow in faith, in knowledge, in love, joy, peace, humility, and all obedience. It is 'in them that believe' that the word of God thus 'worketh effectually:' – 'So, (said the Saviour) shall ye be my disciples' – so 'God will be our God' – so 'the spirit itself will bear witness with our spirits that we are the children of God.' And when at last we shall hear 'the voice of the archangel and the trump of God', and see Christ coming on 'his throne of judgment, with power and great glory,' we shall 'have boldness, and not be ashamed before him at his coming.'

I remain, your affectionate and dutiful Son, Thos. Dicker

When he wrote that letter Thomas had just reached the age of twenty. That was ten years before the chapel was built on the piece of land immediately adjoining his father's house.

After a short time in London he moved to Sheerness, on the banks of the Medway, and obtained a job as a schoolmaster, but the damp atmosphere turned out to be injurious to his health, and in 1780, at the age of twenty-six, he returned to Buxted, and was employed as a Clerk of Excise, or tax collector, for the eastern division of the County of Sussex, but was shortly transferred to a similar post for Kent, in Canterbury. This occupation consisted partly of the apprehension of smugglers. On one occasion he came across two men with a boat loaded with contraband spirits, and he attacked them single-handed, taking possession of the cargo in the name of the Crown. After attempting to kill him with a cutlass the two men fled, leaving Thomas Dicker in possession of the tubs of spirits. He ascribed his safety to a mightier arm than his own, and adopted David's song of praise: 'Blessed be the Lord my strength – my deliverer, my shield, and he in whom I trust, who subdueth the people under me – who delivereth his servant from the hurtful sword.'

It was at this time, in 1782, that he married Rebecca Davies, daughter of John Davies, a citizen and silversmith of London, and his wife Mary.

At Canterbury his relationship to the established Church was strengthened, and in 1786, at a special service, he made a declaration of faith, and was officially designated to the holy calling of pastoral charge. It seems that this was not a formal ordination, but he became what is now termed a lay reader.

His occupation as a Clerk of Excise was suddenly terminated when his immediate superior, a Mr Lampert, lost his job; he was then offered employment with a bank at Lewes, with Harben, Flight and Company, and after some hesitation he moved to Lewes in July 1787. He was very sad to leave Canterbury, where he had made many friends, particularly in the religious society there, and there was a suggestion that he might return, but this did not take place, and in the event he spent the rest of his days in Lewes. But this was only after a number of episodes in which he was tempted to return to Canterbury. On one occasion he actually gave notice to his Lewes employers, and left Lewes by coach, but was overtaken at Uckfield by Mr Harben, who had been supplied with post-horses. After some discussion, he was persuaded to return to his employment at Lewes, where he spent much time, in addition to his banking duties, preaching in the town and surrounding villages. However, in 1793 Harben, Flight and Company went into liquidation, and Thomas Dicker was appointed treasurer on behalf of the creditors. Another banking firm, Lewes Old Bank, had started in Lewes in 1789, and Thomas joined this firm in 1795, becoming a principal in 1807. Officially it was called Dicker, Whitfield and Molineux, but for a time it was known as 'Dicker's Bank'. Thomas continued as senior partner until within a short time of his death in 1822, although it seeems that he regarded his religious activities as taking precedence over his business. His widow Rebecca, who was greatly loved by all her family, outlived Thomas by sixteen years, dying in her eighty-third year in 1838.

Thomas and Rebecca had four sons, John (born 1783), Thomas (1785), Joseph (1787) and Ebenezer (1789), and three daughters, Elizabeth (1791), Mary (1793) and Rebecca (1797).

John, the eldest son, was sometimes known as John Look and Die, having regard to his good features. He was commissioned in the Royal Artillery, and served in the Peninsular War under the Duke of Wellington. He married Ann Galley, who travelled with him to Cadiz in 1811, but they returned shortly afterwards on sick leave. After a stay in Lewes, they sailed again to the Peninsular at the end of 1812. Ann kept a diary during this time, which gives an interesting description of the life of an officer and his wife in those days. They arrived at Lisbon in December 1812, and spent a fairly comfortable three months there in good billets, walking, dining, and entering into the social life of the British officers stationed there.

*Lieutenant John
Dicker, Royal
Artillery
(1783–1821)*

John and Ann had five children, who did not accompany them to Portugal, remaining with John's sister Elizabeth and their grandparents in Lewes, but the children were never out of their thoughts:

1813 Jan.1 Thursday. Dreamt last night of my darling babes, regret more than ever having left them.

Jan 30. Saturday. Dicker dreamed of our dear children last night. I now never dream of them altho' I every night when going to bed think of them and hope to dream of them.

At the end of January there were great celebrations in Lisbon when Lord (later Duke of) Wellington visited the town.

In March they watched troops disembarking at Lisbon, together with 350 horses. 'Expect we shall soon have to go up the country now.'

March 12. Monday. Rio Maior a very pretty place but like all the other places completely <u>romper</u>. Buying vegetables the old gardener gave me a ripe strawberry.

13 Tuesday. Caevalhos most miserable a good barns floor in England would be preferable to Mr Harris's and our quarters.

14 Wednesday. Leirea we got a good billet at the house of a priest. The town has been a very fine one but those desperate wretches the French have completely ruined it, the Cathedral a fine structure they endeavoured to blow up and partly succeeded, robbed it of everything valuable and it is now a sad memento of its fallen grandeur. I begd a piece of silk part of the garment of one of their saints. The Bishop's Palace is completely burnd down.

15. Thurs. Rode with Dicker and Mr Archdeacon to Battalha a most beautiful cathedral church. There is one arch which for richness and elegance is supposed not to be equaled in all Europe, many of the kings of Portugal are buried here, we saw the body of one that had been embalmed upwards of three hundred years. Shook hands with him and was half inclined to steal a piece of his dried skin, the French broke open his stone monument, dragged the body from the coffin and with horrid spite fractured the scull, another monument of beautiful black marble the burying place of a Vicount and Vicountess was broken to pieces when their sculls and the rest of their bones were lying about. The beautiful arch I have mentioned was not defaced as in the event of their being victorious the French General meant to have it sent to Paris as a present to Bonaparte, the beautiful stained glass windows they fired through with their musketry defaced all the sculpture but one beautiful piece of mosaic work escaped them. At least they had done it very little injury. I had not money enough with me or I should have bribed the old man to give me a piece of the stained glass and he would not do it without.

For some time they were at Coimbra, about 100 miles north of Lisbon, and John was appointed to command the Reserve there, but then they returned to Lisbon, where they hoped to remain for the winter. However, John was ordered to sail for Bilboa, on the north coast of Spain, leaving Ann behind in Lisbon, much to his distress. There, although his health was causing much concern, he was able to ride into France to see the allied armies. He wrote to his father:

> Our army is in beautiful order; and to see the tents thickly scattered amidst the magnificent mountain-scenery of the Pyrenees, with the towns of St Jean de Luz and Bayonne just below them, was a most imposing sight, and (in connexion with the late progress of our arms) highly gratifying to an Englishman. I have also been to St Sebastian, where those horrors which are the lamentable effects of war are seen to an unexampled extent; a most elegant town brought to complete desolation – hardly one stone left upon another, and the effluvia from the bodies of the slain (many of them scarcely covered by their shallow graves) yet too strong to be long endured – Pampeluna has not yet fallen – they have still a few horses left to eat, but it is expected that they cannot hold out more than ten days longer.

Ann's diary ends early in 1814, at which time John Dicker left San Sebastian, returning to England with his wife, his health having given way. He never properly recovered, and in 1821 he died at the age of thirty-eight. Of antiquarian interest is the mention in Ann's diary of a large vellum page taken from an office book, probably of the fifteenth century, in the Cathedral of Batalha, previously sacked by the French. ('Dicker stole two small pieces of painted glass and a leaf out of one of their service books.') Another article of some interest is mentioned above, described as 'a piece of silk, part of the garment of one of their saints'. This seems to refer to one half of a chasuble, of late and somewhat debased shape, known to have been brought from the Peninsula by John Dicker. The half chasuble and the page from the cantor's book remained in the family for over a hundred years – they certainly existed in 1922, but now seem to have disappeared.

Ebenezer, the fourth son of Thomas and Rebecca, was a problem to his parents. He had, at a very early age, caused them much anxiety from frequent indications of a wayward, unsteady disposition, in consequence of which his father, in looking out for a settlement for him, thought it prudent to choose a situation where he would be exposed as little as possible to temptation. He therefore placed him with the proprietor of an old-established business in Hailsham, in whom he had confidence. His father wrote to him, at the age of fifteen:

> I hope you find your new abode comfortable, and trust that its quiet and seclusion will be for your good; there is, however, no place secure

from the wiles of Satan, or some evil example; 'keep your heart, there-fore, with all diligence: resist the devil, and he will flee from you;' and 'if sinners entice thee, consent thou not.' Never seek pleasure at the expense of the first great principle – the fear of God; or to the neglect of any known duty; such indulgence will be dearly bought in the end.

That letter was written in November 1804, and in his new position Ebenezer at first appeared to settle down well. However, in the summer of 1805, he suddenly disappeared, and eventually offered himself for service as a seaman on a sloop of war, then fitting out for service in Portsmouth. On this ship he sailed from Falmouth in May 1807, and spent some time in the Medi-terranean, before being shipwrecked near Corfu, where he, with the rest of

Ebenezer Dicker
(1787–1817)

Martha (Hamilton)
Dicker (1793–1877)

the ship's crew, landed and were taken prisoner by the French. They were sent from Corfu, through Italy, to Briançon, France, and later to Sarre Libre, where they remained in a prisoner-of-war camp until they were relieved by a troop of Cossacks in 1814. He then returned home, and married, although from 1816 he seems to have had a premonition of death. In a letter to his father from Compton, near Guildford (probably the house of his in-laws), he wrote, in September 1816:

> My time in this transitory world, I have every reason to believe, will not be long; I must 'go hence and be no more.' What a scene my life has been! The review of a journey of twenty-seven years yields not a single consolatory or approving reflection.

Thomas Dicker
(1785–1868)

Indeed, he only lived another six months, and his poor wife died shortly afterwards.

Thomas Dicker, born in 1785, was the third of the three Thomases. He was the second son of Thomas and Rebecca, and was my great-great-grand-father. He married Martha, daughter of Rev. Frederick Hamilton (died 1819, aged sixty-one) and Martha his wife (died November 1805), who was the daughter of Rev. Richard and Sarah Winter. This marriage brought together the Hamiltons and the Dickers, and the name Winter appears in the names of some of their descendants.

Thomas was a quieter man than his father, and he appears to have taken a more active part in the Lewes Old Bank. He made the bank his career, but he retained his father's religious beliefs, and supported him for many years, writing his biography which was entitled *The Christian Life Exemplified*, first published in 1852. A second edition of this book was entitled *Life and*

Times of a Country Banker, and was published in 1860, after the author's retirement.

This Thomas was described as quiet and unobtrusive in his habits, and devoting himself with unceasing regularity to his duties as a partner in the bank. He rarely took any very prominent part in public matters, but his name was generally to be found on the lists of subscriptions for the charitable or public objects of the locality, while he acted as secretary to various religious, educational and literary societies.

Thomas took a special interest in the case of an 'agricultural rioter'. In 1830 troubles began all over the country, most of the rioters being farm labourers, or men in similar occupations. Many thousands of rural workers had resented the coming of the industrial revolution and the machines taking their jobs, and their long-established way of life. Of course times were hard in England in the 1820s and 1830s. The Peninsular and Napoleonic Wars had drained the country, there were still thousands of French POWs to be supported and the spirit of change was in the air. In his *History of England*, Trevelyan wrote: 'On first taking office the Whigs had been faced with the peasants' rising in some of the southern counties, to obtain the wage of half a crown a day. The starving agricultural workers rioted, but shed no blood and destroyed little property; they were most cruelly punished by the panic-stricken Whigs, who allowed several of them to be hanged and 450 of them to be transported to Australia from all knowledge of their families.'

In the face of the agricultural riots in the south and industrial riots in Bristol Peel was about to create his Police Force; there was great poverty among the workers and cholera was raging; radical parliamentary reform was to be introduced and the unions were gathering strength. Not everyone was enthusiastic about change, and one of the ways in which they tried to solve the problems was to arrest the rioters and either execute them or banish them beyond the seas.

The disturbances took a variety of forms. Threatening letters were sent to farmers and manufacturers, many of them signed by a mythical 'Captain Swing', stacks and barns were fired, and there were riotous assemblies and demands made for higher wages and reductions in tithes. Bands of men travelled around country villages stirring up trouble, destroying machinery and burning stacks and barns. Some of the leaders were executed, and several hundred rioters were transported to Tasmania.

I have some interesting papers about Thomas Goodman, of Battel (now

Battle) who was sentenced to death for arson in 1830. He was aged twenty-two, and attended a political meeting which was addressed by an activist called Cobbett, who told his audience that nothing but a revolution would do good for the country. Cobbett said that he did not wish the married men to leave their families, but it was up to the younger men, putting his hand on Goodman's shoulder, to fight for their rights and their privileges. He incited them to start fires to demonstrate their opposition to the government of the day. Thomas Goodman was greatly impressed by this, and he set fire to a local stack and barn, for which he was convicted and sentenced to death, arson then being a capital offence. Thomas Dicker took up his case with Lord Melbourne, Home Secretary, and after some pleading the sentence was commuted to Transportation for Life. Goodman was naturally greatly indebted to Thomas for achieving this, and for some years he wrote from 'Hobart Town, Van Diemens Land'. His first letter, dated 26 April 1834, is worth recording here:

Dear Friend,

I trust you will excuse this liberty I am now taking, particularly from the length of time that has elapsed since I had the pleasure of seeing you at Horsham [where he had been in prison] where your extreme kindness recommended me to your friend at Gosport in order that I might have the advantage of his good kind offices in recommending me to his friend in this quarter of the globe, whose name I am totally unacquainted with – the reason I have not let you know of my situation according to the promise I made you has been owing to my being assigned into the interior of the country, where the uncertainty of my situation left me no alternative as it was quite uncertain how long or how short I might remain in any one place, consequently it was scarcely any use in acquainting you as I was not fixed. I am now assigned to a gentleman in Hobart Town the Capital whose name is Lieut. Gunn, superintendent of the penitentiary with whom I have remained since my arrival in the Colony, and with whom I hope and trust I have given every satisfaction. I regret most sincerely to say that at present I see no prospect of obtaining any mitigation of my cruel sentence unless your kind benevolence will induce you to step out in my behalf by petitioning or otherwise get my case brought under the notice of the Secretary of State and by pushing my case so as to claim their attention. I indulge in fond hopes yet of even an humble individual like myself claiming their merciful consideration, the more particularly as my conduct since I have been here has been irreproachable never having any offence aginst me since my arrival in the Colony. This can easily be proved from the secretary's books at home and I am convinced by the kind perseverance of my friends I should not escape their notice.

With respect to the Gentleman's names in the Colony whom your friends benevolence urged him to promise to use his interest on my behalf I am totally unacquainted may I beg as a particular favor that you would have the kindness to request that he would write a letter on my behalf to him here as it would render me the most essential service in having a Gentleman who would have the Christian feeling to interest himself on the spot on my behalf & also if not intruding too much on your well known benevolence to write me acquainting me with the Gentleman's name here in order that I might apply to him personally or any other kind friends whom you might have in this quarter.

I have written my brother by this conveyance. I hope and trust in heaven something may be done for me by way of mitigating my sentence. I trust you will excuse me in requesting an answer stating plainly whether anything can be done for me or not in order that I may prepare for the worst. I am strictly attentive to my religious duties which in fact is the only consolation I have left me, but I am deprived the opportunity of attending divine Worship as I was accustomed in England.

I return you most heartily and sincerely my sincere and heartfelt thanks for the interest you have taken in my welfare & pray heaven to shower blessings on yourself and family

and remain, Dear friend,
Your unfortunate servant,

Thomas Goodman

Please direct to me care
Lieut Gunn, Hobart Town, Van Diemens Land.

That letter, of which I hold the original, does not seem to have been written by Goodman himself, he being semi-literate, but it is signed by him, and is addressed 'Mr Dicker, Banker, Lewes, Sussex, England', being forwarded to 'Oriental Place, Brighton', where Thomas had a second house.

There is no record of any development as a result of this letter, but documents received recently from the Archives Office of Tasmania state that in 1837 Goodman was convicted of 'having had improper communication with females confined in gaol', and sentenced to '6 months hard labour out of chains'. In 1838 he was granted a conditional pardon, presumably from his original offence, but whether he returned to England we do not know.

A friend wrote to me from Australia in 1991:

There must now be tens of thousands of Australians descended from the rioters, but I have not noticed any tendency for Australians to be machinery wreckers (apart from the usual predisposition to kick anything that fails to start or run). So much for the genetics!

In 1847 an event occurred which caused a major family scandal. This resulted in the following letter which was written by Thomas Dicker to the father-in-law of his daughter Harriet.

Lewes Jan 12 1848

Dear Sir,

Perhaps an apology is due from me for not having written to you after my last visit to London on the sad business referred to in your letter, but I concluded that you would hear every needful particular either from John or Mr Dawes (or both) and being pressed with engagements on my coming home I put it off as a thing not of absolute necessity.

I could not have thought it possible, but for the proofs disclosed, that anyone with such a measure of understanding and knowledge of life as John has, could have been so completely gulled and hoodwinked as he has been by one whose very appearance was suspicious – whose known extravagant habits proved him unworthy of trust, and whose open irreverence for all religion should have given him a bad opinion of him, to say nothing of the evidence that had been repeatedly brought before him of his utter destitution of honourable principle. I can only suppose that as John had often endeavoured to reclaim this sinner from the error of his ways, he hoped to give more effect to his spiritual counsel by showing his willingness to serve him in his temporal interests; trusting (alas!) to the assurances and representations of such a man, instead of consulting his own judgment, or asking advice of others.

The mischief however was <u>done</u>, and the object of our interviews with Mr Dawes and Campbell D. was to ascertain whether any steps could be taken that would be the means of recovering a portion of the property either from the sharks who held the Bills, or from any effects of CDs.

I pressed upon Mr Dawes the policy to frighten the usurers into a compromise, but he said the respectability of your son's position and property would make any effort of this kind, he feared, quite hopeless. Had he been so circumstanced that they could have got him out of the way for any indefinite time, they might, perhaps, have brought the parties to terms, but, standing as he did at present he thought that such a proceeding would be a worse evil than the loss of the money. Mr D. seemed to hope, from what Campbell had said, that something by way of security might be obtained on the Birkenhead land, if he could be persuaded to make the needful assignment. John and I afterwards obtained the promise of this from him, together with the most confident assurances of its being more than sufficient to cover, ultimately, the whole amount of his debt. The issue of this boasted security you have doubtless heard. I wrote that night from London to my Brother at Liverpool to acquaint me with all the particulars he could learn respecting this Land, and the incumbrances upon it – his reply I sent to John, with a request that he would forward it to you for your guidance, tho' you had long before, I believe, made up your mind to have nothing to do with it on any terms, that involved a further advance.

I assure you that I feel most deeply for you in this painful business, in which you are made so cruelly, and at the same time so innocently to suffer. It is a great relief to my mind that your son's attachment to JCD never arose from any sanction he ever had from me or Mrs D. and (more than this) that if our advice had been followed, this calamity would never have overtaken him. Even if he had consulted Harriet before doing what he did, he would have escaped the snare.

Notwithstanding this, however, my sympathy for you in the matter would have disposed me to meet your wishes as to sending JPP the £100 had not circumstances put it out of my power to do so. In addition to the extra demands I have had upon me this year, the late panic and its consequences (though it has not at all affected the standing of our House in the estimation of the public) will cause a personal loss to me of an amount fully equal to what you will have to pay for your son, so that I have no option on the point.

Whatever plan you may think it right to propose to John as necessary under altered circumstances he must, of course, submit to; and I hope that Harriet has got good sense and good principle enought to accommodate herself to it with cheerfulness.

Mrs D. unites in kind regards to you Mrs P and Miss Emma with Dear Sir,

Yours very sincerely,

T.Dicker

The principal characters referred to in this letter were John (Rev. John Peckleton Power BA), Mr Dawes (presumably a lawyer in London), Campbell D. (John Campbell Dicker, Thomas Dicker's nephew, whose father, Joseph Dicker, lived in Liverpool), and Harriet (Thomas's daughter and John's wife). It seems that John had got involved in some fraudulent dealings, as a result of which both he and Campbell Dicker had signed bills of exchange which had got into the hands of some other person who had then demanded payment. I have searched among family records and have not been able to find out how this affair ended, but without doubt it cost the Powers and the Campbell Dickers dearly, although neither family had committed any offence, except to be kind to another party who turned out to be untrustworthy.

In 1852 Thomas paid for some improvements and additions to the front of the chapel at Buxted, as a memorial to his grandfather. Shortly afterwards a Sunday School Room was erected at the chapel, and in 1896 a new roof was erected.

It was in early in 1854 that Thomas retired from the bank, and with his wife Martha moved from Lewes to Chichester. To mark his retirement he was presented with a silver coffee and tea set together with an illuminated scroll signed by two Members of Parliament together with ninety other residents, reading as follows:

THE SERVICE OF PLATE WHICH ACCOMPANIES THIS SCROLL is presented to THOMAS DICKER Esquire, as a man of undeviating integrity, and as the one who throughout a long life has adorned his Christian Profession, by a few of his affectionate and admiring LEWES FRIENDS, in token of their deep Regret and Sympathy, upon the Occasion of his Removal, with his entire family, from a Spot endeared to him by the intimate Associations of many Years.

The presentation occurred at Thomas and Martha's new home in Chichester, and a deputation travelled from Lewes for the purpose. This is part of a report of this event:

> In presenting the testimonial Mr Burwood Gotelee made some slight allusions to the feeling in which it had originated, and while assuring Mr Dicker that although a slight, it was not a less sincere tribute of the esteem and regard which the donors entertained towards him, expressed the earnest wish on behalf of the general body of the subscribers that he might long live to enjoy the retirement which circumstances had induced him to seek, and the hope that removal from amongst his old friends might be cheered by the recollection that he had carried away with him the kind wishes and unqualified esteem of those amongst whom he had so long dwelt. Mr M.A. Lower next addressed Mr Dicker, presenting him at the same time with a highly illuminated vellum scroll, containing an inscription expressive of the object of the subscribers to the testimonial, and a list of their names. The scroll, which was the work of Mr Lower's own hand, was executed in the most highly finished and beautiful manner, and formed as elegant and elaborate a piece of penmanship as can well be conceived.

The silver presentation set, and the vellum scroll, are in my possession now, and I hope they will be handed down through future generations of the family.

There may have been special circumstances which gave rise to Thomas's sudden retirement from the bank, and move to Chichester, but I have not been able to find out about these. Thomas died in Chichester fourteen years later.

Thomas and Martha had eight children, all of whom married, and eventually there were forty-seven grandchildren, many of whose families we have been able to trace. The two who interest us most, and who appear towards the end of my Aunt Ella's book in the next chapter, were Eustace Hamilton (called Hamilton, he used to describe himself as Hamilton Eustace Dicker), and Emily Winter, who married Rev. Melville Lauriston Lee, and became the mother of Lord Lee of Fareham. Also mentioned by Ella is Louisa Martha, who married Rev. Richard Henry Killick (Henry) who was at first curate-in-charge of Barley, and later vicar of Stratton, Cornwall. I will leave my great-aunt Ella to introduce my great-grandparents Hamilton and Kate.

Chapter II

Barkway

How certain people living in and near the pleasant village of Barkway, Herts. during the late 18th and early 19th Centuries, had much to do with the Hamilton Dickers of today.

By Eleanor Hamilton Dicker, younger daughter of Hamilton Eustace and Catherine Sarah Dicker, & constant companion of Esther, Sarah and Emma Hope in their old age.

Salisbury – 1931

The Quakers

Few people know so much about their ancestors as we do. Not only can we trace our Dicker ones to the time of Henry VIII, and possibly (with gaps) to the conquest, but our 18th and 19th century fore-parents were kind enough to leave behind a mass of documents, letters, portraits and old treasures. And our mother and her cousins had a great store of memories and legends about their forebears, and a fascinating way of telling them to us when we were children. Only I am now left who remembers these old family histories properly – my sister and three remaining brothers only remember them vaguely so I am writing them down before it is too late; they will at any rate show how certain loved old family treasures came into our possession.

Our mother used to say "These came to us through the Bretts and the Stallibrasses." So the first of our parents to step out of the mists, shadowy but distinct living people (not mere names on a document) are Thomas and Sarah Brett. They were "Friends" or "Quakers", and we are very glad and proud of that when we think of the state of the Church of England, and the morals, behaviour and language of the 18th century. For over 100 years the Quakers had been fighting, in their own quiet steadfast way, against the hideous evils which surrounded them, in spite of bitter persecutions and opposition, during which scores of them died in prison or from their sufferings; but the Society had steadily gained ground, and by 1742 they were honoured and respected and doing a great work in England. Although Elizabeth Fry was not yet born, the Quakers were already working for the reform of prisons and lunatic asylums, the mitigation of the penal code, the promotion of unsectarial religious education, the liberation of slaves, and many other things that bore fruition after many years. Though still debarred from political life, many held good positions and had large fortunes; being so steady and so sober they prospered in any business they undertook. It is said that George III was deeply in love with a beautiful quakeress, Hannah Lightfoot, when he was a young man, and would have married her if she had been allowed to be Queen. So you see the Quakers were not a small despised sect by the middle of the 18th century.

Yeomen

There is another thing that needs explanation before I begin on my histories, and that is the position of yeomen in those days; modern people are apt to confuse them with small farmers, but such a supposition is enough to make them "turn in their graves". I will quote what Lambard wrote about them in AD 1570 – the Kentish yeomen, but equally true of the Essex and Hertfordshire ones – in the 18th century.

> The tenure of the Yeoman of Kent, and in this their estate they please themselves and joy exceedingly, insomuch as a man may find sundry Yeomen (although for wealth comparable with many of the gentle sort) that will not change their condition, nor desire to be apparelled with the titles of gentry. Neither is there any cause of disdain, or of alienation of the good mind of one sort from the other; for nowhere else in all this realm is the common people more willingly governed. To be short, they be most commonly civil, just and bountiful, so that the estate of the old franklins and yeomen of England either yet liveth in Kent, or else it is quite dead, and departed out of the realm for altogether.

Farming was a very paying thing before the Reform Bill, and many younger sons of titled families took up farming in England, just as they do now in the colonies. Our Yeomen ancestors lived in beautiful old Granges, Manors and Halls, which may still be visited by any who wish; they were well furnished, and had plenty of far better servants than could be found nowadays. The food was absolutely sumptuous – we have an old manuscript cookery book from those days, the recipes in which amaze us now. One cake, made for meets, needed 40 eggs!

The Stallibrasses were often described on legal documents as "Gentlemen" as well as "Yeomen" or "Farmers", and they were able, if they wished, to seal these documents with their own seal, a fess between two crosslets, showing that they came of a family that bore arms.

But now for the real business of this narrative – our Quaker and Yeoman forefathers and foremothers.

Marriage Certificates – Sarah I

I have before me two old yellow parchments. They are Quaker marriage certificates, treasured by the gentle hands of one of our many Mothers. The first states that Henry Thorowgood and Sarah Reed had been made man and wife on May 23rd 1742, and the second, which is worded much the same, and concerns us more, is as follows:

> Whereas Thomas Brett, of Anstey, of the County of Hertford, Yeoman, son of Hester Brett of Chisel Hall in the County of Essex, and Sarah Thorowgood, Relict of Henry Thorowgood, late of Hitchen in the aforesaid County of Hertford, having publicly declared their intentions of taking each other in Marriage before several Meetings of the People called Quakers in Langford in the County of Bedford according to the good order used among them, whose Proceedings therein, after a deliberate consideration thereof (with regard to the Righteous Law of God, and example of his People Recorded in the Scriptures of Truth in that Case) were allowed by the said Meetings, they appearing clear of all others, and having consent of Parent and Parties concerned.
>
> Now these are to certifie all whom it may concern, That for the accomplishing of their said intentions, this nineteenth day of the First month called March in the year One Thousand Seven Hundred and Forty Six They the said Thomas Brett and Sarah Thorowgood appeared in a Public Assembly of the aforesaid People and others, met together for that purpose in their Public Meeting Place at Clifton in the said County of Bedford and in a solemn manner, He the said Thomas Brett

taking the said Sarah Thorowgood by the Hand, did openly declare as
followeth – Friends in the Fear Of God and the Presence of this
Assembly, whom I desire to be my Witnesses, I take this most esteemed
Friend Sarah Thorowgood to be my wife, Promising through Divine
Assistance to be unto her a Faithful Loving Husband until it shall
please God by Death to separate us (or words to that effect).

And then and there in the said Assembly the said Sarah Thorowgood
did in like manner declare as followeth, Friends in the Fear of God
and Presence of this Assembly whom I desire to be my witnesses, I
take this my most esteemed Friend Thomas Brett to be my Husband,
promising to be unto him a Faithful Loving Wife, until it shall please
God by Death to separate us (or words to this effect). And the said
Thomas Brett and Sarah Thorowgood as a farther confirmation thereof,
did then and there to these Presents set their Hands, And we whose
names are hereunto subscribed being present among others at the
Solemnising of the aforesaid marriage and subscription in Manner
aforesaid, as witnesses thereunto, have also to these presents subscribed
our names, the Day and Year above written.

Thos. Brett
Sarah Thorogood

Isaac Sharples. Mary Squire. John Brett. Joseph ·Ransom. Millicent
Thurgood. Samuel Brett. William Baily. Millicent Nottage. Mary
Thorn. Francis Gibson. Mary Crigest. Thomas Brett. Francis Gilbey.
Thomas Hagger. Mary Joyce. Stephen Hagge. Ancy Wilshen. Anne
Pain.

There are a good many points to notice in these two old marriage certificates. The first is the extraordinary carelessness in the spelling of names.
In the first one the bride's name is spelt "Throughgood", "Thorogood",
"Thurgood", "Thorowgood", but our mother always pronounced it "Thor-
oughgood". I remember asking her once "Was he <u>really</u> thorough good?",
and she said "Yes, one of the best – everybody loved him". What an epitaph
to earn! We may regret that he was not a real ancestor of ours, instead of
scarcely a "step" one.

The parchments are about the same size, printed in large copper plate,
with spaces in which the names and dates have been added in ink; although
only four years had elapsed between the two weddings there is a great
difference in the writing that filled these two spaces, the first being of a far
older type than the second. Both weddings were in Bedfordshire; probably

there was no Meeting House licensed for Marriages nearer, but they were a long way from the homes of the bride and bridegroom. Only one of the witnesses appears on both certificates – Joseph Ransome; and though on each occasion the bridegroom's family came in force to support him there are none of the bride's name. Evidently she had no parents living as they are not mentioned on the certificates, and possibly her relations did not approve of the Quakers. There is a legend that her father was a very clever physician at Hitchen. Although Sarah could hardly have been older than sixteen at her first wedding, and twenty or so at her second one there is no tremor or nervousness about either of her signatures. Henry Thorowgood's is rather shaky and excited, but Thomas Brett's is big and bold and clear – splendid writing!

We can picture the "Friends" gathering round the young couple with their quiet earnest greetings – "I congratulate thee, Friend Thomas Brett, and thee, Friend Sarah Brett!" Then they would be warmly packed up in the "chaise" that was to take them on the long journey to Anstey Hall, through the brown March lanes.

Anstey Hall

Anstey Hall is still there, with its moat and the curious mound in the garden – it is worth a pilgrimage to see. And we know that many of the treasures which we now possess were once at Anstey Hall. Our mother's mother (Sarah Stallibrass), who was granddaughter to Thomas and Sarah Brett, used to tell our mother that she remembered the beautiful old Chinese cabinet (of which she was cruelly cheated in later years) standing in the old home of her grandmother and on it four Chinese figures in white Ming china; two of these were broken – I believe during our mother's childhood – but two of them we have still. The dear old man with his kindly smile, and the merry Pekinese dog with his ribbon and ball, still watch the comings and goings of the descendants of Thomas and Sarah, and long may they do so!

The bride, cold and tired after her long drive, probably sat on one of a set of six Jacobean chairs; they had bandy legs and great splay feet, and the backs and seats were covered with embroidery in bold designs on strong linen. Dear old chairs! For many generations they remained in our family, and as long as my mother lived she refused to part with them, though they were far too big and cumbersome for the small houses of later years, and an additional anxiety in our many wanderings. After her death the family

Two Chinese figures from Anstey Hall (1746)

decided to sell them; ragged and shabby and worm-eaten, but dignified to the last, we saw them go to the sale room. They passed into the hands of an old furniture dealer, who no doubt mended and patched and renewed their youth. We heard they had been sold, all together, to a big house – may they find a happy home and kindly people!

When Sarah, the Bride, sat on one of those chairs (old even then), by the blazing fire after the long cold drive in the March wind, her Thomas would draw forward the Jacobean screen, lest her pretty cheeks should get scorched. That was of the same age as the chairs, and possibly worked by the same hands, though the style of the needlework is so different. I am thankful to say that this beautiful old tapestry screen is still in our possession – a very precious possession! We do not know if Sarah brought with her, or if she found already at Anstey Hall, the oriental treasures of which we have still so many in spite of breakages, losses etc. Chinese bowls, and vases and cups, and exquisite embroideries, Indian shawls, the white Ming figures, the lovely old chinese cabinet – how came they to Anstey Hall, in the possession of Quaker Yeomen? There must have been one of our ancestors, a brave traveller or keen collector in those far-away days; or possibly they came to Sarah from her first husband, the good Thorowgood. It is interesting to know that these must have been some of the earliest to reach England, as China was not opened to foreigners till the 17th century, and then only to Dutch traders.

The old pannelled oak chest always called the "linen hutch" was also at Anstey Hall; we still keep our linen in it, as our ancestresses have done for generation after generation. There is also (out of sight) a rougher, unpolished oak chest called the "blanket hutch", which we still use for blankets. In the cabinet in our drawing room there are many smaller things that were at Anstey Hall: patch boxes and silver vinaigrettes, old toilet and working and trinket boxes, laces, fans, books and all kinds of quaint things. When I was a child there were many more, and several wonderful old dresses, but we were allowed to dress up and play with these until they were torn to rags, and many priceless treasures were lost or stolen. I remember a round gold watch, like a billiard ball, in a round tortoiseshell case, which Mother said had belonged to her step-great-grandfather Thorowgood. I wonder where that is now!

Sarah II – AD1754

Apparently Thomas and Sarah were childless for some years, although there may have been little lives of which no record is left. But in 1754 a little girl came and stayed; she was called Sarah after her mother, and became a beautiful girl, tall, graceful, full of intelligence and capability. There is a saying in our family – "No Sarah is ever a fool!" – and it certainly seems true in our case: this part of our history concerns four Sarahs and a Catherine Sarah, none of them fools!

Apparently Sarah II was a great delight and pride to her parents, but at sixteen – a usual age in those days – she was married and went to another home nearby. The bridegroom's name was John Stallibrass, a sterling good fellow, steady, conscientious and hard working; they were devotedly attached to each throughout their long lives.

1st Twins and Mary Brett – 1771

A year later the seventeen year old wife became the proud mother of twins, a girl and a boy, whom she named Ann and Thomas. But it must have been annoying to her – almost exasperating! – when her mother presented her at the same time with a little sister! Poor little ancestress of ours! I fear she did not get a warm welcome from anyone to start with. Her mother, Friend Sarah Brett, must have been about 45 years old, if not more and in that methodical, middle-aged household a new baby must have been a most upsetting inmate. And when the elder sister, young Mrs Sarah Stallibrass, brought her twins to surprise her mother with their perfections, she would find her absorbed in a more wonderful baby of her own. For there is no doubt that pretty little gentle Mary soon became the delight of her elderly parents, and was probably more petted and spoiled than her sister had been. By and by she would be able to notice the white Chinese figures on the cabinet, and one can imagine the mother holding back the eager little dimpled hands that clutched at them. "Thee must not touch them, for they are old and precious, and thee might break them!" The quaint figures and the baby would smile at each other as they and all the family babies have done since – nearly 200 years!

Very soon afterwards, for education began very young in those days (if it began at all), the little ivory "horn book" would be brought out, and the poor mite would have to sit on a stool and learn her letters. Was it she who broke it in half, or one of the other exasperated babies who have held it in little hot tired hands? It has been most beautifully mended; I often wonder who did it and what glue was used. Perhaps it was broken by little Mary's naughty small nephew Tom, for the twins lived nearby, and the three were almost like a triplet, always together.

Tom Stallibrass

As a boy Tom was very handsome, very much like the portraits of the young Napoleon; he was overflowing with high spirits, witty, kindly and mischievous, a general favourite, yet always in trouble. Our mother had many tales to tell of him. He always sat in one dark corner of the Quaker Meeting House during the long silent Meetings, and he used to employ the time by slicing the leg of the form in front of him with his pocket knife. At last one day the leg was quite severed, and a row of solemn Quakers, wrapped in contemplation, suddenly slipped down the sloping seat into a heap on the floor!

Unfortunately he did not improve as he grew older; he could never settle to any work, but was always in debt and difficulties. Even his beauty left him after a bad attack of smallpox. There were dreadful quarrels between him and his father, who in the end left all his money away from him – but all that comes later in my story.

Ann Stallibrass and Mary Brett

A boy like that would find his pleasures elsewhere, but the two little girls, his sister Ann and his little Aunt Mary, who were both gentle quiet children, played with their dolls in the pretty garden of Anstey Hall. Among our treasures are two or three dolls' garments and the remnants of a dolls' teaset that once belonged to these little maids. We do have some quaint pictures worked in silks by little Ann, and a glass bottle and other things that were hers. The legend is that she "made tea" in this decorated screw-topped bottle, but more probably she <u>kept</u> tea in it – it would not do for a teapot.

We are told that Ann was engaged at the age of thirteen, but I never heard anything about the courting of little Mary Brett – I hope it was not arranged by the family as a sensible and convenient business matter that she should marry her brother-in-law's brother Thomas Stallibrass. It is possible that Thomas was a good deal younger than John (who must have been about 40 then), but even if he were not the parents would say the fault was on the right side. Anyway, as soon as they were sixteen the girls were separated and taken away by their bridegrooms: Ann by William Prior to the faraway village of Tottenham, Middlesex, and Mary by Thomas Stallibrass to Cockenhatch, on the other side of Barkway. We only get two or three slight glimpses of Ann after that, though we know there were devoted friendships and frequent visits between her and her young aunt.

John Pryor

We have a curious document that tells one sad piece of news. It says that "John by Divine Providence Archbishop of Canterbury Primate of all England & Metropolitan, to William Pryor the natural and lawful father of John Pryor, a Bachelor who died intestate, to take possession of his goods chattels or credits . . ." The money was under £100. This was Ann's only child, who died in 1801. One cannot help wondering how the little property of a Quaker could in any way be the business of the Archbishop of Canterbury!

Ann Prior died in 1816 aged 45 years; we have a beautiful memorial ring with her hair set in pearls, her initials in gold, and inside her name, age and date of death. Her daughter was brought back to her beloved old home, and laid in Barkway churchyard.

Thomas Stallibrass

I am sorry to say that I know nothing about our forefather Thomas Stallibrass, except that he was brother to the steady sturdy John, who had married Mary's much older sister Sarah. We hope that he was years younger than John, and that no pressure was put on the poor little girl that she should marry him to keep the property in the family. I never remember hearing him mentioned by my mother or her cousins. We have an old document on vellum, dated Jan. 6th 1770, that said he had leased Nuthampstead Bury farm for 21 years "with all the outhouses, edifices, buildings, stables, yards, gardens and pasture grounds thereunto likewise belonging, lying and being in Nuthampstead and Barkway aforesaid, and Anstey in the County of Hertford". But apparently he and his young bride lived in one or two of his other farms first, before settling down "for good" at Nuthampstead Bury.

We do not know when the good old Bretts died, but "Friend Sarah" at any rate lived to see her children's children, for our grandmother – her grandchild and namesake – remembered seeing her (and the white Chinese figures) in her home, Anstey Hall, when she was a little girl.

Division of the Treasures

John Stallibrass evidently took on his father-in-law's house and land, and that was the home of John and Sarah till they grew old. But all the other property, furniture and ornaments were divided between the two daughters, Sarah and Mary. Sarah had the Jacobean screen, the Chinese embroideries, several Indian shawls, a good deal of china and many other things. Mary had the old Chinese cabinet with the four white figures, the six Jacobean chairs, and various shawls, china bowls and vases and oddments of many kinds. Our mother's cousins, Esther, Sarah and Emma Hope left their share to my sister and me when they died.

Now, after more than a hundred years, the remnants of all these old Brett treasures have met again in our house, the descendants of John and Sarah having died out after three generations; whereas we, the descendants of

Thomas and Mary, are still increasing, strong and vigorous. It is strange when we remember that little Mary was a sort of afterthought, born in her parents' old age, and not nearly so strong as her sister, in mind or body, and also that John and Sarah had so many more grandchildren born. But that comes later in my story. What we must remember now is that Mary's portion of the house treasures came with her to Nuthampstead Bury, and remained there for many years, while Sarah's portion remained at Anstey Hall with her and her husband.

Nuthampstead Bury

Both Sarah and Mary Brett began their married lives at sixteen, both married Stallibrasses, and each had a twin boy and girl to start with, but there the resemblance ended. Sarah was seventeen years older than Mary, who was born the same year as Sarah's twins; these first twins were grown up when the second twins were born, and as they married early their children were only slightly younger than Mary's children – a generation was skipped, as it were.

Mary's Twins, 1787 and Sarah, 1780

Mary's twins were named William and Judith; a year later came Sarah and their little Thake, who died young. All four children were born before Mary was twenty – poor girl! Her elderly brother-in-law, John Stallibrass, was progressing well, buying farm after farm all round the neighbourhood, but Thomas, our ancestor, does not seem to have had the same gift for making money; possibly he was in bad health, for he died in 1802, leaving only a small fortune. All he had he left equally between his wife and three surviving children – the twins aged 16 and Sarah 15 – but the legacies were not divided until the children were 21. Their Uncle John Stallibrass advanced to William £600 of his father's money to keep them going, poor things.

We have this document, written in ink on official paper – by the 16 year old William:

> I, the undersigned William Stallibrass of Nuthampsteadbury in the County of Hertford Farmer one of the three children of Thomas Stallibrass late of Cockenhatch in the County of Hertford Farmer deceased do hereby acknowledge to have this day received of and from my Uncle John Stallibrass of Anstey in the County of Hertford Gentleman one

of the executors named in the last will and testament of my said late
father Thomas Stallibrass the sum of Six hundred pounds of lawfull
money in part and on account of the personal estate of my said father
and the rents of his estates to be accounted for when the whole accounts
are made up and settled. 28 July 1802

(signed) Willm. Stallibrass.

But what a burden it must have been for a boy of sixteen, even with the
help and advice of his Uncle John, to carry on that farm and with it support
his mother and young sisters. No wonder he grew up a grave, silent man,
rather alarming to his small nieces in later years.

The poor mother (our ancestress) was – as I have already said – very
different from her sister Sarah, who was a tall, handsome, masterful woman
to the end of her days; she was absolutely sensible, just and honest, but
people were a little afraid of her, and no doubt she treated her young sister
as a mere child even when she was a married woman. My mother used to
tell me that the children, William, Judith and Sarah, being strong, wilful,
spirited young folks got into the same way, so the poor young widow Mary,
who was very pretty but rather silly and incapable, was decidedly snubbed
and bullied among them all. Her married life must have been anything but
happy – four babies before she was twenty (three of them in little over a
year) a delicate unsuccessful husband who died and then to be bullied by
her young son and daughters! It is hardly suprprising that when she got the
chance she burst her bonds!

Mary's 2nd. Marriage

To the shock and horror of all her friends she took as her second husband
a man of lower rank than herself, not a Gentleman-Yeoman, owning his
own house and lands, but a mere tenant farmer – in those days there was
a vast gulf between the two. He was a good, kind man, a widower with one
son, and he took her to a comfortable home where she was "Somebody"
instead of a "Nobody" as she had felt herself at Nuthampstead Bury – if it
had not been for the severing of old ties she might have been very happy
there. But she was never forgiven for having lowered the family, and though
they occasionally visited her she was always treated and spoken of as a
disgrace. Yet my mother, who was her granddaughter, always said there was
nothing really against the Cannons; he was a good, steady, respectable man,
and devoted to and proud of his wife.

Happily they lived some distance away and the family circle seems to have got on quite well without her. We have all their signatures on some legal documents, when the young folks came of age, and their father's money was divided between them; "Mary Cannon", William and Judith signed theirs in Jan 1808 and Sarah in Jan 1809. The handwriting looks almost as fresh as when the young hands held the pen.

William, Judith and Sarah Stallibrass

It must have been a curious household at Nuthampsteadbury, run by a boy and two girls, but they were clever, capable young people, well educated for those days, and they had good servants and labourers; besides their very masterful Aunt Sarah and Uncle John (such a splendid businessman himself) lived nearby, and no doubt enjoyed having Nuthampsteadbury to overlook.

The two girls, Judith and Sarah, were sent to a good boarding school when they were quite young; each one had a tiny hair trunk, with a good lock to it, and her initials in brass nails on the top, to keep her special treasures in. I still use the one with "S.S." (Sarah Stallibrass) on it for my special papers; though the hair is gone and it is getting very shaky it is a sturdy old box and the lock is as good as ever. At school the girls were taught to be exquisite needlewomen, especially Sarah (our mother's mother) who seemed to be able to do every sort of fancy and plain work – her fingers were always busy with something, large or small. We have a sampler (framed) that she worked when she was twelve years old; a wonderful map of England, all in needlework, and some pictures worked in silks.

Judith marries Dr. Proctor

Judith married, probably when she was about 22 or 23, Dr. Proctor, who had a very good practice in London among the rich city merchants who lived there in those days. Their home was in Salisbury Square, a quaint tall old house, where her daughter also lived in later years, when she married her father's pupil and successor Dr. Goude.

This marriage of Judith's made an immense difference in the life of her sister Sarah, for the Proctors' was a delightful house to stay at and within easy distance of Barkway; coaches passed through that village daily on their way between London and Cambridge. The young Stallibrasses of both families were often there, seeing the sights, meeting interesting people, and improving themselves. Visits lasted much longer in those days too, and there was much to be seen and done in London in the early 19th century. Sarah did not miss Judith at home as much as she might have done, as she had formed a devoted attachment to her young second cousin Mary Ann, Tom's daughter; an attachment that lasted all their lives, indeed for two generations!

Tom Stallibrass

As I have said before, poor old Uncle John and Aunt Sarah were made very unhappy by their son Tom, who, though with much charm and beauty (till he had smallpox) grew up ill and dissolute, and quarrelled with his parents. He only cared for fun and amusement, riotous drinking parties, cockfights and practical jokes, and he was always in debt and difficulties. There were awful scenes between him and his father at times.

Tom had married a gentle girl named Mary Smith, and they lived at Standen Rectory; probably the living was in the hands of a pluralist who lived elsewhere. But the legend is that the Parish Registers were left in the room next to that in which little Mary Ann slept and played, and that she used to cut them up to make her dolls' bonnets!

Mary Ann Stallibrass

This little girl, Mary Ann Stallibrass, although not an ancestress of ours, plays an important part in our history. Owing to the death of his daughter Ann's son (young John Prior), Mary Ann, Tom's daughter, was the only grandchild of Uncle John Stallibrass, and the idol of her grandparents. While she was still quite tiny it was arranged that she should spend half the year with her parents at Standen Rectory, and half with her grandparents at Anstey Hall. As her cousins, William, Judith and Sarah were also constantly with the old Stallibrasses, Mary Ann became like a little sister to them, especially to Sarah. I have already told you that we have some dolls clothes and teacups that belonged to our great grandmother Mary and her niece Ann when they were wee girls together; we have also quite a number of things that belonged to the next generation, Judith and Sarah and little Mary Ann. There was a most beautiful dolls' dinner service – big enough for a dolls' banquet; only about half remains now, for we were allowed to play with it when we were small. We still have also the remains of teasets, dolls' clothes, and a number of childrens' books which belonged to those young people. From the very first Sarah had taken her little golden-haired cousin to her heart; she had felt the death of her little brother Thake very much, and seems to have taken little Mary Ann in his place. The Stalli-brasses, as a rule, had very white skins, and dark brown hair (reddy brown, not black hair, very thick and long and soft and fine). But little Mary Ann was a golden child, the loveliest of all the beautiful Stallibrass girls; even when she was fully grown her hair was the colour of ripe corn, not flaxen, and her complexion so wonderful that it made all the other girls in a room look sallow. An old gentleman told her children in after years that he remembered seeing her in the garden at Anstey Hall when she was about four years old: "A little child with yellow hair, in a yellow dress, on a yellow gravel path, dragging a yellow dolls' chaise, with a yellow kitten playing by her". She was the gentlest, daintiest of small girls, carefully trained by her Quaker grandmother; but on one occasion, when some chickens had got into the garden and refused to leave it she suddenly exclaimed "<u>Damn</u> the chickens! They <u>shall</u> go out!" Probably learnt from her naughty father! Mary Ann was sent to the same boarding school that Judith and Sarah had been to; she also had a little hair trunk with "M.A.S." on it (I have seen it, though we have not got it now) to keep her treasures in. She was very musical, and we still have some of her music and song books, and some of the beautiful embroidery and lace she made.

The Fortune-Teller

One day when they were staying with the Proctors in London Sarah and Mary Ann had a most unpleasant adventure. Sarah had a curious gift of second sight and was deeply interested in psychic matters, so hearing that there was a wonderful fortune-teller in a back street not far off she determined to go and see her; naturally Mary Ann, then a lovely girl of 16, insisted on going too. They found the place was a horrible back-alley, and would have given up all idea of going further, if there had not been a beautiful carriage with an Earl's coronet crest waiting at the door of the hovel. As they waited a grand lady came out and drove away in the carriage, and a nice looking young woman in the doorway beckoned the girls in. There they found a horrible old crone sitting by the fire with two packs of greasy cards on the table before her. She at once began to tell Mary Ann's fortune.

She told her she lived in the country about one mile from four crossroads and several other true things; then that she had many admirers, but that she should see her future husband that night, sitting with his arms on the back of a chair. That she should not see him again for many years, but would then marry him and have ten children. Just then there was a thundering knock on the door; the old woman looked terrified and pushed the two girls into a little back place, threw the cards after them, and locked the door. They could hear the police questioning and threatening the old woman, and were horribly afraid that they would be discovered and questioned, and perhaps have to appear in a police court either as accomplices or witnesses! Happily the house was not searched, and the old fortune-teller was let off with a caution. Directly the police were gone she let out her prisoners and wished to start telling Sarah's fortune, but the girls had had more than enough and hurried home as fast as they could.

Stephen Henry Hope

No word was said there of their adventure, but as they took off their bonnets a knock sounded on the front door. "There's your future husband!" laughed Sarah. Downstairs they found Dr. Proctor quite absorbed in conversation with a strange gentleman who sat astride on a chair, his arms resting on the back of it. The girls were thrilled. But Mr. Hope, a handsome, gay, young man of the world, took little notice of the shy, pretty girl, finding Dr. Proctor a far more interesting companion. Mary Ann was annoyed, for most people, male and female, lost their hearts to her at once; said she did not find Mr. Hope at all attractive.

However, he had not been so unobservant as he appeared, for two years later he came down to Barkway, and after a short courtship they were engaged and married. All appeared glowing with happiness and good fortune; he was a young man of good family, handsome, merry and witty, and she was as good as she was pretty, and heiress to her well-to-do grandfather. It was a church wedding, not a Quaker one, for all these younger Stallibrasses had joined the Church of England; probably their long and frequent visits to London had contact with different thought and outlook. But to their lives' end most of them were Quakers at heart, and they had many Quaker friends.

So pretty little Mary Ann Stallibrass became Mrs. Henry Hope, and left behind her three desolate homes. She had been the one great joy and interest to her grandparents at Anstey Hall; to her unhappy mother at Standen

Sarah (Stallibrass)
(Cornwell) Jackson
(1788–1850)

Rectory and to her beloved cousin Sarah at Nuthampsteadbury. The first two were indeed desolate, but Sarah was not easily crushed, she was too active and energetic.

"Mother's Mother"

The third Sarah, whom we always call "Mother's Mother", to distinguish her from Grandmother Dicker, was quite a remarkable woman, and one that ought to be remembered by all her descendants. She was a small woman, only 5 ft 1 inch, very dainty and trim, with tiny hands and feet; she had not the striking beauty of most of her family, though the oil painting of her, when she was about 50, shows a shrewd, kindly, attractive face. Mother said that portrait made her look much too big and imposing. She never sat like that, doing nothing; she was very much <u>alive</u>, always active, brain and fingers. She was rather too quick in speech at times, and spoke her mind too freely, but it was very seldom that people took offence. Clever, witty humorous and full of common sense; a born sick-nurse, an exquisite needle-woman – indeed, people who knew her have told me that she seemed able to do anything she wished to do.

We still have the framed sampler and pictures embroidered in silk that she made, and a few other things, but I can well remember a large knitted counterpane, and some window curtains she netted and darned patterns on, rather like what the Belgians do now. They are worn out and gone now.

After Judith's marriage Sarah kept home for her brother William at Nuthampsteadbury for many years; she had good capable servants, and her brother was not dependent on her, so she was not oppressed by her home duties, and was free to go for long visits whenever she wished. She was in great demand for all her people sent for her in illness or trouble, to prepare for festivities, or advise them in difficulties. Even if her remarks were forcible rather than polite folks soon forgot their smart because of their common sense.

But I must confess that Grandmother Sarah was extraordinarily careless at times, though she was as a rule so capable and methodical; perhaps it was because she had too many "irons in the fire". She mislaid three £50 notes once, and found them after a year among some tissue paper in a band box. Her brother William snatched a £5 note from the fire where she had thrown it as waste paper. She dropped a parcel of invaluable legal documents in the street, but it was picked up by a small boy. She never seemed to know or care what she was eating – her thoughts were always elsewhere. Once, when shoes were worn to match one's costume, she went out in one brown and one blue shoe. Outside things mattered little to her, except that she was exquisitely clean and neat, and dainty in all her ways. She very much wished to return from London to Barkway one day, but no carriage or coach was available; a big covered wagon was going that way, however, driven by a man she knew, so she went in that. She said it was not a bad journey – she played patience all the way with some cards she brought with her. She was an excellent card player, and much in request for chess, backgammon and other games.

I have already alluded to one curious trait in Grandmother Sarah – a kind of second sight which she had all her life. It took the form of very realistic dreams – she would see things that were happening or going to happen elsewhere. I believe she foretold every death in the family, even those that were unexpected – including her own. For instance, one night she saw her mother, who had died some years before, in her bedroom, and when she exclaimed in surprise her mother said "I am not come for you, my dear, but for your sister!" Very shortly after Judith Proctor was taken suddenly ill and died. This is only one of many cases. I will tell one or two more later on.

One very hot Sunday morning a sudden appalling hurricane swept across England, unroofing houses and barns, uprooting trees, and lifting people high in the air; half Barkway was in its path, but the rest of the village untouched. It was in the middle of the morning Service, and all the windows and doors were wide open because of the heat. The hurricane approached with an awful roar, and by some instinct our grandmother realized at once what it was, and the danger of it. Springing to her feet she shouted out "Shut that door!" Several men rushed to the door and with the greatest difficulty closed it, just in time to save the church from serious damage. One old woman was lifted and carried several yards in the village street, and an apple tree in full leaf was torn up, twisted right round and dropped some distance away.

Grandmother Sarah had some very decided opinions, and seldom changed them, though on one occasion she did – on the subject of having teeth pulled out! She had a fine set of teeth herself, and never having tried the dentists of those days she had a great contempt for those who bore the pain rather than have the teeth extracted. "If ever I have toothache I shall have the tooth out <u>at once</u>" she said. One day she felt a twinge in her face so she asked the Doctor to remove a double tooth with his forceps (there were no real dentists in those days).

Dr. Proctor got a good grip on the tooth with his forceps, but the next instant she hit out with her fists and sent him flying; "Touch me again if you dare!" she said. She never complained of toothache again, and died with every tooth in her head quite sound.

There was a family joke against Grandmother Sarah. She had driven over several miles to call on a friend whose cook was celebrated for her cream cheeses, and on her departure did not know that one of these cheeses had been put into the carriage as a surprise for her. Being very rich and soft and squashy she sat on it all the way home, to the great detriment of the carriage, and her own rich silk dress and cloak!

England as "Mother's Mother" knew it.

Grandmother's life was so full and happy that she had no use for lovers, and she drove away her admirers for many years. She was constantly in London, which was full of interest and excitement in those days of the Regency and the reign of George IV. Napoleon was crashing down kingdom after kingdom on the continent, fully intending to get ours too; we were fighting him and outwitting him and picking up useful bits of spoil where we could. The Press Gang and Army touts were seizing every man possible – they were needed for the Peninsular War, for Waterloo, for the rebellions in Ireland, and the United States. At home too, riots were seething everywhere, against machinery, against the Corn Laws, against Roman Catholics etc. The Court and Society were corrupt beyond belief, disgraceful scandals and duels were of common occurrence – there was even one between the Minister of War, Lord Castlereagh, and Canning, the Foreign Minister. There was starvation and misery among the poor; many became footpads and highwaymen in consequence. Punishments were brutal; on the long drives by coach or "chaise" it was not uncommon to see a gibbet with a corpse dangling in chains, or hear the shrieks of some poor wretch being publicly whipped or branded in a Market Place. People were hanged or transported to work as slaves in some plantation or new colony – for quite small offences. Then there was the trial and rude treatment of Queen Caroline; Grandmother Sarah was actually present when that ill-used woman tried to force her way into Westminster for the Coronation! I remember our mother telling us about it when we were quite young, and she had heard it from her mother – an eye-witness! We were told about the great sorrow of the whole nation when young Princess Charlotte and her little baby died; and the interest everyone took in the birth and doings of little Princess Victoria! Looking back it seems impossible that anyone could live a peaceful or happy life in such lurid times, but our Quaker and half-Quaker folks did. Food was a necessity, so Yeomen and farmers did well, and often made large fortunes; and in the London circle Quaker bankers and merchants were respected and trusted when few other men could be. Many of our present richest families and peers laid their foundations in those days, because their ancestors were sober, honest and painstaking. Grandmother Sarah went from one of these circles to the other, wherever she wished or was needed; keenly observant, shrewd, kindly and capable.

Her life was so full and happy that she had no use for lovers, and she drove away admirers for many years, as I have said. She had one trouble which increased year by year, unfortunately; things were not going well with her beloved young cousin, Mary Ann. The marriage had appeared such an ideal one at first, love and beauty and plenty of money, and the only grievance the sweet little wife had was that no babies came for two or three years. Sarah found her crying over this one day, and reminded her that the gipsy had promised her <u>ten</u>. "Some day I shall find you crying because you have too many!" she said. And this came true; babies arrived year after year, but to their great sorrow all the first ones died very soon.

It is a curious fact that the first five (four of them boys) were all baptized at home, in a large oriental china bowl of their mother's (one of the old Brett collection) and they all died. The later children were taken to the church to be baptized – and they all lived, except one still-born. The prophecy came true! The china bowl we have still, in perfect condition.

"The Little Squire"

The eldest boy, Johnnie, was a little grave, ailing child, and his death at seven years old was a grief, but not a surprise. But little Harry Hope's death was such a poignant sorrow that even the sisters who had only heard the tale could hardly bear to talk about it. Owing to the circumstances which I describe later this small boy had inherited all the money and property left by his grandfather, old John Stallibrass, at and round Barkway, and he was always called "The Little Squire". He was an unusually beautiful, intelligent, attractive child, and a favourite with everyone, rich and poor. But one day he was driven over to Anstey, and they stayed longer than they had anticipated; a chill wind had sprung up and they had not sufficient wraps. He caught a severe cold, inflammation of the lung set in, and after a few days he died. He had always loved the bells of Barkway church, and in his honour (as the little Squire) they were always pealed on his birthday. But they were silenced while he lay dying, lest they should disturb him; till their tolling announced his death. Just at the last he looked round on the tearful faces round his bed and murmured, "Big Grandma loves me, and little Grandma loves me; Mama loves me, and Papa loves me, and God loves me!" – those were his last words. There was a wonderful funeral for this little child; everyone, rich and poor, came to it, from miles around. They laid him in the family vault, close to the church door. After the names of his great-grandparents, his grandparents, his great-aunt Ann Prior, and his little sister Mary Hope, aged 11 months, came the words: "Henry Searle Hope, Dec.

20th 1828. Aged 4 years." His death made an immense difference to his sisters, and possibly to us!

The death of her babies, one after the other, nearly broke Mary Ann's heart, and other bitter disappointments had clouded the life that had begun in such sunshine. They discovered only too soon that Mr Hope was mad for speculation, and when he was unlucky only tried again, certain his luck would change. And not only with his own money, which he soon entirely lost: he speculated with his sister's money, which was in his charge, and lost all that, and then with the handsome sum which her grandfather had given Mary Ann on her marriage – and lost that too. I have often heard my mother tell how Grandmother Sarah rushed to her beloved cousin when this awful ruin fell on them; she found poor Mary Ann crushed and broken, for she had heard that everything in her pretty home would be seized by the creditors. Looking round on her treasures she sobbed, "Even this old Chinese bowl, that my dead babies were baptized in!" And Grandmother Sarah said, "They shan't have that, anyhow", and hid it under her cloak, and carried it off. Happily an arrangement was made, and her friends bought up many of her special treasures and necessities. That china bowl is now in our cabinet, in perfect condition.

Ash Grove, Barkway

Great Uncle John Stallibrass and his wife continued to live at Anstey Hall until age compelled him to live a less strenuous life. He now owned nearly all Barkway and the surrounding neighbourhood, and the living was in his gift. He decided to enlarge a small farmhouse on the high road of the village (that had been in the family many years) and make it into an ideal home for himself and his wife. He added dining and drawing rooms with bedrooms over them, laid out a charming garden, with an avenue of oak trees to the gate, and behind made a tiny model farm, with very fine kennels and orchards.

He was specially fond of roses, and these were planted everywhere, soon covering the house and arches and pergolas; all the roads and paths were gravelled and the beds brilliant with flowers. It was said to be the prettiest house the coaches passed on their way between London and Cambridge, and drivers would point it out to their passengers.

Here Great Uncle John bred greyhounds of high quality; he had one quite famous one named "Van de Neulen". They also had for many years a dear old brown spaniel named "Bessy", but unfortunately she took to poaching in her old age, and was shot by the keepers. She managed to creep back to Ash Grove, and died as she reached the doorstep, to the great grief of her owners. Another important inmate of that pretty homestead was the white donkey that belonged to Great-Aunt Sarah. This tall, handsome, masterful old lady had only one weakness about her and that was rheumatism in her knees; she used to walk about the house leaning on an ebony stick (which I still use, for the same reason!), and drive about the village and neighbour-hood in the smartest of donkey chairs, with a trim, well-clipt white donkey in yellow harness. To outward appearance Ash Grove was the very ideal of peace and happiness, but in reality the dear old couple were torn with anxieties and disappointments. They were hardly on speaking terms with their only son, who was a disgrace to their good name, and expected to be constantly helped out of debts and difficulties; and then the marriage of his daughter, their beloved little Mary Ann, had proved such a catastrophe. At times the John Stallibrasses were supporting her and her little ones, or they would have starved. The worst crash – when Mr Hope went bankrupt, and the home was sold up – did not happen till after Great-Uncle John's death; he was able to tide them over the bad times, till Mr Hope had another stroke of luck, apparently.

But in 1820 the fine old fellow, John Stallibrass, was found lying dead among the flowers in his beloved garden, from heart disease – a terrible blow and sorrow to all who knew him. Nearly all his money and property he left to his granddaughter's son – he knew if it were left to Mary Ann her husband would get it and speculate with it. This was before the birth of little Harry, but the elder sons died. Harry was born "The Little Squire", but after four years he followed his brothers, and his mother became his heir. Alas! Most of his property went the way that his Great-Grandfather had feared.

Great-Aunt Sarah continued for many years at Ash Grove, a very impor-tant person in the village and neighbourhood. A tall, determined, rather fierce old lady, but with a kind heart under her severity. My mother and her cousins could remember her at Ash Grove, and driving about in her donkey chair. We have a black silhouette of her, in which her character is clearly shown; she is sitting at a small table, and wears an Indian shawl – we still have the table and the shawl! But bye and bye a new trouble came to the old lady: a servant who had been with her all her life (Mary Turner) and acted as housekeeper, lost her wits when she became old, and was so ill-tempered and strange that she became quite a danger. The masterful old lady and the half-crazed old servant had hectic times, till our Grandmother Sarah took matters into her own hands: she carried off the old lady into her own house, discharged the servants, and let Ash Grove furnished to good tenants. Great-Aunt Sarah, who was then greatly crippled by rheumatism, and unfit to have sole charge of a house and grounds (though her mind was clear to her last hour) only made one stipulation when she consented to leave Ash Grove – that when she died she should be brought back there, and buried near that loved house. She lived for fifteen years after that, but in utterly different surroundings.

Bygraves, Barkway

One of the houses owned by the Stallibrasses in Barkway High Street was called "Bygraves" – I have never been able to discover the origin of the name. They used to let all this house with the exception of two rooms, which they kept always for their own use; when they lived on farms some miles out in the country it was convenient to have a bedroom and sitting room in the big village, on the coach road. At one time a valued old servant from Nuthampsteadbury was pensioned and allowed to live in those two rooms till she died. Later on our Grandmother's brother William fell into bad health and had to give up hard work so he lived in those nice bright rooms until he died. The sitting room is now turned into a village shop, but the rest of the house is unaltered; the owner very kindly let me go all over it when I last stayed at Barkway. It is a nice house for an ordinary family – but it was no ordinary family that was packed into it for a good many years! One wonders how they managed to get in, and to get on together, when they <u>were</u> in!

When the Hope's crash came it was decided that they should come at once to Bygraves; they could have all the house except the two best rooms. Mr Hope was away a great deal (happily), for he had found work which took him to Portugal very often. But besides poor pretty Mary Ann and her babies there was her mother, the wife of naughty Tom Stallibrass – a plain, stout, crushed flat, gentle creature; and also Mr Hope's unfortunate sister. This poor lady had been robbed of a good fortune by her brother's cruel speculations; she was well-born, clever, cultivated and had travelled a great deal, but now she was practically penniless, and embittered by her losses and her narrow uncongenial life.

It was to this house, already so crowded, that old Great-Aunt Sarah decided to come when she left Ash Grove. No doubt her money would keep the household going, and probably they thought that poor William Stallibrass would soon die, and the old lady could live comfortably in his two nice rooms. But he didn't die for a long time, many years; and as more and more babies arrived things must have been horribly uncomfortable in the rest of the house. Old Great-Aunt Sarah took command, and ruled them all with a rod of iron, and yet with kindness and sympathy, and they loved her. The poor children were kept in order by "Big Grandma", "Little Grandma", "Aunt Mary" and "Mamma"; also by "Dear Papa" when he was there. Many, many years after these children would tell me tale after tale of those days. One of them, when she was over eighty, told me how she was taken into William Stallibrass's room by our grandmother; he was sitting by the fire, a white-faced, silent man with dark brown hair, and by his side was a dish full of delicious-looking oranges. She thought he would offer her one, but he did not do so, to her bitter disappointment. She used to remember a lament over that orange (that she never tasted!) when she was getting childish with old age.

Barkway in the early 19th Century

Barkway, Royston, Herts is an uncommon village in many ways. The long, straight Roman road from London to the North, after miles of dead level suddenly climbs a steep hill at Royston, up "The Devil's Backbone"; originally there was a strong castle at the top, guarding this important pass, "the Bergway", but that was destroyed, and is hardly discernable now. From the entrance to the village one looks down a landscape not unlike that from the Devil's Dyke at Brighton, scores of miles of flat, rich, green land, with the spires of Cambridge in the distance. The air was so clean and invigorating that Barkway folks missed it and longed for it when they were away.

The houses are built on either side of a broad road, and in the days I am telling about a large village green in the centre of the village was an important feature. (This was afterwards seized and covered with the schools, to the fury of the villagers.) It was a large, important village, with coaches and a great deal of traffic passing through it; there were several large houses in it, and shops, and a "Young Ladies Academy". The living was a good one, and was generally given to the younger son of a titled or County family; the Hon. & Revd. Peachey was there in the early days of the 19th century.

It was a big, breezy, busy, lively place with hunting and shooting parties, dances and tea parties, and "syllabub" in the hayfields!

I am sorry to say Barkway was celebrated for another reason. It stands on a little spur of Herts, but is almost touched right and left by Essex and Cambs, a useful position for anyone who was likely to have a warrant taken against him in one county, and so wished to be able to hurry into another one; a great many duels and prize fights took place there. I fear all the gentlemen used to encourage the prizefights in "the good old days", and crowd to watch them. Several prizefighters were killed, and were buried on the north side of the church. Dr. Balding, when he was an old man, told me "he happened to be near" (with a twinkle in his eye), at one famous fight, in which the favourite was killed.

The Baldings

Over 100 years ago, Dr. Balding was a young Doctor, who had just built himself a house at the entrance to Barkway, and laid out a nice garden round it. He had a charming wife, and babies coming every year – but he had rather a stiff time at first, for the "gentry" would not trust him for anything serious, and still sent to London for a better-known Doctor. However he, and his son after him, proved themselves clever and capable, and lived long and loved lives.

The Cornwells' House

Quite near to the Baldings' house there stood – and still stands – a good-sized Queen Anne house of old red brick; it stands right on the village street, but it has a beautiful old garden behind, and a field with a pond in it. This house concerns us, very much! It was then occupied by a Mr William Cornwell, a widower with three daughters – bright, attractive girls.

The Jackson House

Some way down the village street, on the opposite side of the road, stood another large house, slightly back from the road, with a lawn in front, and a fountain with goldfish in it. It was then a long, low, grey stone house, very old and quaint looking; it was said to have been originally a large inn, with wings, and a courtyard in front. One of these wings had disappeared (perhaps burnt down) and the other had been turned into a separate dwelling-house, inhabited by an old man who refused to turn out, to the great annoyance of the owner of all the rest of the house, who would have paid almost any price to have the whole building to himself. This was a Mr. Anthony Jackson, who was then making a great deal of money as a land surveyor, planning and laying out the lines for the new S.E. railway. He had an office there, and pupils who paid him large sums to learn his work – and incidentally did much of the work; there were enormous maps in the office, showing every yard of the way the rail must pass, and every house, barn and pigsty. He and his pupils used to tramp over hill and dale, and prevailing on people to sell their land for it.

He had bought this fine old house in the centre of the village (all but the wing already occupied, and that he always hoped to get), and he also bought all the land he could behind it, from the churchyard to the Royston Road. This he turned into a perfect Paradise of a garden; in the centre was park-like field, and all round he planned a series of gardens, groves, wildernesses, bowling green etc., all leading from one to the other, with seats and summer houses, an ice-house that was also a chalet, and "ball-room" where the young folks could dance. There were also kennels, stables, cow house etc., and laundry, brew house and other buildings – as all gentlemen's houses had in those days. At one time Mr Jackson was also Estate Agent to Gen. Sir William Clinton, who lived at Cockenhatch, one of the two mansions which stand just outside Barkway. We have an old notice of a Sale by Auction, dated 1805, on which there is a hasty note in ink signed "Anthony Jackson". But he gave up this agency as his work for the railway increased.

Bygraves, with its crowded occupants, was almost next-door to the Jackson house, and formed a strong contrast to it; pretty Ash Grove, nestling amid its trees and flowers, was further down the wide road. It was a big village, with several other nice houses in and near it, besides the farms and cottages, but these are the houses which most concern us. Altogether Barkway was as gay and desirable a village to live in as young folks could want in the days of George IV and William IV. There were four tall, lively girls at the Jackson house, and three smaller, but attractive ones at the Cornwell house, young people at the Rectory and the Doctor's and elsewhere, and jolly young pupils of Mr Jackson's, and our Grandmother Sarah coming and going between there and London.

It must have added to the sadness of poor young Mary Ann Hope, the loveliest of them all, and the pet and darling until she married, to come back to her old village a penniless "Grass Widow", living in such discomfort on the charity of her Grandmother. She never lost her beauty and grace, perhaps because she was so gentle and yielding that she did not worry as a more active person might have done. She let others take the lead and do as they wished, never interfering even perhaps when she should have done. They say she was so like Emma Lady Hamilton that her husband used to buy copies of all the portraits of that Lady – so utterly different in all but face and form! – and even intimate friends would take them for likenesses of Mary Ann, wondering why she was wearing such strange costumes! Her complexion was so fine and white that it made everyone else took sallow; even when she was an old lady with snow-white hair she had such arresting beauty that few people passed her in the street without a second glance.

Grandfather William Cornwell

One day long before, when Grandmother Sarah and Mary Ann were young, they were walking in the fields near Anstey when the elder girl stopped and wished to turn back. "But why?" asked Mary Ann. "Because Mr Cornwell and Mr Jackson are in front of us, and I dislike them both, said Grandmother Sarah. You may be certain that this turned into a family joke when years afterwards she married first one and then the other!

Soon after Mr Cornwell's first wife died he sent a beautiful set of garnets to our Grandmother with an offer of marriage, but she returned them, saying she could not be stepmother to his daughters, who were nearly her own age. Some years later he again sent the garnets, and begged her to reconsider her decision; the two elder daughters were married, and the youngest one engaged.

This time the garnets and the offer were accepted. Grandmother Sarah Stallibrass was then thirty-nine years old – quite an old lady for those days and considered "on the shelf" by most people. But she was young both in heart and appearance and very lovable. Their short married life was very happy. I wish I could tell you more about our Cornwell ancestors, but what I have heard was mostly legendary. Happily we have a nice oil portrait of Grandfather Cornwell, probably painted just before this marriage. He was twenty years older than his bride, and a typical county gentleman of that date; except that he never never got drunk or used bad language! So I was told, many years ago, by Dr. Balding and one or two others who still remembered him – these virtues seemed quite noticeable in those days. A quiet, self-contained man, fond of riding, hunting and shooting. Either his father or grandfather (I don't know which) had been a naughty undergraduate at Cambridge, had been sent down for all sorts of mad pranks, and had married the daughter of his riding-master. His family (well-to-do people in another part of England, but I don't know where) would have nothing more to do with him, so he bought a farm with a nice house about halfway between Barkway and Cambridge. This was pointed out to me as we drove past when I was a young girl, but I could not describe it or remember the name now. His sons also bought land and settled in that neighbourhood. Our Grandfather, William Cornwell, had a brother, John. It must have been the eldest son of John that my sister Mildred was taken to see when she was a little girl; he also was a Mr. John Cornwell, living in rooms in Cambridge. She remembers him perfectly well, a quiet, gentlemanly old man, with old-fashioned, courteous manners; she also remembers beautiful old silver cups and other things on his big sideboard and the dinner table. The legend is that these Cornwells were descended from "Richard de Cornwall", the famous son of Henry II, and that is why they have the "dancing lion"! Most unfortunately this old John fell entirely into the hands of his housekeeper in his old age, and he left her everything when he died, including the old silver.

Grandfather William Cornwell had bought the farm at Newsells in the parish of Barkway, but having plenty of capital, and being a wise worker, having propitious weather, and the laws of the land then all in favour of the farmer, in seven years he had made enough money to retire from such work. His land and house were bought by a Mr. White, who had married a Miss Wortham of Royston; unfortunately he was a very different man, effeminate and inefficient (people used to call him Julianna); he let the farm go to rack and ruin, and lost almost as much money as our grandfather had made over it. His daughter, Annie White, was a great friend of my mother's and of ours all her life – we have here now several things that belonged to her, including some exquisite baby clothes, made for her by her mother, and her aunt, Miss Wortham.

So Grandfather William Cornwell moved into "The Red House", Barkway, the fine old Queen Anne House already described; I believe it already belonged to his family, but he may have bought it then. In 1827 his eldest daughter, who was married to William Nicholson, had died when her second little boy, Edward, was born. (Her husband lived to be 104 years old! He had been one of Nelson's midshipmen, and had many interesting tales to tell to us when we were children.) His second daughter was married to Mr "Bob" Robinson, and had one young son, Stanley. His youngest daughter, Ann, was engaged to her cousin, another William Cornwell; she was still quite young, and very fond of "Miss Sarah Stallibrass", so our Grandmother consented to marry her father without waiting till she too had married.

And so Grandmother was married from Ash Grove (which had been her principal home, with her Aunt Sarah, since Old John Stallibrass had died) and she became Mrs William Cornwell, of The Red House, Barkway. And with her there went the old Chinese cabinet, and the white Ming figures standing on it, the six Jacobean chairs, and all her mother's things that had been her mother's share of the old Brett treasures. The other half of these treasures belonged to her old Aunt Sarah, and remained at Ash Grove till they were inherited by Mrs Hope.

The fine old silver teapot that we now use, with "W.S.C." on it, was one of the wedding presents. We have a good many things marked "S.S.", because there were two Sarah Stallibrasses living, our Grandmother and her Aunt. It is almost impossible to tell which belonged to which. My Mother inherited very nice furniture from this Cornwell house, but it was all sold or distributed among her children after her death. She had very good table silver, too, that had belonged to her Father, but after her marriage the Dicker crest was put upon it, which should not have been done.

The Red House, Barkway

The marriage of our Grandparents was a very happy one, for they were admirably suited to one another. It is possible the "dislike" of which the girl Sarah had spoken to her young cousin years before was really the dislike of meeting a just-rejected lover in a narrow lane!

The young step-daughter Ann, pretty and vivacious, lived with them, and so did for a time the poor little motherless baby, Edward, the eldest daughter's child. Ann made this little fellow her special charge, both before and after her marriage.

Birth of Catherine Sarah Cornwell

In 1828 a little dead daughter was born, to the mother's bitter disappointment, and in 1829 another baby girl came, also apparently dead. This time our Grandmother was very seriously ill, and the family and doctors were so

Catherine Sarah (Cornwell) Dicker (1829–1903)

worried about her they had no time to take notice of the dead baby. Even a piece of flannel that had been wrapped round it was needed and snatched away, leaving the tiny body cold and naked in an armchair. Here it was seen by our Grandmother's maid, Sarah Cootes (another Sarah, who was "no fool"!), who had been one of the Nuthampstead maids, and had followed our Grandmother when she married. With tender pity Sarah Cootes slipped out of her own flannel petticoat and wrapped it round the baby, nursing and fondling it in her arms. Bye and bye she sought out the young Dr. Balding (who had come to assist the grand London doctor who had come down for the great event) and told him she could see faint signs of life in the baby. Dr. Balding asked the London doctor if he might try to revive it, and was irritably told he might do what he liked with the corpse – it was as dead as a doornail! So Sarah Cootes held the little thing in her warm flannel petticoat, while the young doctor dropped brandy into its mouth (he had babies of his own, at home!), and very soon its limbs began to move, and its voice was heard objecting! If it had not been for these two kindly, painstaking people we should not be descended from Sarah Cornwell. That "dead" baby lived to have eight children of her own, and a dozen grandchildren, who are now starting families in England and abroad. Sarah Cootes remained in our family, honoured and beloved, till she was past work; she was then pensioned and lived in a little cottage at Wenden. I can remember her there quite well, when I was a small girl.

I can give you two or three peeps at our Mother when she was a wee thing. When I was staying at Barkway many years ago I was told of an old bed-ridden woman who wished to see me. I found her a dear old soul, well on in the nineties, and she said she remembered my Mother when she was a baby. This old woman's mother was washerwoman to our Grandmother, and she sent her little daughter to the Red House with a parcel one day. She heard the sound of laughter in the garden and child-like, peeped through the bushes. Our Grandmother saw her, and instead of being angry called out "Do you want to see my baby?", and told her to come into the garden and watch. Little Kate (our Mother-to-be) was then about 18 months old and trying to walk on the lawn, going a few steps, and suddenly sitting down, as all babies do. The old bed-ridden woman said how plainly she could still see the whole scene – the pretty fair baby, the happy laughing mother, the beautiful garden, the sunshine, the flowers – a hundred years ago!

The Wedding of Aunt Ann and Uncle William Cornwell

Another picture has the same sunny garden for a background, but little Kate was then three years old. The Red House was in a great state of bustle, for pretty young Ann Cornwell was just about to be married to her cousin

William Cornwell. The engagement had lasted longer than at first intended, for various reasons, but Ann and her stepmother lived very happily together, and were in no hurry to part. We have a small silhouette of our Aunt Ann at the time of her marriage – a very graceful and attractive girl. As all hands were needed on this wedding day the nurse dressed little Kate early, and left her to play in a room that opened into the garden, charging her not to soil her pretty white frock and red shoes. But when they came to fetch her they found nothing but her little socks and red shoes – she had gone into the garden barefoot! She was very proud of having taken such care of her shoes!

Death of Grandfather William Cornwell

The last baby-tale of our Mother is rather a naughty one – she could actually remember it herself, probably because of what happened shortly afterwards. She could dimly remember the sick-room in which her Father was sitting in an armchair, very weak and ill. There were grapes growing on a vine outside the open window, and naughty little Kate climbed on a chair and tried to pick them. The sick Father was terrified lest she should fall out, but was too weak to cross the room to save her; He shouted in an agonised way for someone to come. It startled the little child and she looked round hastily – the whole scene was printed on her memory; the four post bed and big chair, and her Father's face of anguish. (Our mother was born in that four post bedstead, and so were all her 8 children. When at last we found it impossible in our small bedrooms the carved posts and footboard were made into a hall-table. My brother Assheton now has it in his Rectory.) For years after, when her Father was mentioned, that is how she saw him. Grandfather William Cornwell had, as I have said, a very short but happy time with his second wife. He died on Oct.1st 1832, aged 62 years.

Mother also remembered her great excitement at being dressed in black, just like her Mother, shortly after that – of course not realising in the least <u>why</u> she wore it. This Grandfather of our's had an unusually happy life – he said he would willingly live it again, day by day; that every great wish he had ever had had been fulfilled. Probably because he had such perseverance and determination. His money was shared among his four daughters, except that his widow had the Red House and a comfortable income to keep it up.

For three or four years more Grandmother Sarah and her little daughter lived peacefully and happily at the Red House. At that time Great-Aunt Sarah was still living at Ash Grove, and driving about the village in her donkey-carriage; and at Bygraves, between Ash Grove and the Red House, lived the Hope family. "The Little Squire" was their pride and delight still, when Kate was born, but he died in the same year. His little sister Esther, however, was a strong and sturdy child; she was the 5th child born to Mary Ann Hope, but the first to live to grow up. She was two years older than Kate, but very soon after Kate's birth another girl-baby arrived at Bygraves; she was our grandmother's god-daughter, and was named "Sarah" after her. So you see these records are about Sarah Brett, Sarah and Mary Stallibrass, Sarah Cornwell (née Stallibrass), Catherine Sarah Cornwell, and her cousin Sarah Hope – "none of them fools!" Little Sarah Hope and our Mother were brought up almost like twins, and they carried on the devoted friendship of their two mothers, being inseparable friends (except for one sad break) all through their lives. Though slightly younger, Sarah was always the leader; probably she would have been a very clever and brilliant woman in after years if her home life had been different when she was a child. Happily for her she escaped from her severe aunt, Miss Hope, as much as possible into the glorious freedom of the Red House, where she led little Kate into all sorts of fun and mischief. Kate was a joyous child, with a round face, yellow curls and blue eyes – a real Cornwell; she was never in the least shy, for everyone loved her, and she loved everyone. But she was timid in some ways, would never sleep alone, and hated being brought forward, or having to take the lead. She was quite ready to get into mischief, but it was always Sarah Hope who suggested it. Soon after they learned to walk they cleaned a fireplace with Kate's mother's toothbrush, and a little later they fetched water in dolls' pails and jugs, and made a nice little pond on the nursery floor! Once they had been left in charge of "Little Grandma" (Mrs Tom Hope) they escaped into the wide world of the village, in their indoor pinafores and no bonnets; they were found some distance away by some labourers who knew them, and brought home triumphantly on top of a hay cart. Of course they were both well whipped, but our Mother used to say it was well worth it; she never forgot the soft-scented comfort of that drive. Once, when they were staying with the Proctors in Salisbury Square, London, they discovered a fascinating ladder that led through a sky-light to the roof of the house; of course they went up it, and out into a glorious unknown continent of tiles and chimney pots, and sloping roofs to slide down. There was only a low parapet between them and the precipice, at the bottom of which they could see the busy street. Unfortunately (or fortunately?) for them there lived a fierce old General just opposite, who saw them, and signed for them to go in; but instead of doing so they only danced and pranked more, to his horror and alarm. So he sent his man across with his compliments, and did they know that two little girls in white frocks were playing on his roof? Another time they wandered out alone in the streets of London, and were lost for quite a long time, and at last they were found in St Paul's Churchyard. They did a dreadful thing once – they nearly drowned some of Dr. Balding's children! Behind our Mother's house, The Red House, Barkway, there is a lovely old garden, and beyond that a field with a most fascinating pond in it – you will hear a good deal more about that pond bye and bye. The children had a yellow "chaise" with four wheels and a pole in front to draw it with, which was a very favourite toy of theirs. On this occasion they packed several little Baldings into this chaise, and dragged them about the garden and field, when somebody (probably Sarah) suggested the "horse" needed some water. This was a new and delightful idea, so they ran the chaise down the sloping bank into the pond, intending, of course, only to wet the wheels; but it went too far, right into the pond, and they couldn't pull it out again. They all shrieked at the top of their voices, and help came at once, but the poor babies were wet to the skin. There was an alarming cane hanging in full sight in the Red House, with which the children were often threatened; but though it was sometimes taken down and swished through the air to show its capability it was very seldom used. Our Grandmother's forcible looks and words were enough. And secretly our Grandmother delighted in this naughty pair, and loved to tell of their pranks in later years.

But things were very different for little Sarah Hope when she returned to her own home, Bygraves, at night; the children there were ruled by a rod of iron by their Great Grandmother and Aunt Hope, who had no sense of humour, and their own Mother and <u>her</u> Mother ("Little Grandma") were too gentle and subdued to interfere. Even in the case of medicine there was a marked difference; if little Kate Cornwell required a powder one was made up in a nice little cake by the cook, and Kate ate it without knowing. But the little Hopes were forced to take quantities of gritty Gregory powder or salts or senna tea. Their tender and pitiful mother did her best to help them to bear it; she gave them a little teapot and cups ornamented with senna leaves to drink the senna tea out of, and if they took it bravely she let them turn over a certain drawer in which she kept her special treasures, and which always went by the name of the "Salts and senna drawer" in consequence. That chest of drawers is now in my bedroom, and I keep <u>my</u> treasures in the "Salts and senna" drawer.

Esther, the eldest of the four Hope girls, had an easier time than her sisters; all her elder brothers and sisters had died, and she was three years old when Sarah was born – she always considered herself immensely older, and quite one of the grown-ups. She was a pretty child, the only one to inherit her Mother's wonderful white complexion, but she had dark hair as a girl, instead of her Mother's ripe-corn colour. I can only remember her as an old lady with snow-white hair; she was then a striking figure wherever she went, tall and handsome and commanding, always dressed in voluminous widow's mourning. In appearance she must have been very much like her strong masterful Great-grandmother, Sarah Stallibrass, but she lacked the depth and strength and warm-heartedness that underlay her ancestress's apparent fierceness. When she was very small she was a terrible chatterbox; our Grandmother once offered to give her 6d. if she would keep silent for half an hour, and though she earned that 6d., she confessed in her old age what hard work it had been. She never got into the big adventurous scrapes that Sarah and Kate did, but she was a naughty little thing. Once she was left alone in our Grandmother's dining room, and finding some sweet biscuits and a pestle and mortar, she amused herself by pounding the biscuits to powder! When Esther was about six years old our Grandmother gave a baby party for her little Kate and her toddler friends; there was a tiny Ashford from Anstey Hall, and little Annie White from Newsells, a little Hale Wortham from Royston, Esther and Sarah Hope, and several other wee children, each brought by a nurse who stood behind its chair and waited on it. Kate's nurse was Mary Harrod. Suddenly six-year-old Esther burst into tears – "They all have maids but me!" she said. Those three or four years always seemed to lift her away from the other children; all her tastes were different from theirs, and she preferred toddling about with the grown-ups, chattering all the time, to joining in childish games. She was nicknamed "My Lady Knocklofty" by the others. I have already told you a good deal about her sister Sarah, our Mother's devoted "twin", and I shall have plenty more to say about her. She was about three years younger than Esther, clever, keen and quick-witted, full of droll humour and merry mischief.

About two years after Sarah came a weird little changeling girl named Ellen. Nowadays doctors would say that she suffered from arrested development, and perhaps special treatment might have improved her. To look at she was a beautiful normal child, and in many ways she was uncannily clever, yet she could not do regular lessons, and never learnt to read or write. Her memory was so wonderful that she appeared to remember every word of any book she liked, and would pretend to read it aloud to herself, turning each page at the right word; she would often repeat things she had overheard long before, to the great discomfort of her hearers. She always called the other children "Miss Esther", "Miss Sarah" etc., and would follow them about, peeping and listening, but not joining in anything they did. She loved to frighten them – "Miss Kate, there's a man under your bed!" or "There's a gipsy hiding in that bush!", and the little girls would run for their lives.

Another creepy thing about Ellen was that she did not seem to feel pain; once, when she was leaning out of a window to watch people in the street her elders shut it, lest she should fall out, and she put her head right through the glass, cutting her face and neck badly. She was only much amused at this, and tore off the strappings and bandages, so that her arms had to be strapped to her sides until the wounds had healed. She would eat spoons full of mustard, and other uncanny things to amuse those around her. And yet, as a child, there was no sign of mental trouble in her lovely little pathetic face; she had great appealing eyes and pretty manners – to strangers she was the most attractive of the four girls. But as poor little Ellen grew her infirmity grew too; fits came on, and in one of them she fell into the fire, and was burnt to death, before she was fourteen.

Esther was about eight, and Kate and Sarah about five years old, when they were told they had another baby-sister, and they received the news with the greatest indignation. They asked Nurse Stott what she meant by doing such a thing, when they told her they wanted a brother. "We don't want any more girls!" they said contemptuouly. "Hoighty-toighty!" said the little old woman, "do you think I have time to turn over all the boxes in my loft to choose a boy-baby for you? I just took the first box that came, and you must put up with it. Now you run off and do your tarkses, and don't stub little Miss Emma." And that was the tragedy of poor little Emma's childhood – nobody wanted her in all the wide world. Her Mother cried when she found she was coming; her two Grandmothers and Aunt Hope objected strongly to another brat in the house. Esther absolutely disliked dolls and babies, and Sarah and Kate were too wrapped up in their own doings and each other that they hardly noticed other folk. Emma was a plain, shy, awkward child, with yellow hair, eyebrows and eyelashes – "like a little yellow gosling" they said. Strangers who heard that one of the Hope children was not normal naturally thought that Emma was the one and even her own family looked upon her as stupid almost to idiocy. Emma was always kept with Ellen, and had to share a bed with her at night, though Emma's sensitive mind soon realised the uncanniness of her bedfellow; this became a nervous horror as she grew older, all the worse because she thought herself wicked and cruel to feel so towards her afflicted sister. For Emma was really a clever, highly sensitive child, full of poetry and imagination, with a great warm heart that loved intensely and longed for love in return. Often she has told me of her sad lonely childhood, and the books and dreams and dolls with which she tried to console herself. No one was actively unkind to her except her Aunt Hope, who was absolutely brutal, even bruising her face with her blows, at times, and never saying a kind word to her. "And yet I was not a naughty child" she would say when she was an old lady. "I was far too frightened to be naughty!" Her terror made her dumb, perhaps, for she was not stupid – she could read at three years old! Her father was kind, and used to buy her quantities of books when he came from London – we have many of them now, quaint little old toy-books. Emma found great comfort in her dolls, and she collected and mothered the neglected ones of her sisters; she treated them all like real babies, and loved them passionately. But her greatest adoration was for her sister Sarah, who, alas, "just put up with Emma", but never admitted her into the secret friendship that bound Sarah and Kate.

Perhaps the greatest romance of her life was Emma's devotion to Mr Jackson. As I have said, he was a very tall man, and a very busy one, but he had two hobbies – gardening and little girls! During the week he was very busy with his pupils, mapping out the country for miles round, measuring and planning for the railway that was coming; but on Sunday morning he used to meet the Hope and Cornwell family after the morning Service, and take them round his beautiful gardens. No doubt the elder children would fly off, running and dancing among the winding paths and flowers, while the grown-ups followed in groups, discussing the latest improvements and gossip. But between the tall gentleman and the tiny "yellow gosling" there was a deep understanding and silent friendship, that made the one real joy of her life.

As they came out of the Church door his big hand would be stretched out, and her tiny one slipped into it; wherever they wandered, and whoever he talked to, she never left his side till the walk was over. She has told me he seldom spoke to her, but he looked at her with kind pitiful eyes – words were unnecessary. Sometimes when he sat down he would lift her on to his knee, and she would lie back in his arms in a bliss almost too great to bear. Neither he nor anyone else had the least idea how starving for love and sympathy the poor little thing was; the tragedy was that she could not express her misery, and only appeared to be a stupid and unattractive child. It was not till Ellen became much worse and had to be sent to a doctor's establishment for treatment, that Emma gradually emerged, and became more on an equality with the other children. Many years after, when Kate had married and gone, Sarah and Emma became the most devoted of sisters, inseparable friends and fellow workers.

In 1835 old Mrs John Stallibrass – our Great-Aunt Sarah, and the Hopes' "Big Grandma" – died at Bygraves; all the family stood round the big four-post bed and watched her die, including little Esther, who was about nine years old, and who could recall the whole scene vividly when she was herself over eighty. Perhaps the horror was increased by the fact that "Big Grandma" had been full of sense and vigour, mistress and manager of them all, to the very last. According to the promise made to her when she had left Ash Grove her body was at once taken back there, and remained in her old home until the funeral. Apparently all her family, including even the six-year-old Sarah and Kate, accompanied her on this touching home-coming, for they have described it to me again and again. It was a brilliant moonlight night, and they all followed her silently down the village street, and under the ash trees and roses that her husband had planted, and left her resting awhile in her loved Ash Grove; a few days later there was a very grand funeral from there to the family vault in the Churchyard.

Nurse Stott

Among those who followed in both these processions was Nurse Stott, in her red cloak – a noticeable figure in all village affairs. She was the nearest approach to a trained nurse that the neighbourhood possessed in those days, and she presided at all the births and deaths of the "aristocracy". She was a little dried up bit of a woman, always dressed in the fashion of a by-gone generation, with a big white cap and a kerchief indoors, and a huge black bonnet and red cloak when she went out. She was supposed to have occult powers, too, and the children and cottagers were horribly afraid of offending her. We have a very curious old snuff box, with divisions for different kinds of snuff, which she gave to one of the children as a keepsake.

Ash Grove Again

Soon after old Mrs Stallibrass's death the tenants of Ash Grove left, so the Hopes joyfully left Bygraves and took possession of what to them was the dearest place in the world. Money matters were easier, too, for they inherited what would have been little Harry's legacy, if he had lived. If it had not been for Aunt Hope – perhaps more bitter than ever because <u>their</u> money had come back and her's had not – it might have been a very happy household. But even then there was the tragedy of Ellen, and poor little Emma, unnoticed by all.

Among our many old papers we have the inventories of the furniture etc. in the houses of old John Stallibrass and his son (Ash Grove and Standon Rectory) taken after their deaths. Among the things mentioned we can recognise a good many things that we ourselves own now – the grandfather clock, the copper warming pans and pots, the beautiful old mahogany wardrobe, linen sheets still marked "J.S.S." etc, but we were at first perplexed to miss in the list so many things which we knew had been in Ash Grove. Afterwards we remembered that these were the private property of Great-Aunt Sarah Stallibrass, inherited from her parents the Bretts, and so they were not mentioned among her husband's possessions. Old Great-Aunt Sarah had been particularly devoted to little Sarah Hope, her great grand-daughter and namesake, and the most like her in character. She had wished to leave Sarah the greatest part of her money, but as that was impossible she gave her a quaint old memorial ring, that she herself always had worn – it had been given her by an old friend in Hitchen. There is a death's head and crossbones on it and the name and date. When Sarah grew up she always wore this ring and we have it now in our cabinet.

Although Esther and Sarah could plainly remember the uncomfortable life at Bygraves, Emma was too young to do so; her earliest recollections were of Ash Grove.

The Jackson House, Barkway

In 1836 there was great excitement in Barkway and the whole neighbourhood, for Mrs William Cornwell – our Mother's Mother – at last accepted Mr Jackson, who had been courting her a long time, and they were married. She was genuinely attached to him, and he was passionately in love with her, but one can understand why she hesitated to exchange the solid quiet comfort of the Red House for the rackity life of the "Jackson House", as it was called then.

I have already described this long grey house, probably part of an old Inn long ago, standing close to the village street, with a garden behind which covered a great many acres. There were fourteen bedrooms and many sitting rooms, and underneath were enormous cellars, like dungeons, that had belonged to the old coaching inn. A narrow garden, with lawns and a fountain, divided it from the village street. It was in those days a homely, comfortable, quaint old house, half covered in creepers; the front door (in the middle) always open in the summer, straight into the square wainscoted hall. Since then a new red brick front has been added, and a grand entrance made at one side.The whole house is so altered that only a few rooms on the garden side, and the cellars, remain as they were in the Jackson days. My mother used to weep about it!

But in 1836 it was a most attractive old house, and the home of a most attractive man. Tall, handsome, clever, humourous, full of vigour, and the most hospitable man in the world; he used to call his house "Liberty Hall", and he liked it full of guests, with music every evening, and often impromptu dances. Although he was making large sums of money it was spent as fast as it came, with no thought of the future. Our Grandmother knew it would be impossible for her to alter this state of things, and that it would require the utmost tact and discretion even to restrain them a little, for with all his kindnesses Mr Jackson was a very determined man, and could at times burst into furious anger.

There were, besides, his pupils to consider; there were always a few living in the house, who paid quite large sums to be taught this important work of planning railways, and really did a great deal of the work, measuring and calculating, and making the enormous maps that were necessary.

Although he was very particular about the young men he admitted to his home – for he had any number of applicants – one can imagine that they required a firm hand over them. So it showed great affection and bravery on the part of our Grandmother to leave her own charming and peaceful home at the Red House, and take up what she knew would be such a different life.

Three of Mr Jackson's daughters were already married, and the fourth one engaged. They had lost their own mother early, and their father had petted and spoilt them (as he did all little girls!) so they were just what one would expect in such a home, big and gushing and merry, always dressed in the latest fashion and "in" everything that was going on. The timid little Hope girls had always been afraid of the Miss Jacksons; they have told me how they would run away and hide if they saw these ladies arriving, or met them in full sail coming down the village street. Yet they were really warm hearted and wanted to be kind to the children; they gave Esther a wax doll (a rarity in those days) which they had dressed themselves. It had a green silk pelisse lined with rose-colour, and a little embroidered handbag to carry its handkerchief which was trimmed with real Valenciennes lace! It had several other costumes and changes of linen, and Mrs Hope bought Esther a lovely little mahogany chest of drawers to keep its clothes in – we have that tiny chest still. But the ungrateful children would not love the doll or the givers, and it was passed on to Emma, who adored it and tended it till she accidentally poked its eyes out one day, and grieved herself into an illness. There was a grand funeral, however, which the elder children enjoyed mightily, and the Jackson doll was buried among the bushes in Ash Grove.

But, as I have said, three of these alarming Miss Jacksons had been kindly removed by husbands before our Grandmother Sarah Cornwell married their father, and one can imagine the intense excitement of all the little girls when they realised that <u>that</u> garden, that Paradise, was to be theirs in future, their every-day playground, instead of having too-short visits to it now and then. Also that the kindly giant who owned it, who so petted and spoilt little girls, was to be their own tame giant for <u>always</u>!

Before we leave the Red House, however, there are two more memories to note down; there is an old rusty gate in the railings opposite, never now used, but it used to lead from the village street into a corner of the Jackson garden. An old inhabitant once pointed this out to me, and said – "Mr Jackson had that made, when he was courting Mrs Cornwell!"

And the other a surprising sight that Grandmother Sarah once saw from a window at the Red House. The village pump was nearby, and as Dr. Balding was passing it a village woman picked up a pail of water and emptied it over him! It seemed he had caused great annoyance in the neighbourhood by some sanitary improvements he had insisted on, and he probably made some unwise remark as he passed this angry woman.

So the Red House was let furnished, and as it had good careful tenants there was a pleasant addition to the comfortable income already enjoyed by our Grandmother and her little girl. Some of the more precious of its contents were taken across the road to her new home, the things Grandmother Sarah had inherited from her own Grandmother, the wonderful old Chinese cabinet (alas!), the white Ming figures, the six old chairs etc. These stood in the fine old wainscotted hall in the centre of the house – the centre, too, of that large busy household. There was a billiard table in the hall, and in the winter there was always a huge fire in the big old fireplace, and plenty of cosy chairs around it.

The staircase, and curtains that could be drawn across, divided it from the "kitchen hall", stone flagged and almost equally large, into which the kitchens opened; and there was a wide door into the garden, so that in the summer one could see the brilliant flower-beds and trees beyond the two halls, as one stood at the front door.

We can picture the constant movement of life in that old hall, for it was the general meeting place for everybody, summer and winter; the men came in with their guns and fishing rods and dogs, the ladies with their work or flowers, friends looked in for a gossip in passing, or to discuss business. In the evening they often sang their glees and part songs here, or hunting songs with a good rousing chorus, and all the servants would stand in the kitchen hall, listening and enjoying. How delighted Mr Jackson must have been when little Kate's dancing footsteps and pretty voice became part of the family echoes of that old hall! For of all his little girl friends Kate and Sarah were his best-beloved, and of course if he had one of these he had both!

I want you to remember that for many years there stood in this dear hall our old white Ming Chinaman and the quaint Pekinese puppy with his ribbon and ball; they watched and smiled from the top of their cabinet, as they had watched and smiled a hundred years before on little Kate's Quaker ancestress, and as they do now on her descendants.

Kate and her cousins lost no time before exploring their new kingdom, and soon knew every hole and corner, from the attic to the terrifying cellars underground. Among other surprises Kate and Sarah discovered a huge water-tank at the top of the house, into which a man servant laboriously pumped a supply every morning. This was a great discovery, and the little girls at once undressed and got into it. They had such glorious fun, and sent such showers of water through the ceiling below, that our grandmother thought there must be a leak in the tank, and rushed upstairs to see. Then she crept silently downstairs again, and fetched Mr Jackson, and together they watched the naughty water-babies romping and splashing and dancing in the water, themselves quite hidden. Of course, being a "grown-up", Mother's Mother had to pretend to be very shocked and severe at the mischief these children were always getting into, but she loved them and their pranks. As for Mr Jackson, he never scolded or even found fault with a child, and could not bear to see them scolded by anyone else.

Partly because of this, and the large exciting household at her new home, but also because little Kate was losing her own personality and becoming only Sarah's second self, our Grandmother decided to send her little daughter as a weekly boarder to a Miss Chalklin, who kept a "High Class Academy for Young Ladies" in Royston. Until now – since she was quite tiny – she and all the other little lady-girls in the village had been taught at a small private school a few doors from the Red House; they were brought there every morning by their nurses, some of them in hand-drawn "chaises", and Annie White on her donkey. The teaching there must have been very good as every child was expected to read well at four years old – some did even earlier; also they did wonderful needlework there. The earliest letter of our Mother that we have is undated, unfortunately, but she used to say that she was not five years old when she wrote it. It is on a torn bit of paper, and she wrote it sitting on the floor by her Mother in the Red House –

Kate's first letter

My dear Mamma
I should like if the
horse can and you
will I would like to
go out for a rid
I am yours affectonat.
C.S.C.

It was for no fault in this excellent and happy little school that Kate was taken away from it, and sent to a boarding school. But Grandmother Sarah was a wise and far-seeing Mother. In spite of all their sweetness the Hopes were always inclined to "keep to themselves", and to despise those who did not think as they did. Kate was gradually becoming Sarah's private property, and hardly dared speak to any other little girl; though Kate was naturally a merry, sociable little soul, with opinions of her own when they were allowed to develop. There must have been consternation among the children, when Kate was torn away from them, and carried weeping to a new life among strangers; it must have seemed sheer cruelty. But it was really far worse for Sarah, robbed of her only friend, and left in her uncongenial home. Kate soon became quite happy, and a great favourite with her school-mates. The "exile" did not amount to much, as she spent every weekend at home, and her Mother drove into Royston nearly every day, shopping or visiting, and constantly called to see her.

Here is a "holiday letter" she wrote from there – most beautifully written –

A Holiday Letter

My dear Mamma,

It is with the greatest pleasure I write to tell you our Holidays will commence on Thursday June the 16th, and I hope you will find me improved and a good girl. Be so kind as to give my love to all at home.

I remain, dear Mamma,
Yours affectionate child
C.S.Cornwell.

There is, of course, no envelope; the big sheet of paper is carefully folded and sealed, and "Mrs Jackson" (no address) written on the outside. The letter was either sent by hand, or proudly brought to her Mother by the little writer.

There is another letter from little Kate, written later in the same year; apparently she, Esther and Sarah are on a visit somewhere together – most likely they are with the Proctors again, in Salisbury Square. This letter is entirely her own doing, without supervision, and it is very different from the prim and proper one just copied. Even the pencil lines are of different spaces, and the writing very unequal.

Nov. 16th 1836

My dear Mamma,

I have no doubt you will be glad to hear that I am quite well and very happy. We went for a long walk yesterday and were very tired. Mrs Dixon has brought home my new cloak today. How is the young lady who was ill? Sarah me and Esther send our love to all.

I am your affectionate Daughter
C.S.Cornwell

Quite a good letter for a child of eight!

Kate was at Miss Chalklin's school for about two and a half years; bright happy years, with all the interests of school life in busy little Royston town, and yet hardly separated from her Mother and cousins and her own delightful home.

The Hopes leave Barkway

Then came another great change and upheavel. Mr Hope found good permanent work in London, instead of going backwards and forwards between England and Portugal, so it was decided that they should leave Barkway and that they should live at Tottenham, nearer his work. So after only a few years residence in the pretty home they had inherited from their Grandfather (and that was so full of memories of him) they had to leave it. Esther and Emma had been born there, while "Big Grandma" still lived there; Ellen and Sarah had been born at Bygraves, but to all of them, to the end of their lives, Ash Grove was "beloved over all".

Until this move Kate and Sarah had met so constantly that the Royston school had made little difference in their friendship beyond giving Kate a wider outlook and more independence; she no longer yielded entirely to Sarah as she had done. But with Ash Grove inhabited by strange tenants, and the Hopes far away, Kate was a very lonely little girl on weekends and holidays in that big house and garden. She had never been very intimate with the other Barkway children, though she and Annie White became great friends in later years.

Then our Grandmother thought of a way in which the children might be together again, and also substantial help might be given to the Hopes, with whom money was always scarce in those days. It was decided that Kate should leave her Royston school, and live with the Hopes at Tottenham Green, and that Miss Hope should educate all the little girls. As I have already said, she was an unusually clever and cultivated woman, who had travelled abroad and read in several languages. If her brother had not speculated with her nice private income, and lost it, so that she was dependent on him without a penny of her own, she would probably have been a delightful Aunt and friend; but the daily and hourly irritation of her present life had ruined her temper. She was elegant and interesting, and deeply to be pitied; being reserved and silent she appeared to bear her troubles bravely. Probably even our Grandmother had no idea how extremely severe Miss Hope was with her little nieces – even really cruel to poor little awkward, dumb Emma. She had never treated Kate with undue hardness, or that spoilt young person would have complained to her mother. So it was arranged that Kate would board with her cousins at Tottenham Green, a substantial sum being paid to Mrs Hope for that, and also liberal payment to Miss Hope for her tuition. Every time Kate came to Barkway one or more of the Hope girls was to come too – and these home-comigs were very frequent.

It was always said that wherever Kate went to school her Mother went too, and of course this house at Tottenham had very special attractions for her; her little daughter and her beloved friend Mary Anne Hope, no less loved then than in her girlhood. It is curious how these two Mothers shared their children – outsiders could scarcely tell which belonged to which! The coach from Barkway to Tottenham constantly brought our Grandmother for the day or to spend a night or two; they thought nothing of the drive in those days. And I must add that our Grandmother would not allow Mr Jackson to pay one penny of her daughter's education or clothing, though he wished to do so, and loaded her with presents, being one of the most generous of men.

Whether they loved their governess or not, she was an excellent instructress and disciplinarian, and the girls had an unusually good education for those days. As they grew older other masters and mistresses came, to give them lessons in music, singing, dancing and deportment.

Tottenham Green

Though not so beloved as Barkway, Tottenham Green was a very pleasant memory in after years to our Mother and her cousins. It was then a pretty little country place, with a few nice houses round a village green, and a sprinkling of cottages in the lanes. There were two quite large houses. A Chapel of Ease had been built there, but our party always walked to the Parish Church, except in very bad weather; they had to go through six fields, with wild roses growing in the hedges.

Most of their friends and neighbours there were Quakers – it was a regular Quaker Colony; gentle kind peaceable folk. One Quaker gentleman, a near neighbour, turned teetotaler while they were there; he brought up quantities of bottles of wine from his cellar, and emptied them onto the village green! There was an elderly Quaker lady named Elizabeth Webster, who was very fond of children and often asked them to her house; she was always dressed in grey, and never addressed people as "Mr" or "Mrs", but by plain Christian names and surnames. The children had to say "I thank thee, Elizabeth Webster". They did not much enjoy going there as there was nothing to do but to look at very proper picture-books or walk primly round her garden. The latter was very neat, with narrow paths; on one occasion little Kate was suspected of having touched the flowers, and after that a maid was always sent to <u>carry</u> her round the garden! You can imaging Kate's indignation! It was at Tottenham they met Cornelius Surgey, such a good friend and benefactor to us in later years. And this life-long friendship with the Walducks (Quakers) began then.

Here is a copy of a letter from Sarah to our Grandmother, unfortunately not dated.

Tottenham, Nov.27th

My dear Mrs Jackson,

> *I am very much obliged to you for the pocket book you were so kind as to send me and Grandmamma has found out a great many of the Enigmas. Kate went to London this morning with Papa, and we shall miss her very much. Esther is going to write to you and*

> > *I am*
> > > *Yours truly*
> > > *Sarah Hope*

It is carefully written between double pencilled lines, folded and sealed, and addressed to "Mrs Jackson, Barkway", but sent by hand, not through the post. Probably Kate was going to the Proctors or some of her other friends for a few days.

Here is a note from Esther to her mother which gives a glimpse of the child. Someone has carefully ruled the paper with narrow lines to write in and wide spaces between, but Esther had written on the <u>wide</u> spaces, huge letters, with no room for the "tops and tails" between! There is no date or address.

My dear Mama,

> *Would you be so good as to ask Master Erdale and Miss Erdale to tea on Monday and pray do not forget Master Heath and I am your affectionate daughter Esther Hope.*

It is folded and addressed to "Mrs Hope Tottenham". One could not imagine Kate or Sarah writing such a letter, though they were three years younger; Esther was prettier and more graceful, but she had not half the brains of the other two.

It seems strange to us that they called each other's Mothers "Mrs Jackson" and "Mrs Hope" instead of "Auntie", as they would certainly do nowadays; in those days wives seldom addressed their husbands by their Christian names, and children at school called each other "Master" or "Miss" so-and-so. Our Mother did not even call her beloved stepfather "Papa" except on very rare occasions; he was always "Mr Jackson" to her and her cousins.

The following letter was written a little later when our Mother was eleven years old; it was sent by hand, addressed to "Mrs Jackson, Barkway".

Nov.13th 1839. Tottenham Green.

My dear Mamma,

I have learnt the Nightingale Quadrilles and when I have learnt Giddons March I am to have a new song. I am much obliged to you for the cake, which was very nice. I like my new frock very much and it fits beautifully, except for being a little too short, which can easily be altered by letting down the hem. I have sent a comb which I suppose is your's as Esther and Sarah say it is not their's.

On the 5th of November Master Ward had a large bonfire and plenty of fireworks in his garden and the boys had another on the Green they both burnt with great brilliance for several hours and the next morning the one on the Green was still burning. Miss Hope says she should be very sorry for me to leave Tottenham so soon as the first week in December, as Miss Baird is just come I have no time to write more and now dear Mamma believe me

Your affectionate child

Catherine Sarah Cornwell.

We have also a silly Valentine that came to Kate that year from the children's "Bête noir", Mr Household – the one person disliked and dreaded at Barkway. This gentleman had been accepted and married by one of the Miss Jacksons when she was in a state of "temporary insanity" caused by her being jilted by another man; what she had done in haste she was repenting at leisure. He was a singularly unattractive man. A gun accident had destroyed one of his eyes and greatly disfigured his face, so he always wore enormous black spectacles to hide as much as possible. He had an impish love of teasing and mocking and playing practical jokes, and seemed to enjoy making children cry and men swear. No one was safe except the few he was afraid of, and those included Mr Jackson and our Grandmother, who always spoke of him as "That fool, Household". Not only were the children terrified of his ugly face, but he would snatch their work or their treasures out of their hands and carry them off; would jerk their arms if they were writing, give them sweets filled with cayenne pepper, etc. Once when he discovered the children in the apple-room (probably unlawfully!), which was a separate building in the garden, he locked them in and went for a drive with the key in his pocket; the poor little prisoners never forgot the long hours of dark dreariness, before their anxious elders found them. Mr Household delighted in ringing strange people's bells, in putting cobbler's wax on saddles so that the riders stuck fast; chaffing young girls and men about each other until they were overcome with blushes and confusion, and countless other disagreeable tricks. He rang up the Doctor in the middle of the night and told him to take his chimneys in – they were getting wet. He used to terrify Sarah Hope by swearing he would marry her by and by – she would be big enough by the time he needed a No.2; and the more she cried and implored him not to the better pleased he was. Yet he did really love his wife tenderly and was very good to her, in spite of the fact that she not only disliked him but liked too well somebody else! This was one of her father's pupils, a handsome, clever, artistic young man, only slightly younger than herself. We have a beautiful little pencil sketch he made of Esther when she was a little girl, signed with his name. He was rather too sympathetic with the unhappy young wife, and the children caught him kissing her in an arbour one day. I am sorry I cannot tell you the end of this episode – the children heard no more about it. Probably, having heard of this affectionate scene from the little girls the elders took fright, and the charming pupil would be asked to finish his studies elsewhere. Mr Jackson and our Grandmother were most particular about morality, in spite of all their gaiety and Bohemian ways.

I don't know why Mr Household sent this Valentine (his own composition) to Kate, nor how it came to be kept, but there it is now!

Clapton

I do not know when the Hopes left their pretty house on Tottenham Green, nor why they did so; probably Mr Hope found it more convenient to be nearer his work, in those days before trams, tubes or bicycles. The girls never had the same love for the tall town-house at Clapton that they had felt for their former homes; but they soon had a circle of nice friends, and they were taken to London to see and hear everything of note.

It was a very different London then from the one we know. Gentlemen had to carry sword sticks, and it was not safe for ladies to be out alone in quiet streets or suburbs, for footpads were constantly robbing or even murdering solitary pedestrians. We still have the beautiful swordstick that Mr Hope always used. A girl friend of the Hopes wished to speak to another friend, a few doors off, just at dusk one evening; she ran gaily up the street – but was never seen or heard of again. Though there were houses on each side of the street they were surrounded by high walls, and the entrance doors were kept locked. Besides this, every house was strongly fortified with shutters, chains, alarm bells etc., and they were searched all over every night for possible burglars. This terror never left our Mother or her cousins (and probably others of that date) but to the end of their lives the nightly searches and precautions were kept up. Little Kate thought that the long-expected "man under the bed" had really got her by the ankle one night, and her shrieks rang through the house, but it was only a wicker chair which had entrapped her foot! Another night the little girls rushed shrieking down the stairs, saying there was a man dying in the bedroom cupboard! But this, too, proved a needless alarm; it was only a next door neighbour trying to learn to play a cornet or some other brass instrument.

The Four Girls, 1839–44

Kate

Although there was a strong family likeness between our mother and her cousins she was an utterly different child in most ways. She was a little merry dancing fairy, with long yellow curls which were never tied back; they were just parted in the middle and allowed to fall free, framing her jolly little face – so round in those days that they used to call her "Princess Badroubadour", which means "Moon-face". She had none of the reserve and aloofness of the Hope children, but loved all her fellow creatures and welcomed all new-comers with her ready smile as she did always to the end of her life. She was so used to being loved and petted that she was quite un-self-conscious, and was always ready to play or sing if asked, or do anything else to give pleasure. She was a little thing, with very small bones and exquisite wrists and ankles; so light that in after years her sons loved to pick her up and carry her about! Her only fear was "the man under the bed", and she never would sleep in a bedroom alone; if she had not a cousin with her a maid slept in a second bed in her room.

The characters of the Hope girls were warped by the constant nagging and scolding of their Aunt, Miss Hope; in their infancy they had also their stern strong-minded Great-grandmother (Mrs John Stallibrass), who would not allow any nonsense. No doubt the other two grown-ups, their Grandmother and Mother, though gentle and loving, would fuss and fidget the children too; they were never free from supervision except when they went back to Barkway with Kate. For fear of becoming conceited the little girls were made to believe they were unusually plain and awkward; so much so that they dreaded to be seen by outsiders.

It also produced a sort of allied defiance against everyone else, whom they quizzed unmercifully. How little did the grown-ups who patronised these prim shy little girls guess that they were making notes of any peculiarities of dress or speech or manners, to be reproduced, and nicknames given, later on! Many years later, when second childhood was growing on Esther – a tall handsome old lady with snow white hair – this bad habit appeared again, and she would make most embarrassing remarks about our fellow passengers in omnibuses, or visitors; quite audible, unfortunately! Yet she and her sisters were, all their lives, the most faithful and devoted friends to the few they admitted to their inmost circle, and the kindest of neighbours to anyone in trouble.

Esther

They were not really plain at all – at least, only poor little Emma; they were daintily made, and held themselves well, and were healthy and vigorous.They were unusually clever and well taught for girls of that date, for Miss Hope was a splendid teacher, and they had the best Masters and Mistresses for accomplishments. Esther grew fast, and had the striking pink and white complexion of her Mother; it never tanned or freckled, but seemed to make everyone else look sallow. But Esther had none of the soft-appealing gentleness that made her Mother so attractive. She was inclined to be hard and domineering to her younger sisters and Kate, and resented Sarah's devotion to Kate.

Sarah

Sarah was much quicker-witted than Esther, and although not so handsome, she had a delightfully shrewd, humorous little face, with a quaint little quizzical twist to her mouth at times. Being Kate's inseparable companion she was less enthralled by her Aunt, and the constant visits to Barkway

"Liberty Hall" made her less shy than Esther and Emma. Of course I only remember her in her latter years, but I can quite imagine what she was as a young girl; a clever, witty, delightful companion, full of life and energy – but rather narrow in her outlook, and jealous of her few beloved intimates. She sang and played well, and had a great talent for painting; she always had a pencil in her hand, and sketched everything and everybody (often caricatures).

Emma

Emma was the plainest, though there was nothing repulsive about her; just small and colourless, awkward from shyness, and very quiet. But she was full of poetry and romance, and not only read everything she could, but remembered all she read. Both she and Sarah could read and talk in German and French almost as well as they could in English. Emma had a sweet, dreamy, humble nature, that was properly appreciated as they all grew out of childhood; it was an immense gain for her when she was released from the constant companionship of her afflicted sister Ellen. It was while they were at Tottenham Green that Ellen was placed with a mental doctor instead of living at home, and only a year or two later that she had her fatal accident.

The Four

So, in their young girlhood, Sarah was the daring leader in all that these four did or thought; with Kate following close behind light-heartedly; Esther protesting and disapproving, but following too in the end; while poor little Emma, never consulted but deeply interested, quietly did what the others did – and in any mischief she was probably the one detected and punished!

Holiday Time at Barkway

I suppose there were regular holidays of allotted length and season for these children, but from the way they afterwards dwelt on the joys of Barkway, and hardly alluded to the lesson times, it seemed to us that it was always holiday time in those days. How often our Mother – "little Kate" – has lamented that we, her children, could not have been there too, and we echoed her sighs. And when dear Aunt Sarah was dying, and we gave her oxygen, she smilingly whispered – "Like Barkway air!" All these dear people pictured the Paradise beyond the grave just like the Paradise of their childhood.

Lucky Sarah always accompanied Kate home, and sometimes one or both of the others came too; what bitter tears and envy for those who were left behind! But how glorious for the happy little home-goers, when the coach started off with a clatter of hoofs and wheels and horn, for the long drive along the fine old Norman road, through towns and villages, open country and woods, nearer and nearer, and then up and up into the keen fresh air of the hill-village. With hardly time to return the smiles of the familiar faces they passed the coach would stop at their own gate, and the stiff, tired little girls be lifted down by loving arms. What an ideal homecoming that was! If it were Christmas time an enormous fire would be burning on the wide hearth of the old oak-panelled hall – which never went out, night or day – and holly and misteltoe made the house a bower. If it were summer, all the doors and windows would be wide open, and the children would rush straight through into that most exquisite of gardens. No rigid laws now, no lessons, no eagle-eyed, sharp-tongued Miss Hope, but everything that tender love and delightful surroundings could do to make them happy.

Indeed, Mr Jackson would have spoilt them dreadfully if he had been allowed, and our Grandmother had hard work to prevent him from doing so. Once he had found little Kate in disgrace because she had soiled her clean white frock; this hurt him so much that when he returned from London next time he brought with him a large parcel of white frocks. "There!" he said "Now let the child play naturally and enjoy herself without having to think about her clothes!" So Kate could have several clean white frocks a day if necessary. Happily the washing of them did not matter much, as there was a well equipped laundry and drying grounds in the kitchen quarters, and laundrymaids were kept; another time, when he was to be away from home several days, he asked his "little Kittie" what present he should bring back for her, and she said " a yellow silk dress, please." Sure enough, when he came back, he presented her with a dainty little frock of soft yellow silk, and insisted on her being allowed to wear it at parties. As a rule Kate was very simply dressed, but the materials were of the best, and only real lace was ever used – sometimes made by Kate or her mother. (We have a quantity of this old lace still left; all kinds, from exquisite veils, 1 yd. long to tiny scraps for neck and sleeves, and we have the "berthas" and "tippets" still.)

No real father could have been more devoted to Kate than Mr Jackson was, nor have been more loved in return. One of her happiest memories was how she would watch him playing cards in the evening (with the same skill and energy with which he did everything), she sitting perfectly still and quiet on the arm of his chair, with her curly head on his shoulder. He taught her to be an excellent player of cards, and other games, herself. But there were not quiet games every night; often the furniture would be all pushed aside for dancing, charade acting, or romps like blindman's buff. Kate and Sarah were in such sympathy that when one was playing for a long country dance the other would relieve her at the piano without the slightest hitch in the time and tune; those dancing would not notice the change. Then there were those delightful musical evenings of which I have already spoken, in which all who could joined, glees and rounds, solos and duets, following one another, grave or gay – often the singers did not even stand up, but sang as they sat about the room. Very sweetly too, for they were thoroughly musical, and so used to singing together. Of course there were plenty of sitting-rooms in this big old house, and sometimes these evening gatherings took place in the long low dining room, which opened into the garden; but their favourite gathering place in the winter was the old square hall, with its great furnace of a fire. And there, in the very heart of that home of homes, stood the old Chinese cabinet that our Grandmother, Sarah Cornwell, had brought with her when she became Mrs Jackson; and on it the white Ming figures watched and smiled at the merry crowds that came and went, the meetings and partings, the children's games, the happy evening gatherings; the old white Chinaman and the romping Pekinese smiled down on them as they had smiled on the quiet Quaker ancestors in the past, and on us, their descendants, now.

Grandmother's Sitting-room

Another room in that house needs special remembrance – our Grandmother's own private sitting-room. She must have needed a quiet corner, poor soul, where she could make her plans and think out all her worries and anxieties; what a household it must have been to keep going in peace and comfort! Mr Jackson, tender as he was with children and animals, was highly strung, irritable and passionate at times, while his calling demanded patience and exactitude, and strenuous work for mind and body. He would come home in a state of exasperation, sometimes, all his plans and calculations upset by some obstinate householder refusing to sell his property, just where the new railway line <u>must</u> run, or some careless mistake in a map made by a pupil had thrown everything wrong. And the long tramps over hill and dale, measuring and planning, must have been exhausting as he grew older. Our

Grandmother must have had a wonderful fund of sympathy and tact and patience to keep the peace between him and his pupils who lived in the house, several of whom were over-full of frolic and silliness, and gave a good deal of trouble at times.

Another terrible cause of anxiety was Mr Jackson's carelessness about money; he would live up to every penny of his income, and only her capable commonsense and management kept them out of debt. The house was always as full of guests as it could be, and he gave to everyone who asked him. Happily he had the most devoted love and admiration for our Grandmother, and she could manage him as no one could. It was his loving gratitude which made her own private sitting room so charming. This was on the ground floor, with a French window into the garden (it was taken for granted in that house that everyone wanted to step into the garden whenever possible!). But so that even on bad days she might have the birds and flowers she loved he built out a small conservatory on one side of this door, and an aviary of the same size on the other. This was an ideal birds' home, with shrubs and small trees gowing in it, and everything else birds like; there was a wire door to it, as well as a proper one she could shut if the singing and twittering disturbed her.

She had a crowd of canaries and other little singing birds, some of whom were so tame she would let them fly about her sitting room, where they would perch on her foot or the book she was reading. In the winter she would sit by her cosy fire, and not only enjoy her bright flowers in the conservatory, but watch her little birds among their trees.

Pets

All animals were loved in that household; there were always several dogs, big and little, but most of these lived outside, where there was a proper kennel-yard and dog kennels; only the pet dogs lived in the house. Then there was Mr Jackson's spoilt cat, that used to sit on his shoulder at meals, and would occasionally put out a paw and grab a morsel from his fork. Mr Jackson would only exclaim "See! See! See!" and patiently submit. In the stables were several horses for riding and driving; for some years the pair that drew the big "chaise" were greys called "Farmer" and "Betsy Baker", after an old woman she was supposed to resemble. Kate learned to ride a pony very young, cantering up and down the broad walk, and later she and Sarah rode a great deal, though they never hunted – they were nervous about going too fast, and they hated killing their fellow creatures. But of course all the men hunted, and the girls enjoyed meets (and later, hunt balls) as much as anyone. When Kate was a big girl Mr Jackson gave her a little pony carriage and pair of ponies of her own, in which she and Sarah used to drive each other about. I am sorry to say that often one would be reading aloud while the other drove – with disastrous results, sometimes!

Garden Houses

Besides the stables and kennels there were cow-sheds, piggeries, and a poultry yard, store houses for fruit and vegetables, and a fine old barn where the children used to play in bad weather; all old country houses used to have these things as a matter of course. But this garden had another attraction – an ice-well, deep and dark and mysterious, over which Mr Jackson had built a Swiss chalet, with several rooms and a verandah, where they often had tea, and sat singing on summer evenings. And not only were there arbours and summerhouses and rustic seats all over the huge garden but in one corner Mr Jackson had had an octagonal ball-room built, with a long avenue of trees leading to it on which Chinese lanterns were strung when a dance was on. Mr Jackson gave a servants' ball there the night Chapman Phypers was married. There was always a Phypers as gardener in those days, and generally two or three of them about – "Old Phypers", "Young Phypers" and "Little Phypers" – who began as soon as he could toddle to pick up sticks and weeds.

The Old Family Servants

Our Grandmother, happily, never had any servant troubles, such as are so common in these days, though servants had to work far harder, and for ridiculously small wages, then. In many places they had to rise at 4 a.m. on washing and baking days; they had to drink out of horn mugs, eat only the plainest food, sleep herded together in attics, and were spoken to as if they were an inferior creation. But I need not say that no servant was treated so in the Jackson house! And if one was lucky enough to be employed there he or she never wished to leave. Though they worked hard and were paid low wages they were treated as fellow-humans and gave good faithful work in return. There was dear old Sarah Cootes, who had saved little Kate's life when she was born; she had been our Grandmother's maid before she was married, and had followed her to both her married homes; in this busy crowded Jackson house Sarah was cook-housekeeper and our Grandmother's right hand.

Almost equal in years of service and trust-worthiness was Mary Gilby, who was, I suppose, what we should now call head House-parlourmaid, for all the rooms and linen were in her charge, and she helped to wait at table. Poor Mary had had an unfortunate love-affair. Her lover, really a most estimable young man, had somehow got mixed up in some sheep-stealing affair (some said it was a mere practical joke) and though he was said not to have done the deed, and though the Jacksons did all they could to get him off, he was transported to Botany Bay for a term of years. Our Grandmother wrote to friends out there, begging them to use their influence to help this young man, and in the end he got on so well that he settled down out there and became a well-to-do, highly respected citizen – leaving his faithful love in England to watch and wait in vain. Sarah and Mary were quite part of the family, and they worked together in perfect accord; under these younger maids came, were well-trained, and passed on to other places or homes of their own, but as long as this family remained Sarah and Mary never left them. Neither did Joseph, the footman and general factotum, with – as far as I know – only one failing; he could not help listening to what was said when he was waiting at table, and laughing at the jokes, to the rage of Mary, who waited with him, but was never seen to smile. Of course this delighted Mr Household, who would say the funniest things at dinner on purpose to upset Joseph. On one occasion this happened when Joseph was handing a vegetable dish to Mr Household, and the unfortunate footman was so tickled that he bolted out of the room with the dish, leaving the spoon in Mr Household's hand. Mary, in terrible wrath, snatched the spoon from Mr Household's hand, and rushed out after Joseph; a deep hush fell on the dinner party – all were wondering what she was doing to Joseph, and what she would do to Mr Household if she dared!

As for coachmen, there were two who took the post in turn, for unfortunately both had a weakness for drink, and were invariably turned away after a short time for drunkenness, though they were excellent in every other way. Neither would take any other place, but just worked at odd jobs till his rival committed the same fault and was dismissed. Then he would humbly plead with Mr Jackson to be taken back, full of promises of amendment. For many years this went on, and seemed to answer quite satisfactorily.

Perhaps old Camp was the one they preferred, on the whole, but both were faithful and devoted.

Maidservants were always dressed in lilac print gowns, with large plain aprons and caps tied under their chins; their wages were unbelievably small, and young girls were often paid nothing at all till they had been trained under older servants. No one would ever dream of addressing a servant's letter to "Miss –" but just her name "Sarah Cootes" etc. Poor women were never called "Mrs" in those days; they were "Neighbour" or "Widow so-and-so". Cottages were horribly crowded and insanitary, often quite unfit for habitation; and although there was beginning to be a stir about education most people mocked at it as being absolutely unnecessary for servants and labouring folk. The one thing "the gentry" liked in poor people was <u>manners</u>, deep respectful curtsies and touching of caps, to show their humility and obedience to "their betters".

Intoxication was not looked upon with the horror that we feel now, and the amount of wine and spirits drunk would seem to us impossible. The big cellars at the Jackson House were kept well-filled – everyone drank wine as a matter of course, though Mr Jackson was very strict, allowing no hard drinking in his house, and keeping a tight hand on his pupils. But in other houses it was quite common for gentlemen to be "not themselves" in the evening, and it was taken for granted that poor people would get drunk if they had the chance – they had hardly any other way of enjoying themselves then!

Barkway Church and Village

Old Phypers was Parish Clerk as well as gardener at the Jackson house; one might almost call him the Comedian who helped the unfortunate congregation to bear the long tediousness of the Sunday Services. Everybody went to Church in those days, for it was considered a deadly sin not to do so, but they did not seem to have much idea of worship. The Morning Service consisted of the whole of Matins, the Litany, the first part of the Communion Service, and a very long sermon; the hymns were a few old favourites we still use at Christmas, Easter and Ascensiontide, and Tate and Brady's Metrical Psalms. We still have the prayer-book, with these hymns bound with it, that our grandmother used.

As in everything else, the gentry made themselves as comfortable as possible in Church, while the poor were left to hard benches and draughts right at the back.

I have told you that there are two mansions, each standing in large grounds, on opposite sides of the road that leads to Barkway, Newsells and Cockenhatch. One of these, Newsells, had long before appropriated what was intended to be a Lady Chapel, and had turned it into a charming little sitting room, with armchairs and tables, and a roaring fire in the winter – the footmen used to poke it up and put coals on every now and then. Cockenhatch, not to be outdone, had taken possession of the fine old rood screen, which they had widened at the top into a nice little gallery, and had fitted up comfortably. A red curtain was hung across on the congregation side, through which Lady Louise Clinton could peep and have a fine view of the congregation – much to her satisfaction. There was another gallery at the west end of the Church, where the village band performed the music; there were four fiddles, a bassoon and a horn. So much has already been written about these old village bands that I will not describe this one; Mother used to say that it was exactly like what Thomas Hardy tells so delightfully in "Under the Greenwood Tree". The extraordinary thing is that really musical and educated people could have put up with such a state of things for many long years; one would think even as a joke it would grow stale.

There was a huge erection in the middle of the Church, pulpit, reading desk, and clerk's seat in one, and around this were nice square pews for all the gentry and well-to-do farmers; the most important folks, of course, having the biggest and most desirable sites. The Red House pew, where our Mother sat as a tiny child, was immediately under the pulpit on the South side; it had fat red cushions which covered the seats, making a perfect square, for even the door had a seat on it. This door-seat proved a real pit-fall to our Mother once, and caused a great disturbance to the congregation. She used to amuse herself by walking round and round on the seats (being so small, and the pew so high, she couldn't be seen outside) but once the door had not been properly fastened, so when she reached it it flung open and little Kate fell in a heap in the aisle! The next pew to this belonged to a well-to-do farmer named "Pigg", and as there happened to be a knot of wood out in the partition, leaving a small round hole, Kate and the little Piggs were always peeping through this at each other; sometimes there was a little blue eye one side of the hole, and a little brown one on the other, and then neither could see anything. Once a little Pigg put a fat wee finger through this hole, and with joy Kate caught it and held it tight till loud squeaks arose! Some descendants of these Piggs are now clever, well known tutors at Cambridge.

The Jacksons, of course, had a large and comfortable pew, with a thick carpet, soft cushions and stools, and a good sized table in the middle. But it must have been most trying for a number of merry young people to sit there face to face for a couple of hours, especially as the congregation seem to have taken little part in the Service. Most of the time they were listening to a duet between the Parson and the Clerk, the latter reading – all alone – the responses and the alternative verses of the Psalms, mispronouncing every word he could.

The Parish Clerk

Apparently old Phypers was never set right; either they knew it was hopeless to try, or because the occupants of the pews really enjoyed the relaxation. They would have been disappointed if old Phypers had not said "King's daughters were among the horrible women" or "he was a lion (alien) to his mother's children", or complained he was "A Perly-can in the wilderness and a howl in the dessert" (he knew the word "dessert", being a gardener). The unfortunate small boys were all gathered together in the draughtiest, dreariest part of the church, and kept in order by a stern man with a long stick; one could hear the blow of this sometimes, and the sobs that followed. I cannot think why our Grandmother deserted the Quakers, with their silent devotion and very real religion, for such Services as these. Perhaps she had found the Church of England very different in the part of London where she stayed so frequently, and she had felt the need of the sacraments. In many ways she was always a Quaker at heart.

The Vicar

When our Mother was born old Mr Peachey – the Hon. & Rev. John Peachey – was Vicar of Barkway, but later Mr Battiscombe came, whom they described as "a very gentlemanly man, with very white hands, and beautiful rings". He had also a large family of children, who used to enjoy playing "touch-last", and "hide and seek" with little Kate and her cousins among the tombstones in the churchyard. It was an ideal place for such games. But Mr Battiscombe was not just elegant; he was very keen about education, and he wished to reform Barkway. I have not heard that he altered anything in the Church or its Services, but he was shocked at the ignorance of the villagers, and insisted on building schools for them. This was quite right and praiseworthy, but alas! he considered the only place for them was the middle of the village, and he seized on the village green – the common property of the villagers, and greatly valued – and built the schools there, to the fury of the people. I need not say that the Jacksons sympathised deeply with the poor people, but Mr Battiscombe and the other landowners were too strong; the schools were built there, and remain to this day.

Barkway Fair

Not only was this village green the general meeting place for village folk, and the playground for the children, and free grazing for donkeys and geese, but the great event of the year, Barkway Fair, had been held there for centuries on July 20th. and 21st. In those days, when travelling was so difficult, and there were so few amusements, people were very thankful to have merchandise and amusements brought to their own doors; fairs were very different from what they are now. Even the travelling packmen that came at other times brought linens and silks and stuffs, and other treasures, that used to be unpacked and displayed in the halls of country houses, and eagerly bought by the ladies. We have still a polished yard-stick, with silver ends, which our Grandmother used on these occasions. So when the good old traders and gypsies came (the Shaws and Lees, the same families, generation after generation), they brought goods to suit everybody, rich and poor, and everybody came to see and to buy. Old Norman Shaw, the Patriarch of the tribe in our Mother's young days, wore 5 shilling pieces sewn on his coat for buttons; they were quite superior people, playing delightfully on their fiddles etc., and singing, respected and trusted by all. Once a baby boy was born in one of the caravans, and our Grandmother went in to see it, and sent all sorts of things for the mother and baby.

There was great excitement in the neighbourhood when the great day arrived, with its procession of wagons and caravans and merry brown show-people. Booths and stalls and shows were put up all over the village green, and swings and roundabouts, and platforms for contests and competitions. Needless to say all the élite went the first day, and had the pick of the wonderful things on the stalls, and saw the shows without being unpleasantly crowded. The nurse once stupidly let the little girls look into a peep-show that represented the horrible "Greenacre" murder; they saw a great four-post bed upholstered in green, with part of a body on it, while another part was being cut up by two men, and a leg was sticking out of a pail! They could laugh over this when they were four old ladies, but at the time it gave them an awful shock, and nightmares for many nights. When it was possible Mr Jackson himself took the children round, with his pocket full of sixpences, and then both he and they enjoyed themselves immensely. The little girls saved their pocket money for weeks beforehand; choosing fairings for all their friends they wandered from stall to stall, helped by the friendly gypsies. All the grown-ups gave each other fairings too; the beautiful, inlaid tea-caddy that we still use was given to our Grandmother from a stall in Barkway Fair by General Drummond, who was a great admirer of hers.

But when the gentry had had their amusement and made their purchases les autres came on the scene, and then the fun became fast and furious, it was the one gay time of the year for them, and they made the most of it. Our little girls were not allowed to go into the crowd then, but the baker, Burr, had a handy gate close to the village green, and the small Hopes and Kate would stand on this and watch the fun from a safe distance. People came from all the towns and villages within reach, and there were pugilistic and other contests, grinning through horse collars, dancing, and romping games. No doubt as evening came on there was a good deal of drinking, for that was considered the right and proper way of showing enjoyment, by rich and poor. The laughter and shrieks and shouts would echo across the dark fields, and the brilliant light from flaring torches and many lanterns on that hilltop could be seen for miles. But there was never anything disreputable about it, as far as I have heard; the people round about there were quiet and law-abiding, and the gypsies too, as I have said.

The End of the Village Green and Fair

But Mr Battiscombe was a newcomer, and did not realise all that this Fair meant to the people; very likely – hearing the noise from a distance – he thought they were worse than they were, and he decided to do away with the Fair ground. So when the next Fair Day came they found the Village Green being dug up, piles of building materials and scaffolding poles all round, and a strong company of constables and keepers to keep them away. One cannot be surprised to hear that a bad fight took place, in which many of the villagers joined – the building materials were found very useful! But of course in the end the poor rustics were overpowered and heavily punished, and the Schools covered the Village Green; they were conquered, but the wound was a very deep one, and perhaps the peace and friendliness of the village folk never quite returned. Nowadays probably they would have gone to law about it, for the Green was the property of the cottagers, and they had a charter for their Fair, but in those days they were just "dumb driven cattle"; they became sullen and rude, and did small bits of mischief and hindrance when they had the opportunity, and were punished once again.

Among themselves they talked and talked about it, and never forgot it; the old people used to tell me about it when I used to stay there, fifty or sixty years after it happened.

Perhaps it was on the day of this dreadful disturbance that Mr Jackson had the big round-about put up on one of his own lawns! He gave the gypsies £5, and for two or three days that merry household had a private round-about on which they all played like children, young and old! How often have our Mother and the Hopes told us about this, and how jealous we were when we were children!

The Village School Treat

I do not know if Mr Jackson instituted the Village School Treat to take the place of the Village Fair, or if he had already started it, but anyway it became the great event of every summer afterwards. I have described how the Jackson garden was laid out all round a big park-like field, and it was in this field that the Treat was held. There were no excursions or elaborate entertainments for the poor people in those days, so this seemed a much greater thing to them than it would to us, nowadays. It really gave as much pleasure to the givers as to the recipients, for the ladies began to make clothes, dress dolls, etc. weeks before, and Mr Jackson and his friends would return from London with their pockets filled with toys and sweets. When the day came everybody helped to amuse the little guests and their parents; swings and see-saws were put up, races and competitions for the elder children, and easier games for the younger ones arranged, while the parents would rest or watch, or walk round the wonderful gardens. Some of the competitions in those days were rather nasty, like biting at dangling trea-cle-puffs, or trying to catch an apple, floating in a pail of water, with one's teeth. "Bobbing for Apples" is a very ancient game, I believe. There was, of course, a very bountiful tea, all prepared by Sarah Cootes in the Jackson kitchen; if it were fine the guests all sat on the grass under the big trees, and if it were wet there was the big barn to shelter in. But in the memories of the four old ladies who used to tell me these histories it was always hot sunshine in those days, and nothing went wrong, and they were never over-tired! When, in the after-years, our school-children had to be taken on long expensive excursions, and got lost or hurt, and those in authority over them worn out with fatigue and anxiety, our Mother used to say how infinitely better things were in her young days.

How the Dickers Came to Barkway

The Red House, where little Kate had been born, was let furnished when her mother married Mr Jackson, but these tenants left when Kate was eleven or twelve, and the house was empty for a while.

Therefore our Grandmother was very glad when she heard from her lawyers that they had let the Red House to the new Curate-in-Charge of Barley, the next village, as he was unable to find a suitable house in his own parish. Nothing was known in Barkway about the new tenants, but our Grandmother had one of her very vivid dreams about them, and told it to her people in the morning. "I saw distinctly a grey-haired lady dressed in black", she said, and proceeded to describe her appearance, feeling certain they would all see her, like that, before long.

[The Killicks]

However, when the Rev. Henry Killick arrived he proved to be quite a young man, with a delicate girl-wife, utterly unlike the elderly lady of our Grandmother's vision, and she was well teased and laughed at for her false prophecy. Some time later the tables were turned, however, for Mrs Killick's mother, Mrs Dicker, came to stay with the young couple; the Jacksons saw her first in Barkway Church, and our Grandmother was so surprised that she exclaimed almost out loud – "There she is! There is the lady that I dreamed about!" The two soon made great friends – little knowing that they were to be Ancestresses of the same race. Each admired the wit and capability of the other, though in character, up-bringing and outlook they were really utterly different. Mrs Dicker was delighted that her delicate young married daughter should have such charming friends just across the road.

At that time Mr Henry Killick was a young priest full of zeal and enthusiasm; he was one of a group of English Churchmen who were horrified at the state the Church of England had fallen into, and were trying to reform it by extreme Puritanical methods. Life was too serious a thing to be wasted in foolishness and jesting; everyone ought to be constantly praying and preparing for their end. Mr Killick worked very hard among his parishioners at Barley, so our people did not see much of him, but his wife and mother-in-law were not strong enough to go so far, so they always came to Barkway Church, and became very friendly with Barkway folks. Young Mrs Killick was a very pretty and charming girl, who admired and tried to agree with her husband in everything, though some of his laws and regulations must have come hard on her. A little daughter came to the Killicks soon after they came to the Red House; she was called "Annie", and was a great delight to the little girls opposite, as well as to her own people. Our Mother made a beautiful little hood for her.

[Hamilton Dicker]

Then another inmate came to the Red House, young Hamilton, Mrs Killick's brother, who, being a delicate boy, was taken from his boarding school and sent to his brother-in-law as a pupil. And he, too, became a welcome guest at the Jackson House, and a playfellow of the little girls when they came home for the holidays – he was just the same age as our Mother. But the really intimate friendship did not begin till little Emily Dicker came for a visit, and took all hearts – or nearly all hearts! – by storm.

[Emily Dicker]

Emily Winter Dicker, even at eleven years old, had much of that radiant beauty and charm that made her quite celebrated in after years. Her figure had not yet developed; like many young Scotch girls she was too plump (her mother was a Scotchwoman), but her face was absolutely bewitching. I have told you of the soft fair beauty of Mrs Hope, who was exactly like Nelson's Mrs Hamilton in face and figure, but almost too gentle and retiring in her character. Kate and her little cousins were nice-looking, well trained, and nicely mannered children. But Emily Dicker was a brilliant brunette, a daring, lawless little gipsy, with the most wonderful eyes in the world! They were a clear golden yellow, with eyelashes like black floss silk all round them, shading them till they were as dark as a starry night. From her babyhood she was perfectly aware of her charms, and knew how to use them to advantage. I fear she was always in a state of rebellion at school and at home; her mother and four elder sisters always trying to keep her in order, and she defying and out-witting them, aided by a crowd of admiring friends. As she grew older her sisters did their best to keep her at a distance, for

Rev. Eustace Hamilton Dicker (1829–1868)

she deliberately stole all their lovers – for fun! Her grave scholarly father seldom heard of her pranks, but she was both the pride and despair of her mother.

[Hamilton Dicker]

The one person in the world she really loved, and had any influence with her was her second brother Hamilton, who was only about a year her senior, and bore a strong family likeness to her. He had the same wonderful eyes, but the face of a jolly boy; he had what was better than her physical beauty – a most beautiful character. He was born with the great gift of attracting love wherever he went, and seeing something lovable in everybody. In many ways he bore a strong resemblance to that most lovable saint, St Francis D'Assisi; he had the same joyous faith in God and man, the same forget-fulness of himself and his needs. Just as the Saint stood in the Market Place giving away his money and jewels to the crowds around him, so did our Father give away with both hands his sympathy, his talents, his influence, his time, his money, his health – yes, his very life, for he died of over-work before he was forty. One can picture him, like St Francis, walking gaily over stones and thorns, singing aloud "The Canticle to the Sun" – "Blessed be our Lord God" for everything, even pain and death; and the little birds and animals gathering round to hear him.

But when he first came to Barkway, at 12 years old, he was just a jolly boy, with two great devotions, reading and ships! At the Jackson House he found all sorts of delightful books not to be found in his own too-strict home; these included the "Pickwick Papers", just coming out in monthly parts. He loved to find a quiet place in the garden, or out of sight – behind a sofa, for instance, indoors, and there he would become absolutely absorbed in what he was reading. Our Mother's first remembrance of him, she always said, were the roars of laughter that could be heard from the small boy, hidden away. He was not too good, happily, for finding a cigar one day he smoked it, and became very sick; them seeing the pallor of his face, he painted his cheeks with vermillion! But when his sister, Louisa Killick, saw his heavy eyes and brilliant colour she sent for the doctor, fearing he was seriously ill!

[Young Hamilton's Newspaper]

While he was at Barkway Hamilton started a newspaper, which he called "The Barkway Gazette"; he asked for contributions to it, but he really did it all himself, writing it out twice a week for some time. Unfortunately we have only one of these Gazettes, No.10, but that I will copy for you. The title is elaborately printed in old letters.

The Barkway Gazette. No.X

Friday, July 21st M.D.C.C.C.XLIII

<u>Notices to Correspondents</u> *"An Advocate of Hydropathy" is asked whether he has <u>personally</u> proved its efficacy; if he has <u>not</u>, we cannot insert his letter.*
"John Bull's" communication is not worth the trouble of insertion.
"A true Angler" shall find a place in our columns.
"Fire-away" is entreated not to send us any more of his empty communications.

The Fair

For the last two or three days this town has been a scene of gaiety and bustle owing to the annual Fair on the 20th of July. We believe it will close tomorrow, Saturday July 22nd.

Hamilton Yacht Squadron

We are happy to state that two additions have been made to this distinguished club, during the last week. We give the table as it now stands:-

Names	Classes	Guns	Distinguishing Flag	Owners
Ariadne	Yawl	6	White, Red Cross, Red Border	Captain Eustace Hamilton
Sea-mew	Sloop	4	White, two red arrows crossed	Capt. E.Winter
Celeste	Cutter	0	Red	Eustace Hamilton
Mermaid	Sloop	0	Blue with yellow anchor	Capt. E.Winter
Kestrel	Sloop	0	White, Red, Blue, Red quarters	Capt. T.Dicker

Barkway Gazette

We subjoin the rules of the Hamilton Yacht Squadron

Rules and Regulations

I. Any person being the owner of one or more vessels, of above 1/2oz. tonnage, may become a member.

II. Every person wishing to become a member must send his name, place of residence, and profession to the Commodore, Capt. Eustace Hamilton, together with the name, class, tonnage etc. of his vessel or vessels.

III. Every member must choose for his vessel or vessels a distinguishing flag, different from every other in the Squadron.

IV. All the members may bring their friends to the regattas of the Squadron, on receiving a ticket from the Commodore enabling them to do so.

V. That no person shall be allowed to view the aforesaid regattas without such ticket.

The Fair!

We have much pleasure in announcing arrival of sundry pleasant and agreeable nieces of General Jackson, at the Veteran's house in this place; we trust their stay will be protracted.

The Fair

Now that this annual annoyance is over we trust that the minds of our townspeople will resume their placidity, and their hands their employments.

The Fair

- weather we are sorry to say has left, and the foul arrived. We hope for better days.

The Fare

- at this season of the year is to all those capable of enjoying food (like the Editor) very delicious; fruits and vegetables are now at the height of perfection.

Printed and published by E.H.Dicker, Barkway, every Monday and Friday

In later years he always signed his name "Hamilton Eustace", for convenience sake, but he was christened "Eustace Hamilton".

There is no doubt that "the nieces of General Jackson were the Hope girls, come to spend their holidays with Kate; being her cousins Hamilton

> # The
> ## Barkway Gazette
> No X
>
> Friday — July 21st; — MDCCCXLIII.
>
> **Notices to Correspondents.**
>
> "An Advocate of Hydropathy" is asked whether he has personally proved its efficacy; if he has not, we cannot insert his letter.
>
> "John Bull's" communication is not worth the trouble of insertion.
>
> "A true Angler" shall find a place in our columns.
>
> "Fire-away" is entreated not to send us any more of his empty communications.
>
> ## THE FAIR.
>
> For the last two or three days, this town has been a scene of gaiety & bustle owing to the annual fair on the 20th of July. We believe it will close to-morrow, Saturday, July 22nd.
>
> ## HAMILTON YACHT SQUADRON.
>
> We are happy to state that 2 additions have been made to this distinguished club, during the last week. We give the table as it now stands;—
>
> | NAMES | CLASS | TONS | DISTINGUISHING FLAG | OWNERS |
> | --- | --- | --- | --- | --- |
> | Ariadne | Yawl | 6 | White, Red cross, red border | Capt Eustace Hamilton |
> | Sea-Mew | Sloop | 4 | White, 2 Red Arrows crossed | Capt E. Winter |
> | Celeste | Cutter | 0 | Red | Capt Eustace Hamilton |
> | Merman | Sloop | 0 | Blue, with Yellow Anchor | Capt E. Winter |
> | Kestrel | Sloop | 0 | White, Red blue White quartering | Capt T. Dicker |

would naturally conclude they must be his nieces. It is amusing to read the disdainful way in which "The Editor" (used to gay Brighton and Lewes) speaks of the Village Fair; he is evidently impatient that the inhabitants preferred the stalls and shows and local excitement to his regattas.

We also have a letter from him to his mother, undated, but probably written the same year.

A Letter from Hamilton

Barkway. Sept.22nd

Dearest Mamma,

    As Henry will soon be coming to fetch Loney, I thought it would be better to write and tell you the few things I should like him to bring for me. In the first place – with regard to shipping; we have been very busy here lately in making a harbour for our vessels, consisting of two substantial piers, 5 ft. in length, at the distance of about 4 ft. from each other. A commodious harbour is thus formed between the two piers, 5 ft. in length and at the entrance nearly 2 ft. deep. (A "Birdseye View of the Harbour", very carefully drawn, fills the bottom of this page) Then I have recovered the Ariadne, which has been at the bottom of the pond (a depth of about 4½ ft.) for two months and three weeks, took off all the old rigging and rotten sails, and rigged her as a complete steamer, naming her the "Belfast" after the steamer at Brighton before the Dart. Again, I have entirely re-modelled the "Red Rover", the vessel we bought at Cambridge, and rigged her as a steamer called the "Dart". IIIrdly I have rigged the Sea-Mew, Emily's boat, as an Algerine corsair, and she goes like lightning; I made the Dart and Belfast chase her. The names of all my vessels are now these –

Dart		
Belfast	} *Steamers*	
Algiers	*Corsair*	} *Middling size*
Celeste	*Cutter*	
Mermaid		
Vivid	} *Pleasure Boat*	
Lady of the Lake		} *Very small*

Now I very much want to have one good-sized vessel and Henry does too, he told me to ask you if you would get Tom to select one made by a sailor, *they are the only ones that really sail well. I have seen beautiful schooners and cutters, brigs and frigates on the esplanade seats, made by sailors, but the Chain Pier Bazaar is* the *grand depot for ships. Henry says, if you cannot afford one, make a general collection for the purpose. If you would give me a good large ship instead of any more money this half year I should be delighted. Of 1 masted vessels I should prefer a cutter to any other class – of 2 masted vessels brigs or schooners – of 3 masted frigates or merchant ships, or men-of-war.* Please *to see after one, I will take the greatest possible*

Barkway
Sept 22nd

Dearest Mamma

As Henry will soon be
coming to fetch Louy, I thought it would
be better to write & tell you the few
things I should like him to bring for me.
In the first place, — with regard to
shipping: ~~the~~ we have been very busy here
lately in making a harbour for our vessels,
consisting of two substantial piers, 5 feet
in length, at the distance of about 4
feet from each other, a commodious har-
-bour is thus formed between the two piers,
5 feet in length, 4 in breadth, & at the en-
-trance nearly two feet deep.

Bird's Eye View of the
Harbour.

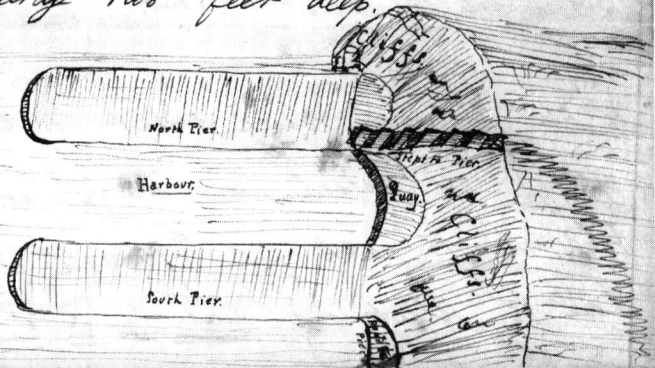

North Pier.

Harbour.

Slipto Pier.

Quay.

South Pier.

care of it, and make it last for years. If they do cost a great deal, yet they are so strong and well made, that they are worth a hundred toy-shop boats put together. The larger the better, it cannot be too large for my harbour. I will press the subject no further – do as you think fit about it.

IIndly A trolling winch – perhaps you have got it already, if not I will, if you like, give it up, and let the price thereof go towards a ship.

IIIrdly a bat, a ball etc. Henry told me you were going to get me one, so as he is coming I think it had better be got soon. But tempus fugit, and the clock from yonder "ivy mantled tower" has given warning to the busy world below that it is 5 o'clock; the postman will in half an hour go forth on his important errand, bearing this letter from, dear Mamma,

Your affectionate son

There is no signature, but a small mark in its place looks as if something had been affixed there – perhaps the words in print or painted, afterwards removed by him, and used again.

I have copied this letter, because it was written from Barkway, but I hope you will all read the original, and very many others written by him, and still carefully preserved by us; letters he wrote as a little child, a boy, a man; delightful letters to his children, and the most touching of love letters to his wife. And you can see hers to him, and the first letters of the children to them both, if you care to.

[The Red House]

There is one more thing I want to impress upon you; that young Hamilton lived for about two years with the Killicks in The Red House – the house that Kate was born in, and that still belonged to her and her mother. The pond where he built his piers and held his regattas was the self-same one that the little girls had played by and tumbled into a few years before, and in which they had nearly drowned the Balding babies! The old pond is still there, but different owners have altered its shape and removed the trees that sheltered one side – it looks shabby and neglected. The Red House itself is much the same, though the Jackson House is now altered out of recognition.

[Emily Dicker]

Emily, of course, was only at Barkway occasionally, on short visits; her mother and older sisters went there before she did, and they used to tell her about a saintly little Miss Kate Cornwell, who never did anything she oughtn't to, holding her up as an example to naughty little Emily. Conse-quently Emily hated Kate Cornwell with a murderous hatred – she told me this tale herself, when she was a beautiful old lady. At last the time came when her Mother took Emily to stay with her married sister, Louisa Killick, and soon after Emily was dressed in her best and taken to call at the big house opposite, the Jackson House. On the smooth lawn in front was a fountain, springing up from a small ornamental pond filled with gold fish; on this lawn lay a little girl full length, her arms in the water, trying to catch the fish. She was soaked with mud and water, and her jolly little round face was flushed and excited, not in the least ashamed or shocked at being caught. Emily and she looked into each other's eyes and became friends at once. To simple little Kate this lovely child, with her dark wonderful eyes, keen wit and daring mischief, seemed more like the heroine of a book than a bit of real life. Fascinated, bewitched, Kate allowed Emily to at once take the lead in their little circle – to the great resentment of the others! Till now Sarah had always been the leader, and the games exciting, but strictly "lady-like"! But Emily did breathless and surprising things up trees and on gates – and nobody minded or scolded in that lovely place, however racketty and noisy their games became. One, that became a great favourite of them all, I must tell you about. The gardeners at the Jackson House had a platform on wheels, on which they stood to clip the tall hedges; it had two platforms, one above the other, and looked like a small four-post bed.

All the little girls would pack themselves on this, and make it run down slopes; there was one especially precipitous one, down on to the levelled bowling green, which only the boldest dared. None of them, our Mother, the Hopes, Aunt Emily, Annie White – ever omitted to mention their joy when they – in their old age – described the beloved garden at Barkway.

When Aunt Emily was a tired old lady, and blindness was creeping over her still beautiful eyes, she told me that those visits to Barkway had been the happiest spots in her life. In her own home she was utterly out of her element; she seemed like a fairy-changeling, with nothing in common with the others – except Hamilton. Her Grandfathers, Dicker and Hamilton, had both been friends and fellow workers with John Wesley, and her Father was a deeply religious, solemn, silent man. Only serious holy people were sup-posed to come to their house, and there were constant long extemporary prayers and Meetings there, besides the long dreary Sunday Services. The older sisters had inherited some of this heavenly-mindedness; they were nice-looking, gentle and rather stylish girls, and happily besides the old family home in Lewes they had a second charming house in Oriental Place, Brighton, where the old Father seldom came, and where the family were able to relax and enjoy itself under the kind wise eyes of their Mother. I am sorry to say that the eldest son, Tom, broke away very early; he brought home a wife (with a baby imminent) while he was still in his 'teens, I believe, and in other ways he behaved so badly that he was packed off to Australia, with his wife and child, and the family almost lost sight of him. Emily was another rebel, from her babyhood; only terror of her tall severe Father kept her from showing what would have broken his heart. Her Mother had a hard time trying to hide the child's naughtiness, and keep peace between her and her sisters, pacify governesses etc. And she was so beautiful, and so clever and fascinating really! There is a family legend that Aunt Emily, when she was a naughty little girl, made a grove in her garden with an image in it, to horrify her sisters!

And yet at Barkway Emily was not <u>naughty</u> at all, only full of tomboy tricks and high spirits. To begin with, she found there a second love, almost as great as her love for Hamilton – she simply adored our Grandmother, Mrs Jackson! Happy as she was romping in the garden, she found her greatest happiness on earth sitting alone with her new friend in her pleasant room (with the birds and flowers) or walking or driving with her. Aunt Emily told me that every good instinct she had came from my Grandmother Jackson, and if she had had more of her influence her life might have been very different. But I must enforce the fact that there was never anything <u>evil</u> in Aunt Emily; nothing low or false or the slightest bit immoral. She was an outrageous flirt; men found her absolutely irresistable – even when she was an old lady every man, at a party, would gather round her if he could, leaving younger ladies lonely and deserted. Not only for her exquisite face and neck and eyes, but for her deep understanding of men, her tender sympathy, or roguish repartee.

At 11 or 12 years old Emily was practically a little heathen, believing in nothing and nobody (except Hamilton) and resolved to have a good time at all costs. At Barkway she came in to an entirely new world, a world where religion was never talked about, and yet was a real force, controlling each one; a world of merry hearted young people, playing and dancing and singing songs and glees, without a thought of such things being sinful. And the mainspring of all was Mrs Jackson, our Grandmother, with her keen kind eyes and wise heart; with her Quaker faith, reticence and tolerance ("if thee thinks a thing is <u>not</u> wrong it is not wrong for thee") and her sympathy for the little child with such great gifts and great temptations. At the same time, I must confess that Emily showed a different side of her character to the Hopes and other little Barkway girls, from the one she showed to Kate and her Mother. Kate's old friends hated and distrusted Emily, and she mocked at and mimicked them, to the end of their lives!

It was really very funny to stay with the Hopes, and then with Aunt Emily, and hear what the dear old ladies said about each other, though they had not met since they were girls!

[The Storm Breaks]

It was wonderful that Emily had been allowed this happiness so long, for if her elders had noticed what the young folks did at the Jackson House their visits would have been stopped long before. Young Mrs Killick was very delicate, and much occupied with her baby daughter; she was glad that her little sister would spend most of her time playing with the good little girls who lived opposite. Hamilton, probably, was deeply absorbed in his boats and harbour works, and if he did go to the other house it was to devour books in quiet corners. Emily would be far too clever to mention dancing, billiards and cards before her sister and brother-in-law. Henry Killick was intensely busy rooting these and other deadly sins out of his parish, Barley, a few miles off. So the storm, when it fell, was like a "bolt from the blue". It was a hot summer evening, and Mr Jackson having come across his old friends the gypsies, he invited them to bring their fiddles and flutes and play more dances for the children; very possibly some grown-ups were dancing too, Mr Jackson's married daughters, the pupils, perhaps Mr Jackson himself. Anyway, Mr Henry Killick, returning from an earnest prayer meeting, was horrified to hear the sounds of ribald merriment, actually <u>dancing</u>, in the hall of the Jackson house. And when he went into his own home, and his wife told him that Hamilton and Emily were actually there, in the midst of that shameful wickedness, he rushed straight across the road into the midst of the sinful thing, and told them what he thought of them! The music stopped with a crash, the terrified children clung to the grown-ups and each other, the pupils came forward prepared to fling him head-over-heels out of the door. But Mr Jackson stood quietly face to face with the white excited clergyman, and no violence took place. A short conversation took place, but the listeners were too excited to remember what was said, except that as Henry Killick dragged the weeping Emily and Hamilton out of the house he said bitterly "I will <u>pray</u> for you!" and Mr Jackson answered "Thanks – I think I can get to Heaven without your help!"

Poor little Emily! Sent home in deep disgrace, never again to come to Barkway, home of her heart. Hamilton, too, was packed off to boarding school, away from those dangerous temptations. A curtain fell between the Red House and the Jackson House for a while; but bye and bye old Mrs Dicker (admirable woman!) came again to stay with her daughter. She showed no sign of having heard what had happened, but came across at once to see her dear friend Mrs Jackson! Dear old Grandmother! Can't we imagine the scene! Both had the blessed gifts of courtesy, and tact, and true Christianity, though they were so utterly different in other ways.

Shortly after that Henry Killick was made Rector of St Clement Danes, London, so the Dickers came no more to Barkway. But (probably through old Mrs Dicker) Kate was sent before long to a fashionable finishing school in Brighton, and as the Dickers were constantly at Oriental Place, and their home at Lewes was only a few miles off, Kate and Emily were able to continue their friendship.

The End of Kate's Childhood

I know very little about our Mother's school life at Brighton, except that the School was in a Crescent opposite the sea, and only older girls were taken. She was very happy there, and made several nice friends. But the terrible tragedy that ended her happy childhood when she left school blotted out all that had gone immediately before it.

She was coming home "for good", her school days ended, and great preparations had been made at the Jackson House to celebrate this great event. Her room had been papered and painted, and new chintz coverings and curtains made for it; a lovely little piano had been bought for her own use, and friends had been invited to join in the festivities and welcomes. Kate herself was wild with joy and excitement. But when her train arrived at Royston station, instead of her Mother's smiling face, old Camp the coachman was on the platform, hardly able to speak for sorrow. His beloved master, Kate's dearly loved step-father, Mr Jackson, had just been found lying unconscious in a field that he had been measuring; probably he had been struck down by a sunstroke or a fit, and he had lain for hours, unnoticed, in the blazing sunshine. He had been carried home, doctors summoned, and everything possible was being done, but there was no hope whatever. Poor little Kate drove back to the distracted house with no one to welcome or notice her; her Mother was watching by the bed of her dying husband. Only Sarah Cootes, the kindly servant who had saved her life when she was born, took her into her loving arms, and soothed and tended her. For a few hours the agony went on, and then the great kindly soul was released from its tortured body.

All the world Kate had known and loved seemed to die when Mr Jackson died. It was so utterly unexpected, for he was a strong man in the prime of life; he had made no will, and no preparations, and had lived up to every penny he earned. Besides the heartbreak of losing him there was the utter confusion and misery all around, for everything was to be sold and the money divided between Mr Jackson's children – not one penny came to his second wife or stepdaughter. And it was in this terrible upset and confusion that the old Chinese cabinet, that had been in our Mother's family for many generations, was lost to us. I have told you how several pieces of the Cornwell furniture had been brought across to the Jackson House when our Grandmother married, and I told you how the cabinet stood in the big square hall with the white Chinese figures on it. When the Jackson sale took place all our Grandmother's things were marked "Not for Sale", but for some unaccountable reason this beloved old cabinet was sold with the Jackson things. When our Grandmother discovered that it had been bought by Mr Adams, one of Mr Jackson's favourite pupils, she at once offered to buy it back, but he refused to part with it then – and ever after, for many attempts have been made by us to regain that dear old family treasure. It was Mr Adams who succeeded to Mr Jackson's work, and lived in the Jackson House. He altered the house out of all recognition, and called it "Barkway House", as it is to this day. But in that house, passed down to his daughter Mrs Arthur Hall, and now to his granddaughter you still may see our old cabinet! Thank God the white figures had been safely packed away before the sale, and they have been with the family ever since, in all their many homes.

After this dreadful upheaval our Grandmother decided to take Kate abroad for a time. They went to Paris, where Kate was sent as weekly boarder at a school, to polish up her French; her mother and a friend from Barkway who travelled with them stayed in rooms near by. After about a year they went touring in Switzerland, where they had a lovely time, and they settled down for several months at Geneva. But Barkway was calling to them, and hearing that the old family home, Ash Grove, was to let, they took it, and joyfully took their furniture out of store to make a charming home for themselves there. A lovely little house it must have been in those days, just big enough for two people – with Sarah Cootes, of course, to preside in the kitchen. A happy and peaceful life the mother and daughter led there, surrounded by old friends and within easy reach of London and Cambridge.

I believe I said that the Dickers came no more to Barkway, but I have a letter (envelope and all!) which proves I was wrong! It is addressed to Mrs Jackson, Barkway, and the post date is May 1849.

7 Parker Street, Cambridge. Thursday

> Dear Mrs Jackson,
>   *Being so near the scene of so many happy days of my life –*
> *Barkway – I cannot resist the favourable opportunity of re-visiting it. Ac-*
> *cordingly I write you a line to say that I think of taking the liberty of coming*
> *over tomorrow about the middle of the day if it should be fine. My friends*
> *Pringler and Crewe would have come with me with much pleasure, but are*
> *prevented from doing so by an impending examination. I believe my sister*
> *Emily mentioned my intended visit, but still it is a very unceremonious*
> *proceeding! I am looking forward with great delight to the pleasure of seeing*
> *you once more in your old village; and trust that my doing so tomorrow*
> *(Saturday if Friday is wet) will cause you no inconvenience.*
>
> *Meanwhile, believe me, dear Mrs Jackson,*
>
> *Most faithfully yours,*   *Hamilton Dicker*

At that time he and Kate were both twenty.

Few people could have had such a joyous childhood as our Mother, Kate Cornwell. Perfectly healthy, surrounded by devoted relations and friends, with no need to think about money; exceptionally well-educated for a girl of those days, and with no real pain of mind or body until the tragic death of her step-father. And during those years when she and her mother were alone they became nearer and dearer to each other than ever before. The life at the Jackson House had been too noisy and crowded, and Kate had always had one or two of the Hope girls with her; she could seldom be alone with her mother there. But now the two lived in absolute harmony; books, music and painting and most marvellous lace-work and embroidery, beside the endless other calls on two such popular people – they were always busy and always happy. Kate would not permit love making from anyone – she was <u>never</u> going to leave her Mother. But the wise Mother often spoke seriously to her daughter on the subject of marriage, advising her to choose a good, kind, husband to take care of her. And the one she mentioned as the kind of man she would like for her was young Hamilton Dicker! At that time they were just good friends, no more.

Alas! Kate's happy girlhood, and her home at Barkway were swept away by a blow more terrible to her than even her step-father's tragic death. Early in 1850 her Mother complained of severe pain in her side; probably it was appendicitis, or something else that could be put right easily now-a-days. But though London doctors as well as local ones, and everything that loving care could do was done, the bright brave spirit passed away on March 6th. Up to the last she was sensible and even cheerful between the agonising spasms of pain. The evening before she died Mother and Sarah Cootes went outside the door for a minute to confer about something, leaving the dying woman apparently quite helpless in her bed. When they returned the bed was empty! – the invalid had got out of it alone, and walked across the room carrying her pillow; she was seated in the armchair by the fire, smiling at their dismay.

One hardly dares picture our Mother during the days that followed. She was too young to live alone, so of course the Hopes claimed her – she should be just one of themselves again, and their home her home. Her favourite step-sister Ann, Mrs William Cornwell, also very much wanted her; so she decided to spend half her time with each of these. Pretty Ash Grove was empty again, and all the furniture and old treasures stored.

Crushed in heart and spirit, not caring what now happened to her, Mother went to the Hopes; their father was dead, and they were now living at Brighton, Esther, Sarah and Emma, with their pretty old mother. They remained just the same, but she had changed; her travels abroad, and her intimate association with her mother had widened her outlook, and set her free from narrow conventions and prejudices. Besides, I am sorry to say that friction began at once between the Hopes and the Dickers. Though living in the same town they moved in utterly different circles, and the Hope girls had never got over their dislike and jealousy of Emily. But naturally old Mrs Dicker came at once to the motherless child of her friend, and Emily felt our Grandmother Jackson's death more than she would one of her own relations. Mother dearly loved both families, and was nearly distracted at the miserable discord between them. I wonder if the struggle would have ended if young Hamilton Dicker had not suddenly returned from abroad! (Curiously enough, on the day of the Brighton Races, as the gipsy had foretold long years before!) He had been in Germany, and he returned to find his merry little Barkway friend dressed in deep mourning, with all the merriment crushed out of her. A few days later the Dickers took Kate for a long drive; several of them went in the carriage, and Hamilton and Kate sat in the "dickey", the little seat behind. There was a family joke afterwards that Hamilton's hands were stained deep black, from holding tight another little pair of hands in black kid gloves! I do not know if it was settled then, for that was too sacred a time for mother to talk about. Her eyes filled with tears as she thought of it.

There was no need for a long courtship – had they not known each other from childhood? She had her own small fortune and a houseful of furniture; he was working in the Lewes Old Bank, where his father was, and Grand-father had been partners, with full intention of taking his place, in time, as the "Dicker" in "Whitfield, Molineux and Dicker". What young people could start married life with happier prospects? They naturally wished for a quiet wedding, but the beautiful Emily had at last consented to marry one of her many suitors, and nothing would satisfy her but that it should be a double wedding, and as grand as it could be! Her lover was an absolute contrast to Kate's; though he was a clergyman, the Revd. Melville Lee, Rector of Bridport, he came of a long line of naval men, and was much more like an Admiral than a Parson! A good and conscientious man, but with very strong passions, and great ideas of discipline, method and order. Of course he knew naughty, bewitching Emily had none of these things, but he was madly in love, and expected to train her into a model clergyman's wife as he had drilled and trained other folks. Of course Emily had her way about the wedding; an empty house at the corner of Brunswick Square was engaged for the reception, and crowds of people were invited to the breakfast etc. There were two carriages with four white horses each for the two brides, and Emily had six bridesmaids in pale pink, and Kate six in pale blue – her two child bridesmaids were little Annie Killick and little Chattie Adams from Barkway. There was a long drive for the string of carriages (all white favours and gay frocks!) to old Hove Church where the wedding took place; at that time the Church stood in a large Churchyard amid fields, with only narrow lanes leading to it. Mother always said she couldn't recall a single thing about that wedding morning, except the infinite comfort of Sarah Cootes, who mothered and petted her, and kept off the noisy crowds. I am sorry to say the Hopes refused to come to the wedding, and spent the day, I believe, in bitter mourning and tears. Of course there were many of

Mother's relations and friends there, but the poor child was too dazed and bewildered to realise anything or anybody.

Then the two couples drove to the station; a carriage had been reserved for them in the train in which they were to start together on their honeymoons, but the Melville Lees were to change into another train after a few stations. It was here that a startling event took place. Aunt Emily seemed suddenly to realise all that this parting meant; she turned quite hysterical and clung to her brother, begging to be allowed to go with him and his bride instead of with her own new-made husband! It was dreadful for all of them, for the train could not wait, and the weeping girl had to be dragged from her brother and from the carriage. Mother said it nearly broke her heart to see her. For herself this was the greatest moment of her life – she and her Beloved going out into the unknown together – together till "Death did them part".

A short history of what happened to the Hamilton Dickers afterwards

[But sadly, here the book ends, the writer dying shortly afterwards; the piece of blotting paper still lies on the last page of the notebook in which this fascinating story was written.]

Chapter III

Dunkirk

So Ella's story ends with the emotional scene after the double wedding of Hamilton and Emily, to Kate and Melville respectively. No doubt eventually all was calm, and the pairs went their respective ways. That was in 1852, before which Hamilton had already made a name for himself in the Lewes area as a student of history and ecclesiastical subjects. At the age of nineteen he was a prominent member of the Sussex Archaeological Society, giving talks on 'Chalvington Church' and 'Ecclesiological Nomenclature', and other diverse subjects.

Much earlier, as a very small boy, he developed a remarkable imagination, and a love of learning. When he was quite tiny, and too small to write, he dictated these verses to his mother:

> *Oh Lord my Friend and Saviour*
> *The Devil's vile behaviour*
> *Shall never make me stray*
> *From following in thy way.*

A Character

> *Mark was a wanderer o'er hill and dale,*
> *He loved to wander, and he loved to roam.*
> *You oft might meet him in a silent vale,*
> *In solitary mediation sad.*
>
> *He was not ignorant of everything,*
> *He was not ignorant of sense.*
> *He was so sad, he could not hear bells ring,*
> *But would retire within himself.*

It is almost unbelievable, but when he was only nine Hamilton wrote this 'Juvenile Sermon':

St John XX 1.2.

We are here assembled, dearly beloved, on the solemn subject of Christ's resurrection. May God instil into our minds that delightful blessing which always accompanies when two or three are gathered together in His Name. This is an interesting as well as solemn subject; may it be blessed to us; may we converse and hold the faith with as much unity of spirit as the holy persons who are chiefly concerned in this text. We will then, if God please, divide this subject into two different parts; 1st. the action of this text – 2nd, the exclamation. Then, my dear hearers, may we receive the blessing of God with the action of these holy people, being the first part appointed for our discourse. 'The first day of the week cometh Mary Magdalene early, when it was yet dark, to the sepulchre'. So do we find Christ's real people that, even when dead and laid in, as they supposed, his last grave, they came to greet him. You would think it a strong emblem indeed of attachment were a person to go to visit a deceased friend when laid on his last pillow, the cold and dreary grave. Yet this was done by Christ's real people; then you have a conception, and that is all you can have, of the love of Christ's people to Him, and His to them. If we really love Christ, Christ will assuredly love us. Oh, blessed thought! Oh, humiliating thought! – Christ came down from Heaven to notice, and what is infinitely more – to love us. When we contemplate this, ought it not to make us immediately cast off those sins which we have made – as our Poet beautifully expresses himself,
'His very eyes weep blood,
And every breath he breathes is big with horror'
Is not this deeply affecting? Suppose, for an example, that a King of whom you were extremely fond was to take all your chains upon himself – every torture which had been inflicted upon you by your cruel enemies, & thus release you, would that time, however long, be happy? No, you had brought upon your mind, your doatingly kind sovereign a deep agony which cannot be expressed, & which was manifested by fond & frequent exclamations of 'My God, my God, why has Thou forsaken me?' Thus I have by an example endeavoured to show you the agony which your kind Saviour must have suffered, but you can only have a

distant idea of it; sins and chains are infinitely different, besides being on a Saviour who was too pure for sin, and who knew not what sin was. But let us return; this deeply interesting subject has led us away. 'Mary seeth the stone taken away from the sepulchre'. What must her feeling be when she finds the entrance taken away from that sepulchre in which she was seeking her beloved Saviour? What do we find she does on seeing this? 'Then she runneth and cometh to Simon Peter'. She cannot be satisfied with containing the anxiety which was experienced in seeing the sepulchre thus treated, but she goes to inform her brothers in the Lord of it. Here is love, and love indeed; and though it may seem such strong love, yet it is no more than anyone should have who knows she has such a Saviour. But, dearly beloved, the precious time wastes away, and I think we had better now contemplate the 2nd part of our discourse, viz. the exclamations which were used on this distressing occasion by this same servant of Christ. It is highly expressive of the love she had for Him, & is very interesting. Here we see, in the eye of our minds, a young virgin, very probably beautiful (as in the East in the present day most of the young virgins are handsome) saying the following beautiful and emphatic words. 'They have taken away my Lord, & I know not where they have laid Him.' She evidently shows that she loved Him exceedingly or she would not have said the words; though few, they are interesting. My dearly beloved, I am induced by my love for you to make no distinction between you & my best friends. You cannot tell with how much interest this fell upon my mind when I was searching the Holy Book for a subject for this discourse; it fell upon my heart as a powerful weight & I was induced from the intense interest I felt in it, to make it the subject of this day's delightful & heavenly admonition to you. I cannot hide it from you; such I never felt before, and as far as I can tell may never feel it again, uncertain as life is.

No one can tell the interest I felt when I had written a few pages of this sermon; an interesting occasion this is indeed. It is the present prayer of your dearly beloved Pastor that should your lives be mercifully spared to another Easter Sunday you may feel as deep an interest in this subject as your beloved Pastor does in addressing you on this subject. Remember, my dear brethren, that you are here assembled on the day of the resurrection of a Saviour whom should you gradually forget and forsake his laws, could plunge you in the instant into an eternal and burning hell. Should you take His Name in vain, ere the words were out of your lips, your breath might be stopped, and you, on the ground whence you came, might be an awful warning to your fellow sinners.

Hamilton Eustace Dicker (About 9 years old)

It is indeed difficult to believe that this document can have been written by a child, although the grammar is undeveloped. Without doubt, it was written by Hamilton, and even if he were in fact a few years older it exhibits the powerful thoughts which were going through his mind as a boy, and which were reflected in his future career.

A few years later, at the age of twelve, even before his visits to Barkway and the formation of the Hamilton Yacht Squadron, he had shown the serious and industrious side of his nature. Here is a letter to his mother from school in 1841.

Stockwell Green, 5th March 1841

My very dear Mamma,

I received your very kind letter quite safely on my birthday & with great joy, as I had not had one for a long time. I have had a slight sore-throat, which began on last Monday but is now well. I am much obliged to you for those lovely wafers that you sent me. I think now of hardly any-thing but the joy & the happenings I shall experience at Brighton with my flagstaff, which with dear Papa's consent I shall place on the Summer house. I intend to buy two new flags, viz. a Royal Standard & a Union Jack, neither of which I at present have. Will you be so very kind as to get Mr Duplock to paint my flagstaff white. I have a class of small boys in Dr. Daltrey's Sunday school, at which, you may guess, I am delighted. I have delivered a lecture on Magnetism, & almost prepared 3 more, 1 on Coloured Fires, 1 on Modern Inventions, & 1 one the Structure of the Eye. Will you tell me in your next letter when Margaret & Harriette [his sisters] will come to Stockwell? I am all expectation to see them. I often hope & pray that I may not be so wicked & ungrateful to you & dear Papa as Tom was. I hope most sincerely that I may always be an obedient dutiful child. Every morning I read a chapter in the Bible & I think I can feel the good influence of it as I have lost but few demerits as yet & have only been turned down twice with a lesson during the whole time I have been here. Pray write often & also write <u>very</u> long letters. Let Emily and

Josephine [his two younger sisters, aged ten and eight] also write. Give my best love to all, to dear Papa, Louisa, Emily, Josephine & also to little Fripon, & as I have no more time, I remain, your most loving son,

Hamilton

The reference to his brother Tom was about a 'black sheep', who at an early age had married and gone to Australia. But his name does not appear in any further family archives. 'Little Fripon' was not one of his siblings – perhaps it was a family pet.

It seems remarkable that at such an early age he could deliver lectures on such diverse subjects as Magnetism, Coloured Fires, Modern Inventions, and the Structure of the Eye.

On leaving school, Hamilton spent a short time in the 'Indian Marine', an organisation involved in marine survey. He was promoted to it from the Pilot Service, and rapidly rose to Third Officer, which was an honour at such an early age. But his ambition was always to go into the Church, and this, coupled with his feelings for Kate, which dated back some years to his visits to his sister at Barkway, he set out to develop.

We have already heard about Hamilton's courting days in Barkway. Not surprisingly, he asked his brother-in-law, Henry Killick, to perform the marriage ceremony, and received this reply:

Devizes   March 17th 1852

My dear Hamilton,

I need not assure you that it will give me no ordinary pleasure to officiate at your wedding. To promote the happiness of those we love is a piece of sweet selfishness that is very allowable.

Give Kate my kind love and tell her I shall rejoice in linking her to our family for life.

It is thoroughly in accordance with my long cherished wishes that I feel unmixed pleasure in the connection.

Excuse a very short letter, for I am quite overwhelmed with work.

Your truly affectionate brother, R. Henry Killick

P.S. Your stingy partners have not sent me an invitation.

*Emily Winter
(Dicker) Lee
(1831–1918)
Mother of Viscount
Lee of Fareham*

After her wedding at the age of twenty-one in 1852, the wild and emotional Emily settled down as a rector's wife in Bridport, and had five children, the youngest of whom, Arthur Hamilton Lee, became prominent in the Army and in politics. He acquired 'Chequers', and gave it to the nation as a residence for the Prime Minister, and became a Viscount. But that is another story.

Immediately following his marriage, Hamilton lived with his wife at Lewes, or rather Southover, a suburb of Lewes, and then, after brief visits to Ilfracombe and Newick (the latter close to Lewes) he attended Chichester Diocesan College in preparation for the Ministry. Kate's first child, Mildred, was born at Southover, and her second, Charles, at Chichester. Hamilton

Extract from Kate's Diary, March 1855

was ordained Deacon in 1855, and Priest a year later. His first appointment was as curate at Seaford, but a year later he went to Bridport, where Kate's third child, Maitland, was born, and shortly after he was appointed Curate of Warminster, and Chaplain of the Warminster Union. His interests were many, and he was always ready to speak to gatherings on various subjects. At the formal reopening of Warminster Athenaeum in 1858 he addressed a large audience on the Study of Art:

Mr Dicker concluded his remarks by reminding his audience that recommendations to the Study of Nature came to us on the highest of all authority. The Book of Psalms contained evidences of the delight experienced by David in beholding the beauties and wonders of God's handiwork; and we were actually directed to the study of these things by our Lord's memorable words – 'Consider the lilies of the field.' We are told to <u>consider</u> these things, – not the lilies alone, but all the marvellous works of our Creator which surround us. With this high sanction, and with this high view of the meaning and importance of Art before them, the members of the Institution were entreated to avail themselves of every opportunity it offered to increase their knowledge and appreciation of a pursuit, which might lead them on, through elevation and refinement of their moral and intellectual character, even towards the greatest end of man, acquaintance with the great Maker of all – true intercourse and communion with Him whose we are, and whom we serve.

We have already seen Hamilton as a boy, enterprising and imaginative. Now, as a young man, recently ordained, he was able to speak in a refreshing and passionate way about his religious beliefs, which had, perhaps, been partly inherited from his father and grandfather. He was also an accomplished singer, taking part in and organizing many concerts in Warminster. Sadly, he only lived another ten years, but if his life had not been so shortened without doubt he would have risen to high rank in the Church to which he was so dedicated.

He was also immensely dedicated to his wife and large family of seven children. There was an eighth, Arthur, who died from whooping cough in Warminster before his first birthday. In December 1860 another son, Assheton, arrived, shortly before Hamilton was honoured by being appointed British Chaplain at Dunkirk, after only three years in Warminster. He took up this prestigious appointment early in 1860, and the residents of Warminster were sad to see him go. On his departure he was presented with a purse containing thirty-five and a half sovereigns and a letter including the following:

> While the Committee feel that the testimonial in itself is too trifling to carry an adequate expression of their sentiments, they are assured that it will be grateful to you to receive even such a small parting token, from those with whom you have so much reciprocated that Christian affection and those genial feelings which will, it is hoped, leave long remembrances on both sides. Nor would the Committee

forget how earnestly and cordially Mrs Dicker has thrown her unos-
tentatious kindness into the active associations which have fallen
within her proper sphere. Not only the Committee and your personal
friends, but the Town, regret your leaving us; and were I not restrained,
on this occasion, by the remembrance that I am representing others, I
should indulge my heart in warmer expressions of personal regard than
I may venture now to do.

In acknowledging this parting gift of £35.10s., Hamilton told the donors
that he had spent part of the amount in the purchase of a complete edition
of the works of Wordsworth, six volumes 'to be inscribed with the circumstances of their coming into my possession'.

After settling in Dunkirk, where there was a large British community,
Hamilton took a particular interest in the English and Scottish students
who were attending college there, taking them on long, agreeable and
instructive rambles, encouraging them to get up a cricket club, and joining
in their amusements and sports. The situation regarding the Anglican
Church in Dunkirk not long after Hamilton's arrival was set out in the
following article in the *Guardian* of 10 December 1862:

It will be interesting to those who have visited the fine, healthy, 'quaint
old Flemish city' of Dunkirk (and may the more dispose others to make
its acquaintance, so near as it is to our shores, and so full of stirring
histories), to know that our Church there established shows, both in
its services and material fabric, signs of vitality and zeal. Great interest
was felt by the congregation on Advent Sunday, in the improved
appearance of the ancient building in which they have worshipped for
about thirty years; it having been to a great extent refitted through the
exertions of the Rev. Hamilton E. Dicker, H.M. Consular Chaplain.
This work is only considered as a necessary instalment of the greater
design which it is foreseen will demand accomplishment – the providing
of further accomodation for the increasing demands of British subjects,
either in the present building or in another, to be bought or erected.
All the present fittings have been procured and arranged with a view
to this probable exigency; and their possession will greatly relieve the
strain that will then have to be made; while in the interval it was
absolutely needful to obtain them, in consequence of the meanness,
inconvenience, and insecurity of the hitherto existing arrangements
for divine service. In these respects the English Church at Dunkirk has

hitherto borne a sad resemblance to those fabrics occupied by most of our congregations abroad. Happily it does so no more. The church itself is an ecclesiastical structure, having been the chapel of Les Soeurs Blanches, and though dated 1672, and now curtailed by part of its height by an intervening floor, has with its handsome vaulted roof and good proportions, a very church-like effect. The effect was, till lately, much marred by the seats, which pressed on every side close up to the holy table, so that there was hardly space to pass by it; by the two mean pulpits, of nearly equal height, one on each side; by the miserable rails, and dingy black hangings. Now, by the recent arrangements, room has been gained for about sixteen places, and yet sufficient space obtained at the east end to make a large addition to the sanctuary, which has been enclosed with handsome wrought-iron rails, blue and gilt. The level has been raised, and the holy table, new and massive, is adorned with a beautiful crimson velvet covering, embroidered by the ladies of the congregation, who have also executed a device for the recess above – a cross in gold, with a scroll twining round it bearing the words, 'Jesus Christ, the same yesterday, to-day, and for ever'; the whole upon a ground of deep blue. They have also executed illuminated scrolls, which go at intervals round the church. Crimson damask hangings line the east wall. A stall seat has been provided for the prayers, and an oak lectern for the Lessons. The new lights are of handsome brasswork. The appearance of the whole is now solemn and church-like; and a clear gain is effected not only in places for the congregation, but in the order and conveniences with which the divine services can now be celebrated. The rareness of restorations of this sort in our churches abroad, and the importance of their aspect towards foreigners, as well as to our own people, may be sufficient apology for this somewhat detailed account of the church improvements lately effected, with the unanimous approval and sympathy of the British residents at Dunkirk.

So, in just over a year from his arrival, Hamilton had transformed the church in Dunkirk, and had set his sights on further improvements and perhaps a new building. He worked hard and successfully to improve conditions for his parishioners, and sponsored an application to the Town Council for permission to erect a new building to replace the existing one, of which the lease was due to expire in November 1868.

While at Dunkirk, three further babies were born to Kate – Eleanor (who wrote the last chapter), Seymour (my grandfather) and Gilbert. During those seven years the older children spent a great deal of their time in England, Charles (Charlie) and Maitland went to boarding school, while Milly and Assheton were at local schools in Dunkirk, but during the holidays there were many visits to their cousins, particlarly to the Hopes and to 'Aunt Ann' Cornwell, who was Kate's stepsister.

It was comparatively easy to cross the Channel, with two or three ferries a day travelling between Dover and Dunkirk. When he was only ten, Maitland, who was a pupil at Miss Wilkin's School, Warminster, was elected Chorister Boy at All Saints Church, Margate Street, London. This was a most valuable appointment, and was eagerly striven for by a number of candidates.

There was some excitement in 1867 when the Emperor and Empress of France visited Dunkirk, and a special invitation went to Hamilton to attend the reception. Hamilton described this event to his mother:

It was the grandest thing which has happened for Dunkirk for many years, and I hope will indirectly be considerably to our advantage, as it seems certain that the Emperor has resolved to have executed vast works for the improvement of the port and town, which will make it one of the most important places in France, and much more frequented also by English people – all, as we may hope, <u>bringing grist to the mill</u>. The royal visit here was rather suddenly announced, and not having many days for preparation the whole population set to work in a most enthusiastic manner to prepare for their arrival. I never saw anything so successfully done. The French certainly have a marvellous genius for such things; the whole town was transformed into a sort of fairy scene; especially the main streets they were to pass through. Blue and white draperies were hung in festoons across the streets, with crowns and garlands and venetian lanterns in the centre, all the houses each side being hung with flags, and triumphal arches of various kinds at intervals. There was such a demand for flags and other decorations that a great many had to send to England for them, and I had to do so, and got a splendid Union Jack only just in time. And now let me pass to what particularly concerned myself; I had the great compliment of being invited by the *Sous Préfet* to attend the 'Reception Officielle' held by the Emperor and Empress on their arrival. I did not expect this, as it might be supposed that only French subjects were concerned in this visit, and we had nothing whatever to do with it; even the Consul was not sure he would be invited; but however the invitations came in good time, and of course we were very much gratified, as it is a new mark of respect on the part of the authorities. I think you will see something about it in the French news in the next 'Guardian' this week. I was fully intending to go in my usual clerical frock-coat etc., – but the Consul told me only a day or two before that I must go in my gown and cassock, as at an English Court – and he would have me to do so; so not having a silk gown etc. I was obliged to send off poste haste to London and hire them, which I happily succeeded in doing in time, and was able to present myself in 'silks that whistled', and had a most imposing effect. I put on my robes at the Consulate and went over to the *Sous Préfecture* with the Consul, of course in his uniform. We waited in the room where all the authorities were assembling; and I was told I was to go in with the clergy of the town, which I thought was an additional compliment to my clerical office. We were almost the first to be summoned into the imperial presence; I of course let the Curés and Vicars go first, and as they went in I had a good look at the Emperor and Empress, who stood on a dais before the throne. The Emperor looked much younger and better looking than I expected to see him; and I had the pleasure of seeing him with a most pleasant and beaming manner present the Cross of the Legion of Honour to the old *Doyen-Curé* of St Eloi. His face in speaking, at least on such an occasion, is very pleasing. He gave me the impression of a rather fair man – not dark and swarthy as I had imagined; but they say his hair is getting grey, which at a distance makes it look rather a light colour. We were all marched before him and the Empress, making our bows, and then marched out again.

The Minister of Public Works, with Chamberlains, Aide-de-Camps etc., in grand uniforms stood on each side. I could not look up at their Majesties when exactly opposite them; but after passing I got a chance of seeing the Empress very nicely; her face and manner were perfectly charming; – so much more warmth and '*empressement*' in her manner than I expected to see; I was also surprised to see her with such a decided colour, strong colour, I might say; I thought she was so very pale. They say she is sunburnt. Mr Vesson was very near to me in passing in, and I thought it was my duty to let him pass before me, as he was the Emperor's subject and I a foreigner; but there was no recognition of him in any way more than me. I thought that when he first caught sight of me in the waiting room he manifested some

dissatisfaction, but perhaps this was imaginary. It was remarked by many
that his seedy bombazine gown presented a great contrast to my 'whis-
tling silks'; though alas they were only borrowed! But it is most rarely
that I need a silk gown; and they can always be hired in such cases.
The ladies were received by the Empress previously to our reception;
a number of young ladies, amongst whom were the Pringles, Emily
Carlie and Marie Gilling! were chosen as '*demoiselles d'honneur*' – all
in white and blue – to receive the Empress, and present her with a
magnificent bouquet. Mrs Pringle had the honour of being called
forward from the other ladies by Madame de Jessaint, and presented to
the Empress; who spoke to her in very good English, and asked her
how long she had been at Dunkirk etc. This was of course very pleasing
to Mrs Pringle. After the reception, we had a very good view from the
windows of the Consulate of the departure of the Emperor and Empress,
with their splendid escort of Cent-Gardes, which are very rarely seen
outside of Paris. In the evening I was invited to dine at the Consulate,
on a haunch of venison, which came from Lord Ashburnham's near
Battle, so that we were very grateful to the 'Battle friends'. At night
the Park was beautifully illuminated with coloured lamps, and there
was an open-air ball in it.The streets were a perfect miracle of graceful
beauty, owing to the tasteful way in which the illumination was done
– principally with Venetian lanterns of coloured paper, which give a
soft and dreamy light; and the weather being perfectly beautiful and
calm there was no hindrance to the complete success of the whole.
There were fêtes and amusements the whole of the next day also, and
at night a grand display of fireworks beyond anything I have ever yet
seen. I and the children saw them to great advantage from Mme
Tumerel's. Of course poor Kate saw nothing of the grand doings, but
she had been rather overtired before, and she said the two great days
were welcome to her on account of the quiet, as everyone was out, and
she did not care much about the sightseeing. An amusing episode of
the affair has been the sensation caused by the presentation to the
Emperor of a London Alderman, Mr Cotton, an immensely rich man,
now staying here with all his family with carriage, horses etc. Milly
was introduced to them by Lizzie Goude and her husband when they
put her on board the steamer on returning from London, and they have
been very civil to us here. Mr Cotton had his uniform as Deputy
Lieutenant here, and said he would like in some way to take part in

the proceedings; so I took him to call on the Consul, and mentioned his wish to the Adjoint du Maire and others; and it all ended in its being telegraphed by the *Préfet* from Lille that Mr Cotton (whom they thought was a <u>mi-Lord</u>) was to be first of all amongst the presentations; – besides which he was authorised to go in his carriage and meet the Emperor at the station – the only carriage besides the royal cortege. As you may suppose all this was rather distasteful to the aristocratic tastes of our <u>chief residents</u> – to whom a city magnate, however wealthy and respectable, is nobody. But it was only a very well-meant compliment on the part of the *Préfet* towards the City of London, which is always so hospitable to the French.

Perhaps this letter calls for a few explanations. Although the monarchical system had been abolished by the French Revolution, it had been restored by Napoleon during the 'First Empire' in 1804. This lasted until the 'Second Republic' of 1848, which became the 'Second Empire' in 1852. In 1870, three years after the events here described, Napoleon III (nephew of the Great Napoleon) was deposed and the 'Third Republic' was set up.

Mrs Pringle was, I think, the wife of the British Consul, which would account for her special treatment.

The one reference to Kate is curious, but this event had occurred only a short time after the birth of her youngest child Gilbert on 9 August 1867, and this probably explains why she did not take part in the celebrations.

The year 1868 brought much tragedy to the family. Early that year Hamilton's father, Thomas Dicker, died aged eighty-three, leaving his wife Martha on her own after a long and happy marriage.

Hamilton wrote to his mother after the death of Thomas:

Dunkirk, March 10 1868

My dearest mother,

We were delighted to receive your last kind letter, as it appeared a very long time since we had had any tidings of you, but we could certainly believe that your time must have been fully occupied. We are sorry to hear of your bad cold, and hope it is now quite well. We are also sorry to hear that Josephine continues so poorly [Josephine was his youngest sister, who had married Braithwaite Skeate]; the best plan will be for her to go off to the German Baths as soon as the season permits, & for you to come with her by Dover, by easy stages & stay with us while she goes on to Germany (which is a direct route from here). We would take the best care we could of you, & do everything in our power to console your comfort, quiet and convenience in every way. You little know how happy it would make us to have you so near; and I can answer for it that you would find Kate truly unto you 'as a daughter a faithful <u>Ruth</u>'. You should have practically your own sitting room (our present pretty drawing room) as well as a bedroom for your own quiet use, and as to the objection of the children, that really diminishes on consideration to almost nothing, for in the first place the two eldest boys will be in England (I will explain further on as to Charlie). That reduces the number to five; and of these Milly and Assheton are at school nearly all day, & most likely Ella will be in the summer, leaving only our dear little Seymour, whom we call 'the poor Lamb', who is of a quiet thoughtful turn; and our sweet, noble, heavenly tempered little Gilbert; & these two, under the care of our respectable Warminster nurse, & with a well shut in nursery of their own would not molest you much. We notice very much the freedom from noise in this house, even when the children are at home; owing to the arrangement of the rooms, & the thickness of the walls. Our house is only a few steps from Mrs Pringle and Madame Carlier; and we have now some other excellent and superior friends; but of these and of society in general you can have as little or as much as you choose, & no more. We could get you the newspaper every day & we have always nice books circulated from a London library. I think that the objections to this plan are thus reduced almost entirely to the crossing from Dover; certainly nothing <u>else</u> in the journey, which is as simple, expeditious, & inexpensive as almost any journey you could take; as I proved when I came to Worthing so quickly on my late visit. And, after all, the Dover package thus examined by itself, – what is it more than crossing to Cowes, which people think nothing of?

There is no need to go by any particular boat, if the weather should prove rough; you could stay at your favourite Lord Warden & rest a few hours until it was calmer, as there are boats two or three times a day; and I would joyfully come over and keep you company for the package & the rest of the journey. On the whole, admitting every drawback there may be to the proposed plan, yet consider that if Josephine goes to Germany – as she <u>ought</u> to do, you must go <u>somewhere</u> to be with <u>some</u> of us.

We still trust that when your more important affairs are settled, & your mind tolerably at ease, you will be able to manage the little journey as proposed, & find a quiet rest for a time with us. Gladly would I send 'the waggons' to bring you, as Joseph did, all the way if possible, but I would come myself as far as Dover. The difficulty about the church, we may consider now past; it was simply a very trifling and contemptible step taken by the owner of the adjoining property (probably in vexation that we had not bought <u>her</u> ground) to get the town to rescind their concession of the site; but it has done us good rather than harm, by drawing out a vast amount of respect & friendly feeling towards us. With best love from both, and hoping Josy is better, ever your most affectionate Hamilton.

Then Hamilton himself became ill – indeed he was frequently unwell during his time at Dunkirk. He died at Lindfield, Sussex, on 21 September 1868, aged thirty-nine. His will, dated 20 September 1868, reads:

THIS IS THE LAST WILL of me HAMILTON EUSTACE DICKER Consular Chaplain of Dunkirk in the Empire of France and of Lewis (sic) in the County of Sussex Kingdom of Great Britain I give devise and bequeath all my real and personal estate whatsoever and wheresoever it may be either in this Country or in France or to which I may be entitled in possession or in expectancy or in reversion to my dear wife CATHERINE SARAH DICKER for her own absolute use and benefit and I appoint my said wife sole Executrix of this my will In Witness whereof I have set my hand this twentieth day of September one thousand eight hundred and sixty eight Hamilton E.Dicker

There are two points of interest about this will, apart from the mis-spelling of 'Lewes'. Hamilton described himself as Hamilton Eustace, which are the names he adopted, whereas he was baptized Eustace Hamilton. Secondly, the will, probably his first, was made the day before he died. The exact amount of his estate is not known, but probate was sworn at under £450. Hamilton was buried in Worthing Cemetery, Sussex.

In his short life Hamilton showed remarkable talents, and he was sadly missed, not only within his own family, but in the communities where he had lived and worked. Here is a letter from his successor in Dunkirk, Rev. F.W. Kinxton, to his mother Martha, who was then living in Hove:

Dunkirk, France
28th May 1870

Dear Madam,
    Your polite note, enclosing one from a lady at Boulogne, reached
me this morning, and I am happy that any circumstances should have
occurred to enable me to communicate, even by letter, with the mother
of my good and worthy predecessor in the Chaplaincy. I assure you
scarcely a day passes without affording me fresh proofs of the devoted
zeal and earnestness of, as you with just hope and reason say, your now
blessed son. From high and low, the same tale of kind conciliation, of
unwearying exertion in his Master's Service, & of consistent Godliness,
is being perpetually repeated. Very often I have felt the sincere desire
that those who were nearest and dearest to him on earth could hear
what I have heard in his praise, especially from the lips of the poorer
class, in whose welfare he seems to have taken a special interest. It
would be a sad but yet cheering solace to their sorrowing hearts to
know how truly he was beloved & how deeply his loss is felt, how
greatly his memory is revered by all who had the pleasure & happiness
of his acquaintance
    With every sentiment of respectful sympathy for your own deep
grief, and those of his beloved widow & family, I remain, Dear Madam,
yours very faithfully,

F.W.Kinxton

Then disaster really befell the family. The seven children ranged from
Millie, aged fifteen, to the baby Gilbert who was barely one. There was
little money available for Kate to bring up this young family, and Kate had
a terrible time making provision for their maintenance and education. But
somehow she managed to arrange for her children to complete their education. She did receive a small income from a trust which her father-in-law
and mother-in-law, Thomas and Martha, had set up in 1847, the income
of which was divided equally between their seven children and their families.
The Trust Accounts are interesting, since they exclude the eighth child of
Thomas and Martha, Tom, who had disgraced himself in some way, as I
have mentioned earlier.
    Kate herself survived her husband by thirty-five years, and most of that
time she lived in lodgings in various parts of London (Lime Grove, Catford,

Acton, Walpole Terrace, Aldrington, Portslade, and South Norwood,).
Kate's last letter, just before she died, was to her cousin Esther Hope, at 39
Norfolk Square, Brighton:

16, Eldon Park, S.Norwood   March 6th 1903

Dearest Esther,

I am indeed very thankful that you are able to send a better report of
dear Sarah. I trust that now she will rally, & not 'worrit' – as we can
slowly get in order with brighter times before us. I feel that once the
real move is over I shall take life quietly – & she must do the same.

I did not know how ill she was – or I should have worried still more –
& could not have done any good – for my mind and body seemed worn
out. <u>Sleep</u> was the only thing for me – not quiet resting – but with
troubled dreams – jumbled together. It has been a terrible season to so
many.

We still have a sick house. Poor little Tam has a bad cold and cough,
and is kept in bed, hoping to cure it before his father comes next
Thursday.

Thank you very much for wishing to see me at your new house – but
it would be impossible just now – I am to be taken in a fly to the
Goodes & left there till the Charminster house is ready for me. Millie
can come to me every night as I still need her help. Charlie can only
be here from Thursday to Saturday, but Addie Crallen [her late husband's niece] is coming to help Ella here, and the real turnout will be
Monday & Tuesday 16th & 17th. I cannot write more, but hope to
finish my letter before long. My eyes and fingers get so tired.

Much love, & earnest prayers from your afft. cousin, Kate S. Dicker

As we shall see later, little Tam was her grandson, the 7-year-old child of
her eldest son Charlie.

Kate died on 15 March 1903, aged seventy-four, at Streatham, the house
of her friends the Goodes, just as she was about to move to Charminster in
Dorset.

Kate's great comfort over her latter years was her family, who kept in
constant touch with her, and helped her financially as far as they were able.

Family Group 1900. Left to right: Emily Winter (Dicker) Lee (1831–1918);
Charles George Hamilton Dicker (Tam) (1886–1977); Emily's maid;
Catherine Sarah (Cornwell) Dicker (Kate) (1829–1903); Rev. Charles
William Hamilton Dicker (Charlie) (1855–1912); Eleanor Hamilton Dicker
(Ella) (1862–1932).

She also had support from William Cornwell, her cousin, who lived at
Wenden Place, near Saffron Walden, and only a few miles from Barkway.
He was her father's nephew and had married her half-sister Ann. Kate and
her children were made welcome by William and Ann Cornwell at Wenden
Place, and the children spent many happy days there. Part of the premises
were used as a small school, and both Millie and Ella were there for a time,
Millie taking part in the housekeeping.

Kate's two daughters, Millie and Ella, never married. Millie, the elder,
was the linchpin of the family for many years, and the two sisters spent
most of their lives together. They were devoted to their mother and their
brothers, and they were, as Ella has recorded, the constant companions of
their cousins, the three Hope sisters, in their old age. They both lovingly
cared for their mother until her death, after which they moved to Dorset,
and helped their brother Charlie to bring up his son Tam.

Chapter IV

Australia

During the twenty years after the premature death of their father, Hamilton's children grew up and were educated in their various ways. And then, towards the end of the century, three boys, Charlie, Seymour and Gilbert, decided to emigrate to Australia, where the prospects of a secure future were exciting.

Charlie

Charlie, the eldest, had been ordained in 1881, and spent some time as curate in the parish of Pensnett, near Dudley, Worcestershire. He was not happy there, complaining that the vicar left him far too much work to do. He was expected to preach seven or more sermons a week, in his own parish and in surrounding villages, and altogether, although still in his twenties, he never really settled down in the urban surroundings. Like the rest of his family, he was always short of money, and on one occasion he was desperate to borrow £4 to last him from 2 December until the end of the month.

In 1886 Charlie was elected to a minor canonry at St David's Cathedral, Hobart, Tasmania. Of course he travelled there by sea, and, being a keen artist, on the way, through the Mediterranean, Suez Canal (only seventeen years after the canal was opened), and calling at Ceylon, he produced some sixty-five paintings, which still survive, in excellent condition.

He spent two years in Hobart, working at the cathedral.

While he was in Tasmania Charlie wrote many letters to his mother and sisters in England, and kept fascinating diaries.

Shortly after arriving in Hobart Charlie wrote to his mother:

14.4.87. On Easter Monday I had a delightful holiday. I went down the river in the 'Southern Cross' for a trip to 'East Bay Neck', the second of the narrow isthmuses of Tasman's peninsula. All the worst convicts were at Port Arthur, at the southern end of the peninsula, so that to escape they had to run fearful risks The whole peninsula with the exception of the cleared villages (townships we call them here) is covered with dense bush, affording no means of subsistence to human beings. At the first isthmus, 'Eaglehawk Neck', which is only two or three hundred yards wide, bloodhounds were kept on a platform which ran into the water on each side, and even if a man had tried to swim round he would have had to run the gauntlet of men in boats with blunderbuses, and plenty of sharks. Then came another large densely overgrown peninsula, then the second narrow neck guarded in the same way ten miles further on. In spite of all these difficulties men often did manage to escape, but they generally died of starvation or gave themselves up. There are abundance of bloodcurdling stories of the horrors of Port Arthur, of incredible cruelty on the part of the officials, and so forth. But I have always found that the inhabitants say that the evils are much exaggerated, and that as a matter of fact the system was not half as bad as the modern books make out. Certainly a good many were hung in those days for crimes of violence, as our registers show. All the well-behaved convicts were sent out as labourers or domestic servants, and the plan seems to have answered on the whole very well. Then all over the island there were small stations or depots, for those who were out of situations, or sick, or refractory – the worst of these went to the stations on the peninsula, and the very desperate ones to Norfolk Island, where the restraint was very severe . . . we hear accounts of little children, sometimes only 8 years old, being transported for crimes committed in England . . . can there be any truth in these stories?

His work at the cathedral seems to have gone down quite well, although he was very outspoken, and at times critical of both the Bishop and the Dean. He tried to improve the standard of music in the cathedral; he had no good words for the organist, and at first few for the choir. Here are extracts from some of his letters:

21.3.87. [after 3 months in Hobart, during which time he was trying to organise the cathedral choir] The choir are utterly vile in their singing, although people think we are improving. But the stupidity of boys, men and women is awful. They can't get through a service right. The boys are half gentle folks, none really poor. The girls are very grand, some of them, but want smashing sometimes.

14.4.87. Of course the choir and organist did their very abominablest on Easter Day morning, as they always do when the Bishop is there. He thinks I am a very dunce at music, and doesn't know how much better we get on when he isn't there. The organist lost his place in the Magnificat, and spoilt things generally. But the Bishop, who is a very severe critic, congratulated me publicly on what had been done.

[Whitsuntide 1887.] Our choir is getting better now – the utterly good for nothing ones have gone. I told them it was no good their coming at all if they were not to be depended upon.

He also became involved in local society:

14.4.87. [The Governor and his wife, Sir Robert and Lady Hamilton, had arrived from England] I went last week to Government House and took the bull by the horns – or rather the cow (don't put this in the Parish Magazine please) – and asked for flowers for the cathedral. Whilst I was waiting Lady Hamilton's little girl came in and talked to me – a dear little thing, full of fun. She told me all about their voyage, and about her brother at Cambridge, Trinity Hall, who they hope will get into the varsity boat. Lady H. is young and very pleasant – she told me of her plans for teaching the Hobart people 'etiquette de la cour', and how she evaded dancing in Lent etc., – she is just the person for Tasmania, and both she and Sir Robert are becoming very popular.

6.7.87. I have sent some acres of newspaper accounts of our Jubilee festivities [Queen Victoria's golden jubilee]. This event has probably done an immense amount of good in the colonies. It has taught the colonial mind that there is a Queen of England – a fact that was entirely denied before – that the colonies are really ruled by, and dependent upon, the mother country – another thing that wanted teaching out here. But the thorough way in which the Tasmanians have done justice to it has shown that the lesson was not thrown away on them.

[He went on to describe some of the celebrations.] The great Ball at Government House was a complete success. The rooms were beautifully arranged so that there was no crowd. I felt rather out of it at first – however I made a dash at last to the dais and was favourably received by the swells, and had a grand lady to take in to supper amongst the vice-regal party, to the awful envy of the hungry crowd.

Rev. Charles William Hamilton Dicker (1855–1912), Hamilton, Tasmania, 1894, with Kit

There are references in his letters to many people who were sick, and perhaps the following extract from a letter provides some explanation.

12.5.87. I have had a very sad case to deal with – a young fellow called Silver, a graduate of Magdalen, Oxford, came out to Melbourne in a sailing ship for his health; arrived here a month ago; in a week took to his bed in the Carlton Hotel, first Bright's disease and then typhoid set in, and I buried him yesterday. He was very patient and gentle, and I communicated him a fortnight ago. He seemed very happy and resigned, although the knowledge that his father expects him home again restored to health was a terrible grief to him. The doctors at home are much found fault with here, for sending so many hopeless cases out, to get them off their hands.

Early in 1889 Charlie was involved in a dreadful accident when sailing off Hobart. He was on a boat with a young friend, who was drowned, and this event seriously upset him, although he always maintained that he was not to blame. But this remained greatly on his conscience, and for a time he could not make up his mind whether to remain in Tasmania, accept an important curacy in Melbourne, or even to return to England. Eventually, after much discussion about his future, two years after arriving at Hobart he was appointed to Hamilton, a country parish about forty miles from Hobart. This was a curious coincidence. His third name was Hamilton, which had been in our family for three generations (and still remains), and later in life he adopted it instead of Charles, although his letters are signed 'Your loving son (or brother), C.W.H.D.' So far as I know there was no connection whatever between this name and the parish, or with Sir Robert Hamilton, the Governor.

Charlie spent eight years at Hamilton, and his many letters provide a very full description of his life there. Here is one which he wrote just before his official appointment to Hamilton:

27.3.89. I am spending the week in Hobart, as Synod is sitting. It is pretty certain now that I am to have Hamilton (unless some other living falls vacant in the next fortnight). I have had charge for three weeks now, and am getting quite the country parson. My predecessor, Mr Gray, has left the work in a very bad state – he has broken down through the use of chloral etc., and has had to give up work. The country air and riding and driving have already done me good – in fact I am as well as I could wish to be. I have been staying at the parsonage and using Mr Gray's horse etc. The house is very comfortable, and there is a very fine garden, though at present shamefully neglected. I shall set out to work at it next week; everything grows so fast here that there will soon be something to show.

There seems to be no opening that will bring me anywhere near Seymour [his brother Seymour, in Brisbane], so I shall stick to the idea of a home in Tasmania. and it grows more and more attractive to me. I long to get you out here. I am sure you would like it. There are so many English families in reduced circumstances who have made a bush home and 'do' for themselves in comfort. Wherever I am, we could make a nice home and support ourselves, as I should always get a better stipend than I should in England and you [his mother], and Milly and Ella would make no difference – rather a saving probably – in the expense of housekeeping. The country is not nearly as dull as one would think – there are many nice people scattered about, and all are very socially inclined. It is quite the thing for people to 'drop in' for a bed, as in England for afternoon tea. I rode or drove 80 miles last week, and called on 40 families. There are two townships with churches in the parish – Hamilton and the Ouse, 10 miles apart on a good road. Hamilton is a decayed agricultural place, the ground for miles round having been turned into a sheep run; but the Ouse is flourishing and contains a lot of nice people.

I send £10 today. I <u>must</u> keep a balance just now for necessary expenses if I am inducted; and Gray may want ready money for his buggy, which I could do well to buy – perhaps the piebald cob too, though she is almost too fat even for Dr. Grub!

Cheer up mother! What does it matter whether we have money or not, if we can live? It is not likely that any of us will be very rich, but so much the better. Hardly anyone has more than enough to live on here, but they manage to live very happily. If Ella were here now I could have got her a very good place as a governess – there are a good many opportunities for <u>ladies</u> in her position. I wish you would come out as my housekeeper. I could offer you £100 a year and beer, wherever I am. If Milly came, she could have a cow and keep chickens, as hundreds of ladies do here. Uncle W. will give her a lesson in milking!

I feel certain Gilbert [his brother, who later went to Queensland] could get something if he were out here, but there is nothing that would immediately pay his passage, or that would be kept open for him. Everybody fights shy of having young men out, as so many turn out badly.

You might tell the Killicks that a Major Holmes of the 60th has a large farm – and family – in Tasmania, and that one of his sons is a schoolmaster in my parish. They seem to have spent their all upon a start in the bush, and are now doing everything themselves – clearing, ploughing, dairying etc. It is uphill work, and will not pay, in money, for some time yet. But I think it is a splendid life.

Tasmania at that time was a British Colony, and as can be seen from his letters there were many colonists who had gone out to make their homes there. The population was about 132,000, and good agricultural land was sold by the government for £1 an acre. The climate was so temperate and equable, and the quality of the soil so rich, that it produced almost any kind of vegetation. Among Charlie's many interests were music, architecture, archaeology and botany. He was a competent artist, and painted over 200 pictures in Tasmania, landscapes and plant life. A century later these paintings came to light in England after his son's death in 1977. These were improperly obtained from me, and were subsequently exhibited and sold in London. I believe that many of those paintings found their way back to Tasmania.

His letters from Hamilton are too numerous to repeat here, but this one provides a description of his new parish:

16.4.89. I have just returned from a pastoral journey in that part of my parish called the 'New Country' – i.e. the open plains and marshes opened up by the new track to the West Coast. I went on horseback about 130 miles, and visited 12 large families and several shepherds' huts besides, during the week. In 3 places I baptized children, and held a short service; I also did a good deal of examining copy-books etc. It was surprizing to see how civilized and well looked after the children are – the smallest family consisted of 6 children, the largest 12. Without exception they were strong and hearty – in some cases beautifully cleaned and adorned for the occasion.

The day's work may be described thus. Accompanied by a Police Inspector on his rounds (no uniform; but a drab wide-awake turned down, a yellow oilskin coat (except when he preferred to ride in shirt-sleeves) – enormous leggings up to his waist, and a large stockwhip)

I started off from a sheep station about 8. I had my luggage on my saddle bow, and a bag on my back, which soon got filled with presents of skins etc.

We passed along a track, first marked on the turf of a sheep run, with here and there a fence with a 'sliding panel'.

Then through a forest of burnt scrub – all the trees dead and dying, their trunks looking bleached and like an overcrowded cemetry in which the tombs have taken root and shot up a couple of hundred feet, with white arms wildly twisted against the blue sky – we had miles upon miles of that sort of thing. Then the scenery gets green and we emerge upon a marsh, all dark rushy grass with lagoons, with the wheel tracks spreading all about to find hard ground, and crossing deep boggy creeks. Then a sort of rocky oasis, with gum trees and brush, and enclosed paddocks of good grass for a mile, surrounding a shepherd's hut. A dozen dogs bark, and children swarm out (sucking the bones of mutton chops – boiled mostly). We have come a dozen miles perhaps, at a slow walk, and are hungry. Horses are 'hung up' or let loose, a second edition of boiled chops – very nice – with beautiful camp-oven bread, put on the table; we sit on stools and set to work. Tea is the universal beverage – out of an enormous iron teapot which stands in the fireplace, always ready. We are beyond the region of fruit, so must not look for jam; but often a nice sweetened Damper is forthcoming, or pudding even, to finish with. Then I interview the children, while my companion catches the horses or smokes a pipe; and off we go. More marsh, then a rapid river to ford. Then up steep hills and through more burnt forests till the sun is low, when the barking of dogs, and children with mutton-chop-bones announce another hut. This time, after hand shakings, the saddles and bridles are taken off, and off the horses go, to hunt for themselves till the morrow. No question is asked about accommodation. There is the hut, a log building with two rooms; all wood except the enormous chimney of piled up stones. Skins hung up to dry all round – opossum, kangaroo, rabbit etc. One side of the interior taken up by a settee, one side by fireplace, one by rows of shelves for household utensils – and the larder; a door into the family sanctum. At tea, another stranger comes cantering up – his horse is set loose, & more hand shakings – no one has a surname here except the Parson, who is most ceremoniously treated. Tea cleared away, talk round the fire of about six logs the size of a man's body, for an hour, during which the children are being mysteriously stowed away. A bed is made up for me on the settee, several opossum and wallaby rugs thrown on the floor, and about 8 o'clock all turn in. My two friends on the floor go to sleep with pipes in their mouths, and I watch their bearded faces in the firelight for a very few minutes, & then off too.

At daybreak piercing frosty air comes in through the fireplace, and I hug the rug till I hear a welcome crackling there. By the time I have read the Psalms and a lesson things are ready for me to get up. I go outside and souse myself with a pail of water, & come in to breakfast, whilst the grey morning is still opening its eyes, and the white frost on the marshes, with mountains frowning beyond. Cold boiled mutton chops and bread and tea; then the family breakfast, while I go after my horse. He has gone clean out of sight. I give chase to somebody's I see a mile off – cross a river, then find it the wrong one. Back, across another river, there he is, but would rather not be caught – but I had very seldom much trouble that way.

The children are now cleaned, and I hold a short service; drawing illustrations from their father's occupation – branding the sheep etc., I teach them something of the Good Shepherd, to which they listen attentively. Then off again for another 30 mile ride, promising to call again. There is a great deal of snow in the New Country, and I was fortunate last week in having such bright weather. We came across one splendid house, inhabited by the owner himself. I had dinner there twice, in most luxurious fashion – English beer etc.

He has his sister and daughter up there in the summer I am told – he was not at home when I called, but his servant made me very welcome – and also the policeman; sounds of hilarity proceeded long and loud from the kitchen – more like a London Square than a bush house ten miles from the next neighbour, and 40 from the nearest settlement. Everything comes up from Hobart on a bullock dray, some-times with 'ten yoke' to it; no horses could draw on such a road.

I hope to make that journey every two or three months.

The week before, I rode over the hills beyond the Derwent towards the S.W., to a lovely new settlement called Ellendale, 12 miles off. I was guided by Douglas Bethune, a sheep-farming Saint. He is one of the most admirable class of men – his family owns a great many miles of sheep-run and forest, and he has acted as lay-curate to the whole district, magistrate, head of the rifle, cricket and football clubs etc. for years. His children are getting big, and he has bought a new place nearer Hobart in order to bring them up better, to the great sorrow of the neighbourhood. We called at a great many houses, held a service; I presided at a meeting of the building committee of the new Church, then galloped home through the dark bush late at night. I could see nothing for a great part of the way, but the white of his breeches, and even then I ran into his horse sometimes in the gloom of the forest – of course he knew every inch of the way, and avoided the 'logs'.

I have begun 'Litany and Catechising' every Sunday afternoon, alternately at Hamilton and the Ouse, and it takes well at present. In fact all my new services succeed – the Sunday <u>morning</u> service is the failure.

Holy Week is very uneventful here. One or two services are all one can expect people who are so scattered to come to. On Good Friday I go to the Ouse, to Ellendale, and back for evening service here – some 40 miles, and have been promised the loan of three horses to do it with, as mine wants a rest,

Last night (Monday) I had a communicants' class and choir practice at the Ouse; here very differently – hardly any are confirmed. I am trying to organize the Sunday School etc. We have a great Treat, or picnic as they call it here, on Easter Tuesday; with a concert in the evening, at which I am chief accompanyist! (All the talent is at the Ouse).

Here is an extract from a further letter:

15.2.94. I made a very pleasant trip to Lake St Clair. Some men from Melbourne – chiefly connected with the University – had a camp there, and I put in a couple of days with them. I took two of them up Mt Olympus, but they got so tired coming back that darkness overtook us in a scrubby place in the Cuvier Valley, where the track is hard to find by daylight. I took them into the river, which is rather rough – filled with boulders – and told them to follow it down. I pushed on, and lighted a fire where the ford is, for them to stop at until help arrived. Then I pushed through the scrub to the lake, and got to the camp. It was pitch dark and raining hard, so I sent some of the fellows with lanterns and supper to the ford, but the two men gave it up about a quarter of a mile higher up the river, and spent the night under a rock.

So the search party ate the supper and drank the grog by my fire, and then came home. They did not seem any the worse for their wet night when they turned up next day to receive the customary chaffing.

I was determined not to spend the night in the bush if I could help it because two stupid parsons have done it lately and brought the order into disrepute. One of them was so upset that he got a carbuncle on his nose and was ordered to go to England for a change, to the great disgrace of the cloth.

Five years after moving to Hamilton Charlie met Mary Margaret (May) Swan, the 33-year-old daughter of a Tasmanian family, and he staggered his family in England by announcing that they were to get married. The wedding took place in January 1895, and the best man was his younger brother Gilbert, who had travelled from Queensland for the occasion. After the wedding Gilbert wrote:

I couldn't tell you what costume was worn by anyone present except that I myself was trussed up in a tail coat and white waistcoat and top hat – a costume of a bygone barbarous age which I sincerely hope never to be condemned to wear again. When the fatal day arrived I drove from Hamilton to fetch the Bishop from the coach and drive him to the Ouse as quick as possible in order to give the poor man time to get some lunch, and then we adjourned to the church. The bride did not keep us waiting long and everything passed off without a hitch . . . Charlie was as unconcerned as a hearse horse. Just as the bride was coming up the church he leant over and told Miss Latham not to forget to put on the green altar cloth for the next Sunday.

Charlie's life thereafter was sad. He and his wife lived at the Ouse for just over a year, and in January 1896 she gave birth to a son, following which she became ill and died a few weeks later.

Charlie wrote to his mother on the day after May's death:

My poor poor old Mother,

I feel that this sad letter will be an awful blow to you, but perhaps my last may have in some measure prepared you for it. <u>It is well with</u> my darling – far far better than it could be if our wishes had been literally granted, and it may be that it is well with me and Baby too – though at present no happy path shines out through the impenetrable forbidding Future. But hitherto hath God helped us, and to that Help I am looking to bring me through the rest of my day's work, to the blessed call which bids me join her again.

You would like to have the whole story. Last Saturday Jones told us that, taking advantage of a favourable opportunity of sounding his patient more thoroughly, he had once more come across what seemed like an indication of <u>Hydatids</u>, and begged that Dr. Butler might be sent for from Hobart for a consultation. So next day the two came out, and after sounding the spot again (between the 5th and 6th ribs) they passed an exploring needle in, with the expected results. Dr Butler then said that the whole history of the case was plain, and the outcome of it certain if it were allowed to go any further. The supposed 'abcess' was a very large suppurating cist of Hydatids, which having burst from the liver through into the lung cavity was rapidly progressing in such a way as must soon end her life. So, weak as she was, they opened and drained a cist which must have contained pretty well two quarts of hydatids and pus. The effect was that she at once began to breathe freely and lost all pain. But the operation was too late – she never <u>quite</u> recovered consciousness, and although she readily took quantities of nourishment and stimulants she gradually sank, and the Day of the Annunciation came upon us as she took the last turn.

Her vitality was so wonderful that she lived 12 hours after the Doctor had given her up, and the struggle was a dreadful one. We find it very hard, after all these weeks of battle and suffering, to think of her at all as the dear sweet smiling little May that everybody fell in love with. And this helps us in a measure to make our thank-offering to God for a life so pure and single hearted and unselfish as hers has been.

I was reading to myself the 2nd lesson for the day: '<u>And Mary said, My soul doth magnify the Lord</u>' etc, when it flashed upon me how wonderfully my darling Mary was like my ideal picture of the Blessed Mother, and I shall always count Lady Day as a <u>very happy</u> day, one I can understand, better than other Saints' days.

The day before, there was one brief lucid interval, although she could not express herself rightly, and I mentioned to her that I had just had a letter from my dear old friend Mrs Davies in Hobart. After some struggling with her poor tongue May told me to 'save Mrs Davies's letter'.

Earlier in her illness the lucid minutes were generally employed in talking over our plans when she was well again, and plans for bringing up the little Charlie. She had such hopes that the liver trouble was passing away, and that she would ride and drive about with me again. One day she said 'Poor old boy, my liver spoilt your wedding tour last year; we'll have such a happy one this year to make up for it'.

I told you, I think, how she commended the child to Julia to nurse when she was gone. A day or two afterwards, when she was so much better she said 'I think now we shall have Baby to ourselves after all'. Now and then she would call for him, and would touch him, and would call him so sweetly 'Mother's little darling', 'Be a good little boy', 'Mummy's little treasure'. Then the excitement would prove too much for her, and she would break into murmuring exclamations. Once when she was quite herself she told us how very glad she was that she knew she had to die – that it had come rather as a surprise to her, but that she was willing to leave herself in God's hands.

So there is the ending of a life so precious that I can't estimate my loss. No one but God knows what she was to me.

After May's death Charlie gave much thought to his future, and that of the baby. His sister-in-law Julia Swan was willing to take care of the baby, but he was not happy about this although he had a great regard for Julia. One possibility was that his mother and sisters might join him in Tasmania, but in the end Charlie decided to give up his living and he returned to England with his baby son early in 1897.

He lived with his mother at Portslade and Norwood until just before her death. After a short time at Charminster he was appointed to the living of Piddeltrentide in Dorset, where he lived with his sisters Millie and Ella, who helped him to bring up his son.

While at Piddeltrentide Charlie took an active part in local organisations. One spectacular event which he conceived, created and presented in July 1910 was the 'Pydel Pageant'. (The name of the village, now known as 'Piddletrenthide', has been spelt in different ways over the years). The pageant was performed to a large audience including the Bishop of Salisbury, in the vicarage grounds and was adjudged to be a tremendous success, ending with 'The Dorset Shepherd's Song' composed by Rev. C.W.H. Dicker.

He died in August 1912 following an accident when his new motor cycle, which he was riding, skidded under a lorry.

After his death the *Church Times* reported:

Charles Dicker was one of the most versatile of men – an artist and a wood craftsman, a poet and a writer, a musician and a composer, an antiquary, a natural scientist, a pageant organiser, a lecturer, a photographer, and much more besides. Such clergymen as he do not stagnate in small country parishes; indeed his wide interests and many studies made him all the more efficient as a parish priest. Busy in his home, busy among his parishioners, busy in his rural deanery, busy in the county, he was one of those strenuous souls who alone find time to get things done and to get them done well. For the last three years of his life he was very happy in holding the office of honorary editor of the Proceedings of the Dorset Natural History and Antiquarian Field Club, of which club he was also a vice-president and a much valued member, and not a few of his confreres journeyed from far-lying parts of the country to be present at his funeral. At the close of the service the Archdeacon of Dorset read to the assembled congregation a telegram from the Bishop of Salisbury sending his deepest sympathy to the mourners, and expressing the grievous loss which the county of Dorset and the diocese of Salisbury had sustained in the death of this single-minded parish priest who had so many talents committed to him, and had used them so faithfully for the glory of God and the good of man.

Seymour

My grandfather was the sixth of the children of Hamilton and Kate, having been born in Dunkirk in 1865. His life was centred round music, and before he was ten he went to St Paul's Cathedral School, where he became head chorister. In 1881, at the age of sixteen, he was appointed organist of St Michael's, Sydenham. He was an organ pupil of Sir John Stainer, and won an organ scholarship to Christ's College, Cambridge, where he was a founder member of the 'Footlights' Club. On leaving Cambridge he was appointed organist of St George's Church, Perry Hill, London. He composed a number of works, and at the age of twenty, with his eldest sister Milly he wrote the Fairy Operetta *Little Snowdrop and the Seven Wee Men*, which was first performed at Forest Hill, Kent in 1886. Later that year, on the recommendation of Sir John Stainer, he went to Australia as organist and choirmaster of Brisbane Cathedral. He was a different character from his elder brother Charlie, vague, jolly, unmethodical, but always great fun. What I remember most was the enormous wallet which he used to carry in his inside jacket

Mr. Seymour Dicker.

MR. DICKER was born in France in 1865, but has nevertheless always considered himself an Englishman. Before he was ten years old he was singing as a chorister in St. Paul's Cathedral, and in 1881, when only sixteen years of age, he was appointed organist of St. Michael's, Sydenham. The following year, however,

Photo by Poul Poulsen, Brisbane.

MR. SEYMOUR DICKER.

Seymour Fane Hamilton Dicker (1865–1938)

pocket, full of papers, but not money, in which he never had much interest. While in Brisbane he became musical director of a number of societies, and continued to compose, although his works did not become well known. He directed the Musical Union and two amateur opera companies in the city, and conducted the festival concerts given in connection with the Queensland International Exhibition in 1897.

In Brisbane he met Ethel Margaret Buckeridge, daughter of Charles Buckeridge of Hampstead, England, and in September 1890 a double wedding took place in Brisbane Cathedral – Seymour and Ethel on the one hand,

*Arthur Seymour
Hamilton Dicker
(aged 13 months)*

and on the other Ethel's brother John Buckeridge was married to Ada Stanley. In the official report of the wedding it was said: 'That Mr Dicker must be popular among the musical fraternity of Brisbane is evident from the fact that every musician of note was present to assist in the choral ceremony.' The Bishop of Brisbane and Seymour's brother Charlie were the officiating clergy. After the service Seymour and his bride were conveyed in the Governor's carriage, which had been placed at his disposal for the occasion, together with coachman and footman, to the reception at the Masonic Hall for the wedding breakfast. The report also stated: 'Mr Dicker having received handsome presents from the Governor, Sir Charles and Lady Lilley, Sir Samual and Lady Griffith, and hosts of others, the young people seem to commence their new career under very happy auspices.'

Seymour was a member of the 'Johnsonian Club', a strictly exclusive club

Richard Maitland Hamilton Dicker (1900–1965), Arthur Seymour Hamilton Dicker (1892–1974), Gilbert Charles Hamilton Dicker (1894–1974), Seymour Fane Hamilton Dicker (1865–1938), Ethel Margaret (Buckeridge) Dicker (1869–1950), Mildred Ethel Hamilton (Dicker) Biden (1891–1961), Violet Ella Hamilton (Dicker) Morrison (1897–1988), Dorothy Catherine Hamilton Dicker (1902–1964), Nancy Hamilton Dicker (1895–1922)

in Brisbane, described as a delightful Bohemian assembly, Scientific, Artistic and Literary. Seymour was said to be: 'the chief object of worship within its precincts, and the most popular man in Brisbane'.

On 8 September 1890 a 'Seymour Dicker Benefit Concert' was held in the Centennial Hall, Brisbane, under the immediate patronage of His Excellency the Governor, His Honour Sir Charles Lilley, and other distinguished members of the local community. The programme, conducted by Seymour, included Mendelssohn's 'War March of the Priests', Mozart's 'Overture in C', and ended with a March 'St George', by S. Dicker.

Seymour remained in Brisbane for twelve years, and during that time his wife Ethel gave birth to five children – Mildred (Millie), Arthur (my father), Gilbert, Nancy and Violet. When the family returned to England there were two further children – Richard (Bobs) and Dorothy. Seymour entered the service of London University at the London Day Training College, a training school for teachers, and during his long service there it was said that he possibly assisted in training more teachers in music than did any other man. For several years he lived in Dulwich and was organist and choirmaster of Chelsea Old Church. He was Director of Music at various colleges under the London County Council, and a member of the Savage Club.

While in Australia Seymour had been able to save some money, and again on his return to London where he was able to earn a fair amount. Although he always regarded music as more important than money, he managed to send his three sons to boarding school at Ardingly.

Seymour became a freemason while in Australia, and he continued to be an active mason on his return to England. He was a member of several lodges in London and Brighton, and of course he was usually appointed organist.

In 1920 he and Ethel moved to Brighton, where he remained for the rest of his life. There he continued his musical activities, arranging and assisting at concerts and deputizing as organist at churches, and he was, at the time of his death in 1938, organist of Christ Church (Unitarian), New Road, Brighton. He was aged fifty-five when they moved to Brighton, and thereafter life became difficult for them. In 1932 he wrote to his sister Millie:

> The musical profession is very much depressed just now but everybody else is too, and we manage to keep our heads above water. I go to London every Wednesday for my organ recital and give Musical Appreciation lectures every week, with gramophone recitals for the 'Columbia' Company, to Associations of various kinds, and in schools,

all over Sussex. It is very interesting work and each brings me in £1.1.0 and expenses, and the idea will develop, I hope. I got over £50 last year.

But his optimism did not continue, and his work brought in less and less. He got depressed but had wonderful support from Ethel and his two unmarried daughters Nancy and Dorothy, who started a small school called 'Nurseryland' in their house at 3 Crescent Place.

In 1938 he became very ill at his home in Brighton, and his last days were plagued with worry that he had nothing to leave to his family, who were immensely helpful in supporting him and Ethel in their old age. He died at home on 20 June 1938, aged seventy-three.

Gilbert

The third brother to go to Australia was the youngest of the family of Hamilton and Kate. Before that, he was educated at Trinity College, Stratford, and in 1892, at the age of twenty-four, encouraged perhaps by glowing reports from Charlie and Seymour, he went to Queensland and took up cattle farming in a remote place called Conobie, about 400 miles from the east coast, and 200 miles from the north coast. Conobie was a cattle station, which mainly consisted of one large building in which all the inhabitants lived – not more than ten or so perhaps. Most residents of Queensland lived on the coastal strips, but this station was far from them. Conobie was almost cut off from civilisation. Mail from England arrived at Normanton, on the north coast, about once a month, and thence by coach to Donors Hills Post Office. Letters and newspapers were then carried by horse mail to Conobie, but parcels had to wait until someone was passing who would take them. So Gilbert was very much out of touch with home, letters sometimes taking as much as two or three months to reach him and vice versa.

At the station they had mainly bullocks, which were taken each year to the nearest port at Normanton, or to Townsville on the east coast. There were also some milking cows and pigs. It was very hard work for Gilbert, and indeed all the residents at the station. He wrote regularly to his mother in England, and kept in touch with Charlie in Tasmania, but he had some difficulty in communicating with Seymour in Brisbane, who never wrote letters, and all the family complained about this.

On one occasion they were visited at Conobie by an Afghan hawker with a camel, a survivor of past years when such animals were fairly common.

According to Gilbert one of the workers thought that the camel was a cross between an emu and a kangaroo, and the horses were very frightened by it.

In 1894 his brother Charlie asked him to go to Tasmania and act as his best man, so he decided to go, thinking that he might not return to Conobie. Gilbert described his journey:

Arthur Hillcote and I, and the little black boy 'Tommy' left Conobie on 7th Dec. Our cavalcade consisted of six horses, two for me, two for Arthur, one for the kid, and one carrying the pack. The first day we only made a short stage of 25 miles to a hut on the plain. The next morning we started in earnest about 6 o'clock, and that was the only time we had any trouble with the horses. Our packhorse started bucking, and I began to think that all my savings of 20 years were going to spread about the country promiscuously – but luckily he was caught in time. Then I had a turn. A strap was broken, and I went back to the hut, about 100 yds, to get another one. Much to my surprise my little mare started off full gallop straight into a clump of timber, and when I got a pull on her, she down with her head, and imitated the pack horse. I thought I was going to be squashed against the trees, but I steered between them somehow, and got back all right. By the end of the day we had done 45 miles and there wasn't much buck in any of the animals. Thence we travelled on without any incident to Hughenden in just 7 days – 280 miles. We had some rain almost every night and towards the end the road were terribly heavy. We had a small fly with us, but that would not stop rain from beating in, and once we got wet through, blankets and all. Once we had to travel about ten miles before breakfast, as we had eaten all the cooked food and everything was too wet to make a fire and cook more. Two of the horses we sent back with a drover we met on the road, returning to Conobie, and the other four we left at Hughenden.

Then we spent one whole day in the train to Townsville. I stopped the Sunday in Townsville with the Hillcotes and started on Monday by the Arawatta for Brisbane, where we arrived on Friday at daylight. The boat was due on Thursday, and poor old Seymour waited all night on the wharf! He drove me out to his house at Rocklea – 8 miles, where we had breakfast, and I was introduced to my nephews. The baby is a fine little chap, with big eyes – never cries, and will amuse himself for hours on the verandah (caged in so that he can't fall), perfectly happy so long as he sees someone occasionally. Millie and Arthur are both bouncers, fat and strong and look twice their age! Certainly they have lungs strong enough to supply the wind to the Crystal Palace organ! They are the most irrepressible little beasts but dear little things for all that. I presented them with a go-cart, and they have not yet succeeded in breaking their necks out of it. We got up a Christmas tree for them, it was grand to see their facial expressions on seeing it. Seymour is much the same as ever, only more so. He always seemed as if he were on wires, and the wires seem to have tightened. Ethel looks very well. They have a very comfortable little house with a garden and two small paddocks. Plenty of big blue gum trees all round them, with stumps of hundreds of old trees. Their neighbours seem very pleasant people.

I left there on 2nd January, and came on to Sydney, where I saw Gooch again, and renewed the recollections of my youth by going to see a pantomime. I was only one night there, catching the Tasmanian boat next day.

Ouse Jany.10th. Here I am once more in Tasmania. I have seen HER. She has certainly a very sweet face and nice figure. She seems very quiet and rather reserved – but I shall be able to say more about her next time. I only saw her for a few minutes last night. The brothers and sister seem very nice too. I haven't seen the father yet. Charlie is not changed at all – a little more comfortable I think, and more satisfied with life. He has developed a liking for sentimental songs!! a very bad symptom. The sacrifice takes place next Monday and our time will be pretty well taken up till then. After that I am to stay a week or so at Dunrobin and then join the happy couple at Port Arthur for the last few days of the honeymoon, and then Charlie wants me to come back and play in a tennis match, but my subsequent doings must depend on circumstances as the 'cheque' won't last much longer. I am afraid I shall have to go back to Conobie. All inquiries I have made result in the same answer.

I shall feel rather ashamed to do so, as I felt pretty sure when I left of being able to improve my position. The boss was really most kind – he wrote two letters for me – one to myself and one to Mr Grant. Mine was very satisfactory, but the one to Mr Grant was most complimentary and flattering – the more so, as I was not supposed to know what it contained. But after all, what good is it! The old man insisted on sending a present to the bride and commissioned me to get it for him in Sydney – as well as sending a couple of paper knives made by himself out of some pretty wood that grows out there. It is a treat to be down in this climate again. I spent yesterday trout fishing with George Swan in a lovely mountain stream shut in by high hills. Such a difference to what I have been used to. The whole place too seems so homelike and pleasant. Not the glare and worry and generally unsettled and unsatisfied feeling that there is up north. The people here seem content to settle down here, whereas up in the gulf everyone believes that he or she is only stopping for a time, though like me many return to it.

I will write again after the wedding. Your loving son, Gilbert

After the wedding, as expected, Gilbert went to join the happy couple in Port Arthur, sailing in a storm from Hobart to Taranna, and found Port Arthur itself in flames, with everybody in a wild state of excitement. A bush fire had been burning in the hills for nine days, and the storm through which Gilbert's boat had passed had driven it towards the township. A splitter's hut was the first to go, and after that the model prison. Then the lunatic asylum, the hospital, the police station and some private houses caught fire, and eventually a large part of Port Arthur was destroyed.

Charlie and his bride were living in the old officers' quarters next to the hotel, which had been the commandant's house in the old days. These buildings caught fire several times, but the fires were put out without a great deal of damage. It was a sad scene as all the old buildings had gone.

Eventually Gilbert came to the firm conclusion that he could not find employment in Tasmania, and he would have to return to Conobie. Shortly after his arrival at Conobie he experienced another disaster – the whole station house was destroyed by fire. Like the buildings in Port Arthur, everything was built of wood, and once the fire got a grip there was no stopping it. Gilbert lost all his personal possessions, and in those days, and in such a place, there was no form of insurance. Gilbert was in charge of the station at the time, the owner Mr Palmer being away, and although Gilbert was not blamed it was very much on his conscience.

Gilbert stayed on at Conobie for a short time, but his health gave some cause for concern, and he moved to a more civilized part of Queensland, Oona, near Gooray, about 100 miles inland from Brisbane. This was after Charlie, and also Seymour and his family, had returned to England. He was really wanting to obtain a small farm of his own, but for the time being he obtained one or two jobs as a bookkeeper. He regarded himself as a 'plodder',

Conobie, Queensland, May 1895

and never really settled down. Then came the First World War, and after a time he decided to join the Army. But he was too old, so he gave a false age when he enlisted in April 1917. His attestation paper gave his age as 44 years 7 months, but he was born on 9 August 1867, so in fact he was aged nearly fifty at the time, and if he had disclosed this his application would have been refused.

In June 1917 he travelled to England in a troopship and then to France, where he served as a private soldier for several months. Although Gilbert passed his initial medical examination his health was never good, and he suffered a great deal during his army service. Shortly after the Armistice in November 1918 he returned to Australia suffering from 'chronic rheumatism' and was discharged in March 1919.

After the war Gilbert remained at Oona doing odd jobs and running a smallholding, where he grew maize, cotton and wheat, but although quite happy he was never very successful. He wrote long letters to his sisters in England, most of these describing the weather which was of such great importance to everyone there. One experience in 1920 is worth recording from a letter to his sister Millie:

> You were always a good letter writer and lately you have developed a very keen humour of a rather satirical variety. What a blessing it is to see the funny side of things! What must life be to those who can't? It was want of a sense of humour that made the Germans so objectionable.
>
> The great event of the day is that the rain has come at last! After numerous threatenings and beginnings we have now had something to last some time. Of course the drought made itself as obnoxious as possible and chose its time of breaking just when there were 70 people gathered together at Oona – the long looked for Bachelors' Dance. All the week we had been busy getting things ready and all was complete. The Dining and Sitting Rooms were carpetless and furnitureless and opened into one big room. The extempore supper room outside looked splendid, roofed with tarpaulins, sides covered with bagging, a long table supported on stumps, sunk in the ground with stools likewise – the whole very nicely decorated with greenery (real) and flowers (artificial). The tennis court was swept and garnished and the lines freshly marked with mathematical accuracy. Friday was a beautiful day, clear and pleasantly warm and the guests began to arrive in the afternoon, nearly all in motors. Friday night's dance and supper were a great success but were not kept up much after midnight in consideration of the hard

day's tennis and more dancing that was in front of them. Alas! Man proposes etc. At daylight next morning an ominous rattle began on the roof. At first very light, the rain got heavier as the day wore on till at night it was coming down in sheets. The tennis court was under water, half the supper room was flooded so we had to have meals in relays. Still, everyone was happy, delighted at the end of the drought. The young folk danced all day (I never saw such endurance) while the elders played cards or swapped yarns about former droughts.

However, the question was – how to get home? Motors wouldn't be able to travel along our roads for (possibly) weeks! It was important for most of them to get back, besides how was the Oona commisariat to stand the strain of that mob for a whole week? The only train was one passing Gooray at 3 a.m. on Sunday morning, so most of them decided to go home by that. Then another trouble arose. Gooray is 3 miles away, and the track goes through low-lying and heavy blacksoil country which would be utterly impassable after such a deluge. Luckily we had the telephone so we rang up the station master at Goondiwindi, and prevailed upon him to instruct the train to stop at 'Burke's Grid'. This is a level crossing (they call them all grids on account of a gridiron arrangement on both sides of the crossing to prevent cattle straying up the line) only about 2 miles away and the track to it goes through better kind of country. We thought we could get there without much difficulty. So it was decided to try, and at 1 a.m. just 40 people (nearly half of them girls) set out. We had a large buggy, a sulky and a spring cart which carried the girls (or most of them) and the men had to walk. It was pitch black dark and raining harder than ever. I was the pilot and walked in front with the lantern. Just away from the homestead there is a watercourse that has been dry for over two years. I had inspected this an hour earlier and found only a few inches of water, but now it was waist deep. However there was no going back. In the middle some part of the buggy harness broke and the horse walked out of the shafts. No matter, 20 men shoved the buggy out, the harness was fixed up, the horse put back and on we went. Then for a few hundred yards we were on a good main road and thought our troubles were over. Then we came to the turn off and from there to the railway we never saw land! The road which Mr Evans had described as a 'good hard track' and the country all round were all under water, mostly knee deep. We kept to it by following the cleared line of timber and battled along slowly. Every 100 yards or so the horses had to be rested, and then several men would have to shove behind to get the vehicles started again. It was indeed the 'End of a Perfect Day'.

Then the spring cart stuck up, and had to be left till the buggy could come back and take its passengers. However, at last we all reached the railway at 3 a.m., having been just 2 hours over the two miles! Just now the rain eased up a bit and the folks began to recover their spirits and started singing, though every one was wringing wet. So they amused themselves till the train came along at 4.30 (our trains are very casual – an hour or so is nothing). Then we yelled and waved the light for fear the guard wouldn't pull up. The sleepy passengers must have thought they were stuck up by Red Indians. However it stopped all right, and in they bundled leaving me alone to wait for daylight. Jack McArthur was coming back with me but it was hopeless to tackle the return trip in the dark with 3 vehicles and only two men so he went on to Gooray to get our mail, afterwards walking back along the line. I had tied the horses to trees, standing in water, poor brutes. I was wearing my old military overcoat, and finding an old bag to lie on, I lay down and had a snooze for an hour. It was quite like some of my experiences in France. When daylight came Jack and I had little difficulty in getting home with the three traps, and arrived just in time for a good breakfast, a bath and then to bed.

They are expecting to hold the whole affair here again in a fortnight's time. Mrs Evans is indeed plucky. When you consider all the work it entails without any paid domestic assistance, though of course there are plenty of voluntary helpers. There were fourteen motors that arrived on Friday. Two of them went away on Friday night, intending to come back on Saturday. Mac Ross got back to Callandoon on Sunday morning but he had only 4 miles to go and a comparatively good road. Besides he has a very powerful car. The other 11 cars all had to be left at Oona. A few thousand pounds worth!

[In the same letter there was a reference to prices.] Queensland is certainly cheaper for butter this year. I think it is 2/3, but I never have to buy it. They make a lot at Oona and Mrs Evans always send me some. Sugar is just raised to 6d. now. Both sugar and butter are 'fixed prices'. Tailors prices have jumped terrifically. I enquired the other day for a pair of trousers (gabardine) similar to what I got in January 1917 for £1.11.0. The present price is £3.15.0. I'm simply not going to give it. I'll wear fig leaves first!

Gilbert continued to live at Oona until, in 1932, having always regarded himself as a confirmed bachelor, he met and married Elizabeth Jane Taylor, a widow whose maiden name was Rolfe. She was known as Bessie, and she and Gilbert were very happy together for about ten years. This marked a major change in Gilbert's life. When he married Bess they set up their home at Morningside, just outside Brisbane. He was then in his mid-sixties, and neither he nor Bess were in good health. Perhaps because of his severe rheumatism, which was noted on his discharge papers in 1919, he gradually lost the use of his right hand, and although he continued to work in his garden all his letters in his later years were written with his left hand.

Bess died on 12 December 1941 and was buried in Toowong Cemetery, Brisbane. Gilbert lived another ten years, and died in Eventide Home, Sandgate, Brisbane on 26 May 1952 at the age of eighty-four. He was buried beside Bess in Toowong Cemetery.

What kind of a man was Gilbert? He was the youngest of the seven children of Hamilton and Kate, excluding little Arthur who only lived for less that one year. He never knew his father, and was brought up in circumstances of some poverty. At an early age he decided that there was no future for him in England, and followed the call which attracted so many in those days, to seek his fortune overseas. But unlike his brothers, all of whom obtained some professional qualifications, he never progressed far in any job which he took on. He described himself as a plodder, and he really enjoyed the tough life which he chose, or perhaps which circumstances forced him to adopt. He worked hard, at times incredibly hard, and in his early days he always hoped to better himself by obtaining some more profitable employment. In many ways he felt disillusionment, but he continued quite happily until in his latter years he settled down with Bess to share a home. He never lost touch with his family in England, writing frequently to his mother until her death in 1903, and also to his two sisters Millie and Ella, who died in 1939 and 1932 respectively. Strangely enough, I never heard my father mention him, and indeed he may never have met him.

There remains a mystery. In his will, drawn up in 1951, he left legacies totalling £550, including two to his nieces Nancy and Dorothy Dicker in England, but the residue of his small estate he left to Mrs Eunice Mary Forsyth Dicker, and a legacy to Robert George Dicker. Both Robert and his wife were said to be living in the same house as Gilbert, but I have not been able to trace whether there was any relationship. Robert George was certainly not Gilbert's son, and Gilbert's death certificate shows as informant 'R.G. Dicker, friend'. Possibly in his declining years, after the death of Bessie, Gilbert met Robert George, and found him to be descended from his (Gilbert's) uncle Thomes Frederick, who was said to have disgraced himself and gone to Australia about 100 years before. He was the 'Tom' mentioned by Hamilton in his letter to his parents of 5 March 1841. Thomas Frederick certainly had children, including Claude Hamilton and Emmeline Hamilton.

But perhaps Robert George was no relation at all, and just met up with Gilbert in his old age.

So Australia saw a lot of our Dicker family at the end of the nineteenth century and the early part of the twentieth. There are many Dickers living in Australia now, no doubt all descended from Dickers in the last 200 years. There was an Arthur Dicker, a convict from Sussex, transported in 1821, and executed for slaughtering a bullock in 1824. And an Arthur Seymour Dicker (my father was Arthur Seymour Hamilton), born in Hackney in 1883, who went to Australia in 1903 (not as a convict!), and was killed at Gallipoli. More recently George Dicker retired as bursar of Canberra University, and we became good friends by correspondence, although we never met, and never established any relationship between our two families. Sadly George died in 1994.

Chapter V

Millie, Ella and Tam

Apart from the three brothers who went to Australia, there were three other sons of Hamilton and Kate.

Sadly, Arthur died from whooping cough on 15 April 1860, one week before his first birthday. I have a little copy of 'In Memoriam', inscribed 'To much loved M.H.D. from Hamilton & Kate on behalf of Arthur Wrey Hamilton May 18th 1859'. Martha Hamilton Dicker (M.H.D.) was Hamilton's mother, who was probably Arthur's godmother, and the date no doubt referred to Arthur's christening, as he was born on 25 April 1859.

Maitland, born in 1857 at Bridport, married his cousin Hettie Crallen. They had no children, and Maitland died in 1913.

Assheton, born at Warminster in 1860, was accepted at the age of eight for the Clergy Orphan School, Canterbury. This was a boarding school, and he wrote many letters to his mother and his sisters while he was there:

My dear Mama,   21st October 1871

I am all right now. Has Gilbert been to Wenden before? I hope you enjoyed your visit. Did you leave Tamar and the rabbit at Lewisham alone, or did you take Tamar and leave the rabbit with Charlie and Maitland? I am glad it is all right. The time flies away very quickly does it not? did you play cards at Wenden like we did? You did not stay long. We have had some very fine weather till today, we have had drizzling rain all this afternoon. I am glad Ella is happy. has Millie come back yet? I hope she gets back safe. Mrs Harris is very kind, she lets me have meat for breakfast every morning and sometimes gives me an egg for tea. I gave her that note. Give my love to Gilbert and Seymour and my rabbit.

Ever your fond son A.G.H. Dicker

At that time Charlie and Maitland would have been aged 16 and 14 respectively, while Ella was 9 and Millie 18. Gilbert (4) and Seymour (6) apparently accompanied Kate on her visit to her wealthy cousin William Cornwell at Wenden, while the two older boys were left at Kate's house in Lewisham.

Four years later Ella wrote to Assheton, still at the same school, suggesting that he might have forgotten his brother Charlie's forthcoming twenty-first birthday, and she received the following reply:

Dearest Ella (that doesn't seem the right way to begin a 'jawing' letter)

Your base insinuations are highly insulting & degrading. To say that I, A.G.H.D., F.R.C.S., a.b.z.x.y.w.v. & royal knight of Columbiganice &c. &c., had not the honour and welfare of our most gracious family at heart as to forget all about his majesty's coming of age. I am sorry to say that I cannot subscribe to your kind thought for divers reasons. For your impertinence &c. I won't make you my confidante. Take that awful punishment with all the patience & resignment you may, although it is with pain I say it; yet it is my duty as a just & impartial judge to read the sentence. But you will know my awful secret anon; I do not throw you into the bottomless pit of ignorance for ever; far from it; you will soon rise again from it, so don't despair. After all it won't be such a very great secret, but its as well to make as much of it as possible. Sooth to say that I have my own present to give him. If it comes before the time, keep it till Saturday morning for him. It will be a long something I expect. I shall address it to Mr <u>W</u>. Dicker so look out for it. You had better tell Tamar about the address; and she is not to let Charlie see it, if she goes to the door to get it; but mind, you are not to open the parcel till the day comes; anyhow you must let Charlie open it himself. You must write again and guess what it is, and tell me what you have proposed getting. If you had told me before this I might have joined my money to yours to get an album or something like that, but I haven't any money now so I can't subscribe to it. Mind you obey my instructions and don't get sulky about my not telling you; but I never intended to tell anyone, because I am afraid everyone will jaw at me for it; but it was quite a sudden thought of mine to get what I have. I hope they <u>won't</u> jaw. Among other things I should like to know what was that wonderful picture at the end of your epistle; all I can make of it is a <u>very</u> fat man with an immense pair of shears stuck deep into his back and a toasting fork with a huge piece of potatoe or something on it coming out of his back – followed by a little ghost in a winding sheet, with a dog clinging onto one of the corners of the same winding sheet; and lastly a little boy with a long beard looking on with the utmost complacency, as though it were an everyday occurrence! A strange picture indeed; and rather horrible too.

Give my love to everyone, Ever your affectionate Junipper Bow Yow.

Tamar was the faithful family servant, who looked after Kate for many years. About the same time Assheton wrote to his mother:

My Dear Mamma.

I write to wish you many happy returns of your birthday. I don't know whether I have sent one of the views which I send now; I know I sent the entrance, but I don't remember sending one of the Canterbury side. I hope you are all quite well. I am awfully well for my part. I think I shall put 3 bob in the bank, because my money's going so fast. That only makes 15/- though, and when <u>shall</u> I get about £4 to get a gold chain! I suppose I shall in time though; but I wish old Mr Ashton or some covey would tip me a couple of pounds or so like Mr Seymour does; he's an awful brick.

Cecil has been promoted into the 6th form; he is going to college; I shan't go into the 6th at all; because the upper Vth is the commercial form and all that sort of thing and in the 6th they do little or no arithmetic which is what I want most. Toffee making is all the rage in the school now, and I have made three brews already, of different recipes as to how much butter to put in the sugar etc.. I wish you would give a recipe for toffee; do you ever make it? We do a most frightful lot of stuff (I mean work, <u>not</u> eatables!) we do Horace now, besides the old things; we do Horace, Virgil and Ovid; Horace & Ovid repetition, besides construing and in Greek I believe we are going to do Orestes. I shan't be <u>last</u> this time I think.

I can't think of anything else to say; ever your affectionate son A.G.H.Dicker

After leaving school Assheton lived with his mother at Catford, in South London, and took an office job for a short time. Like other members of his family he was always enterprising, and when he was twenty-three he learned *The Canterbury Tales* by heart, after which he proposed, for his annual holiday (in a letter to Millie):

to buy a young hop pole and a scallop shell (I could get several of the latter for 1d., vinegar pepper and fish included), and walk to Canterbury to do homage to St Thomas's – hill worn by the steps of generations of C.O.S. chaps wending their way to Mother Normans! I should like to know Charlie's opinion as to the best plan; I think I shall go by train to Dartford on the Saturday night, walking pretty easily to Rochester on Sunday; (I want to see Stone Church & a saxon tower of which I forget the name not far from Dartford) on the road. Then I should sleep at Rochester & get up early & do the remaining 25 miles on the Monday. Will you ask Charlie if that would be practicable, & if I should find difficulty in getting a bed at Dartford & Rochester?

Then I intend to spend two days at Canterbury, after which I should go home & on to Wenden, Cambridge & Ely; & if it would suit you to come home then, I will come & fetch you & we will call at Rugby & Warwick (if you tell me soon; I will write to ask Miss Johnson what is the best day to go to Warwick Castle. And have you seen Windsor Castle? I particularly want to go there. The 'upheaval' (which becomes more practicable every day) demands it, & besides everyone ought to go there, & I thought we might take it somehow on the way. But anyhow, as old what-dye-call-him in Great Expectations used to say – 'wot larks!

Millie at that time was staying at Pensnett with her brother Charlie, and Assheton wrote to her:

How is old Charlie? is he in highfalutin form, again? Didn't Pensnett Church recall St Stephens? It did to me. How does the air suit you?it had a deadly effect on my appetite; when I was down there I ate ravenously, but perhaps it was caused by extra exercise & not by reason of my constitution being undermined.

Later Assheton was ordained and after a few years as minister of St Barnabas Church, Acton Vale, went to Canada in 1893, where he was appointed Rector of St John's, New Brunswick. He married Helen Alice Dunn, daughter of Andrew Hunter Dunn, Bishop of Quebec. Assheton and Helen came to England for some years, and he was Rector of Stowting, in

Kent, but later they returned to Canada. They had four children, all born at St John's, New Brunswick. The eldest was Christine, who married W.D. Sturgeon, and went to the United States. Their son, Peter, now lives in Vienna. Rev. John Hamilton Dicker, whom I met when he visited England in 1966, was for a time Assistant Chaplain at All Saints Indian School, Prince Albert, Saskatchewan, and died in 1988. The second daughter of Assheton and Helen was Katherine, who married Geoffrey Stott, and whose family now live in England, and the youngest of the family was Ernest George Hamilton-Dicker (the family having adopted the hyphenated name), who died in an accident in 1969, and whose widow Florence now lives in Toronto, near her four children and eight grandchildren.

Millie and Ella were a wonderful pair. Millie was the eldest of the family, and she was aged fifteen when her father died so tragically. She looked after her mother in the difficult years of her widowhood, and was present at her death in Streatham in 1903. Over the years she held the family together – not just caring for her mother, but keeping in constant touch with her brothers, and her cousins. This was probably her first letter, at the age of six:

> My dear Mama. I am very good very happy and quite well I had my cousin Charlotte and Louisa to stay with me from Saturday till Monday I like Charlotte very much today the two little Miss Jones are coming to spend the day with me I am tire'd so give my love to dear Papa and dear Brother and with love to you I am your affectionate Daughter Milly Dicker

At an early age Ella showed her remarkable ability for writing descriptively, and her acute sense of humour. As a teenager she wrote to her mother:

> Dearest Mother,
>
> I am sending you the two things that I know you left behind; if you had only mentioned the others I would have sent them too, but I have puzzled my brains over them in vain. I hope this will reach you in time. Nellie is going to take it at once so that you may get it this evening. No letters have come for you, except an invitation from the Revd. and Mrs Bramley for the afternoon of July 21st. It felt like an invitation, so I took the liberty, not only of opening, but of writing and declining the same in your name & my own! I am very much <u>engaged</u> on that day – Bishops absorb my every thought. I do hope I

shall be able to wear my cream frock. Why can't you come too?

The boys were at home nearly all day yesterday, & were very jolly. In the evening they went to Tim's ship, & did not come home till midnight. I had supper at the Matthews' but did not stay late because of Nellie.

Poor Mrs Cyprus Smith has been very ill again – they called up the doctor on Sunday night, & he did not leave her again till the middle of the next day, she was in such a critical state. I saw her yesterday afternoon she looked dreadfully ill & she does not think she will be allowed to get up again till after the event, but she is very patient & cheerful.

The parcel must go, & there is no news to tell you. Don't hurry home – there is no need whatever. Give my dear love to Auntie – I hope you found her better than you expected.

Ever thine

Ella

P.S. I forgot to mention that the house was burnt down last night, but it really didn't matter much, as burglars got in the night before & stole everything in it. We were also all struck by lightning in the storm yesterday.

The P.S. was typical of her roguish sense of humour!

Three more letters from Ella are worth recording, after she took a job as a governess at Charmouth:

The Cottage, Charmouth   May 15th 1887

My dearest Millie,

I never have a minute for writing now, except on Sunday evenings while I am waiting for the children to go to sleep. You see I have to put them to bed as Emily goes to Church, and they never can be left until they are asleep. Other nights I get no evenings at all, for we have supper at eight – as soon as the children go to bed, & after supper I have to talk to Mrs Boniface till bed time – soon after nine. Talking to Mrs Boniface is not like talking to anyone else, for it is impossible to work, or to talk to anyone else at the same time, & our talks generally end in hot & fierce arguments. She is a dear old thing; we understand each other now, & I love her; she used to stand on her dignity & was very reserved at Lee, but now she pats me on the shoulder and calls me 'my dear' & is awfully jolly altogether. As for Miss Boniface, she is a sort of dream, there never was such a woman. She always gets the best out of people. I positively surprise myself when I am talking to her. She is so sympathetic, & understands before you speak. We have the most lovely talks. She is so sweet about everything – tonight she has been helping me put the children to bed.

Altogether I am very happy – 'my lines are fallen in pleasant places'. This country alone fills one with beautiful thoughts, & this queer little lop-sided mad house is full of surprises & I don't think I shall ever get used to it. There is one big idea in my head that gets bigger every day, and that is that you must and shall come here too. If I pay a sovereign towards your journey expenses & Mrs Martyn asks you, you will come, won't you? I can't say much at present, but it is not at all impossible that such an invitation may come. This place would simply drive you wild; we explore every day, & each day come upon a nook or view more glorious than we have seen before. We scramble up and down cliffs – cliffs covered with velvety grass, with golden flushes of cowslips & clumps of creamy primroses, with streaks of bluebells & dog violets here and there, & in some places impassable with masses of gorse in full bloom. All the trees and hedges are soft pale green, except the pine trees, & the sea looks so beautiful against them. Then great white seagulls flap about quite amiably with the crows & rooks, the cuckoo sings all day, & there are hundreds of larks. The may is just beginning to blossom. We haven't had a dull day since we have been here; every day the same – the glorious burning sun & fresh keen wind – not at all too keen. I hear you have had rain and bad weather at Lee, but there has been no idea of such a thing here.

We don't know anyone here yet; some people called but our maid stupidly said Mrs Martyn had not yet come, & did not say Mrs & Miss Boniface were here, so we remain as we were before. But there is the delightful feeling of being objects of interest, & of being watched, & we invent names & occupations & family relations for the other few interesting people in the village. It is so funny meeting the same half dozen young men & girls over & over again & peeping at each other out of the corners of our eyes whenever we do so. You will be amused to hear that one is already called 'Miss Dicker's young man' & Miss Boniface threatens not to allow me to go on the beach without a chaperon! The best of it is she sat on the beach ever so long the other night, & not a soul came near us, but she had to go home & leave us, & before she had gone a hundred yards she met him coming our way, & hadn't the face to come back again, she says! He took up his position close to us, too! We haven't spoken, of course, but he is a very interesting young man & he takes photographs. Bye & bye we shall have plenty of friends. There is a tennis club here, & a lending library, & all sorts of things. Our vicar is just like 'Great Agrippa' in 'Struel Peter'! He wears such a vestment of a surplice – it falls in huge folds from his shoulders, & touches the ground all round. He also wears a broad black sash round his neck by way of a stole. There is no chancel to speak of, but the Church is eminently <u>clean</u>, as Charlie Fraser would say – everything in the best spic & span order. It is an old Church newly restored, & it stands on a hill overlooking the sea. The bells chime merrily every Sunday morning from half past eight till nine. They have a celebration here (at midday) twice a month. This afternoon we found a charming nook, by walking up a cliff and then scrambling down the face of it, & I read 'Alone in London' all the afternoon to the bairns. It was rather roasting, but we were sheltered a little by the cliffs. We haven't been to Lyme yet, for Miss Boniface has had a slight cold, & was afraid of the drive. We shall most likely go tomorrow or Tuesday. We have developed the most alarming appetites – you would be perfectly aghast if you saw the food disappear! We live on the fat of the land; chickens & new laid eggs & cream & delicious country butter – everything of the best & plenty of it. Tell Mother beef is 8½d a lb here! And the best new laid eggs 12 for 9d! And warm milk 2d a quart.

If she wanted a house for the summer there are heaps of sweet little cottages, furnished and unfurnished, for next to nothing a week. Johnnie already is almost as brown as when I first saw him, & Louie is getting so too. As for me, my nose is a fierce and furious scarlet, & so are my cheeks, just where the sun and wind catch them, but the spots are going, and I am perfectly well. My hat has been very much admired & is excessively useful.

Miss Boniface thinks it is very pretty & ladylike & so becoming! By the by, tell Seymour I have stuck the choir photo up in my pretty room, & Hoddie will call it 'Miss Dicker's Angels'! He loves looking at it. I only wish I had my football photo too, but I should want Frank Smythe cut out of it first. I guess I must go to bed. (I have had supper since I began this, & am finishing my letter by stealth, when I am supposed to be asleep.) You would love my room. It is up in the roof, & has a sort of Church ceiling – brown rafters running across, as well as down each side. It has a sort of very high dado – six feet or more – of artistic pale bluey green paper, then a band of dark wood, & pale cream above. All the woodwork matches – wardrobe painted pale cream & brown etc. The window is very large, standing out from the roof like an attic window, with a jolly broad window ledge I use as a table & stick my flowers & photos in. From it I see a broad strip of sea, behind the cliffs & trees. If just a chosen few of you London folks could come here too, <u>how</u> happy I should be! You really must come, Millie Mavourneen & you would get as fat as Miss Mills or Madame Carlier. Did Assheton tell you that Bernard came to say goodbye to me before I left? You can tell Charlie that he is quite ready to go to Tasmania if there is anything for him to do there, & he says he shall certainly go if we all go.

I really & truly mustn't write any more. Please make everyone write to me – I hate the postman not to bring me a letter. Give my love to everybody.
Ever your very loving sister Ella

Then, in pencil:

(missed first post)I am finishing my letter on my knee, as I sit on the beach. I wonder if it will smell of the sea. I can't think how it is that I have always forgotten to tell you about our nearest & dearest friend here. The very first time we came down to the sea we were hailed as friends by a sweet black puppy, who insisted on accompanying us, & ever since he watches for us, & leaps & barks with joy when we appear, & always comes too wherever we may go. We christened him 'Sweep' because he was like the black puppy in 'A story of a short life' but we have since discovered that his real name is 'Toby'. He much objects to me writing this letter, & tries to run away with my pencil.

There are a few more lines which are illegible.
Then ten weeks later, some bad news:

Shade of a bathing machine, Charmouth
July 1st 1887

My dear Mother,

I meant to have answered your letters sooner – it is seldom enough I have two letters from you so close together; but we have been having a terrible time lately, & I have had no time for anything. Poor Mrs Boniface has been very ill indeed, last Monday we did not know what might happen. She has not been well ever since she has been here, & then she got a severe cold, which laid her up altogether, & they were obliged to call in the doctor. On Monday afternoon at about half past two she woke up with a frightful attack of cramp in her legs, & it continued till past eleven at night. It was the most horrible thing I have ever seen – she hardly ceased shrieking & calling for help all the time, we hardly thought she could live, & she thought she was dying, & prayed it might not last long. Her foot was dead, quite white & shrivelled up, the nails black, & the muscles of her leg gathered up into hard knobs. Sleeping draughts had no effect on her, & we were all hard at work with remedies which gave no relief to speak of. At eleven she was so weak she could only moan, & then the pain, the intense pain I mean, suddenly left her, but the reaction was almost as bad – the tingling and burning all the next day, & she was afraid to move for fear of starting it again. Two people sat up with her every night till last night, when Emily sat up with her alone, & Mrs Boniface seemed much better this morning & was sitting up in bed. Miss Boniface was sent for of course when she was taken so ill, & as Mrs Hurlston cannot well be left alone it has fallen to my share of the work to take care of her as well as the children, & I have had very little time for anything else. You know Miss Boniface has only just recovered from congestion of the liver, & is still very weak, & Mrs Martyn is not at all fit for nursing, & to add to our woes our cook took to her bed with a very severe cold & bilious attack, so everything had to be done by the person who wanted it. No one can manage the children but I, so I could not be spared for any nursing till they were safe in bed, but Mrs Martyn would not let me sit up at night with her, as I had so much to do in the day. That first terrible day I never left Mrs Boniface till past twelve at night; the children were out for the afternoon, so I was at liberty. Have you ever heard of such cramp as that? You see the

old lady is more than seventy, & so very weak to begin with. Mrs
Martyn and Miss Boniface are both dreadfully done up: I had the best
of it, for I got out and about, & they had no change. Indeed I have
never been so gay since I have been here, just because I felt tired and
cross and didn't want to speak to anyone. It was only a few days ago
that I was complaining that I had hardly a soul to speak to (a gentle
soul, I mean, for I know almost every poor man woman & child). On
Jubilee Day I felt rather out of it & lonely, as my only one or two lady
friends were too busy to notice me, but the reaction set in the next
day, & no less than three invitations arrived – for a children's picnic
on the beach, given by one of the swellest ladies in the place – a Miss
Eliot, then a haymaking children's party at Colonel Little's, & for a
real swell garden party at Mrs Pavey's, next door. This Mrs Pavey is
one of my oldest friends here; she has a most lovely ideal garden, in
which I sit & read sometimes, while my bairns play with hers, & she
keeps me supplied with roses & literature. Their house is where the
Montefiores lived, they only took on this cottage when Mrs Montefiore
took pupils & they overflowed the beautiful old house next door. The
garden is not so very large, but every part of it is so cared for, & made
so much of, & there are such shady nooks & walks, such unexpected
gardens, such blazing beds of wonderful flowers; arches of creeping
geraniums, almost as high as those Charlie speaks of, & masses of
blossom, roses such as I have never seen before, & old fashioned borders
of dusky pansies & sweet williams, columbines & pinks. Their hothouse
is perfect – the ferns instead of being in pots grow wild everywhere, &
foliage plants in every crack & corner, great baskets hang from the
roof, & water flowers grow in the tank. The garden party was a great
success, & I enjoyed it immensely. Of course neither Mrs Martyn nor
Mrs Boniface could go, & I was so wearied out & so headachy that I
felt I would rather do anything else, but Mrs Martyn called me a nasty
ungrateful thing, after all the trouble Millie had taken in buying me
those pretty things, & she dressed me with her own hands, looping up
that shabby old muslin, & lending me this thing & that to finish me
off, & as the Montefiores had promised to call & fetch me I didn't like
to be disagreeable. And when they arrived Mrs Montefiore had brought
me five most exquisite half opened roses, pale pink & creamy & white,
they made quite a wreath round my neck, & with one of those pale
yellow Burmese umbrellas I looked a horful swell. There was nobody

very interesting there, the chief feature of the assembly was the number
of parsons. About half the people present were parsons, old parsons,
fat & thin, high & low, with Mr Montefiore jerking his little self about
among them like a very small & shrivelled & ancient mummy just
galvanized. There never was such an extraordinary being. May &
Maggie came with him. Everybody was very nice, especially the straw-
berries & cream, which was unlimited.

 I am finishing this on Sunday evening, not having had time
before. Thank Millie very much for the things, they did admirably.
How much do I owe you now? It must be about 7/- isn't it? Let me
know soon. Mrs Boniface is much better. We are all going to
Bournemouth soon. Ever your loving Ella

Old Mrs Boniface died a few weeks later, and Ella wrote to her sister Millie:

2 Durrant Villas, Avenue Road, Bournemouth
August 5th 1887

My darling Millie,

 Your letter went where I long to be and am not, for we left
Charmouth sadly and tearfully on Wednesday. The parting almost broke
our hearts; it is wonderful how many friends we have made there, &
how we love each inch of the ground in and round that heaven of a
place. When I say 'we', I mean myself and my two bairns, & partly
Emily – the others were mere names, & hardly known by sight in the
village, & Emily didn't exult in the place as we did. To think that after
all my dreamings you never came! But some day you must come there
with me, and see the great monster hills, flecked with fields, range
beyond range till they mix with the clouds – the glorious billowy woods
– the tender little villages – the whitefaced placid cows & horned sheep
– trickling streams & fairy nooks, & beyond & above all, the glorious
bay, bluer than any other English sea, with its peaceful shore & gleaming
white cliffs vanishing in the distance. I have some jolly photos, but of
course they don't do it justice. You really can't realise what it is unless
you have seen it. Sad as are the memories connected with Charmouth,
they only hallow the place more in my mind, & soon, when all the
horrors of this death are worn away my time there will seem once more
the <u>perfect</u> peace over it that struck me the first time I saw it. During
those dreadful days when she lay dying, we three would climb high up

the cliffs & lying down on our breasts look over the soft dreamy sea & talk about things to come, till we could almost see the angels waiting for her in the sunset clouds.

And then to go back to that room, and see that pitiful hand moving, moving – always stretching out for something we couldn't understand, to see that weary face – so horribly changed and yet the same – it was dreadful, & haunts me always even now. And the horror of it – dead, & yet alive – ! And there was one thing I never dared mention in my letters before, but it is over now so I can talk about it. You know it all happened in the drawing room, the largest and pleasantest room in the house. It was there that she fell, & they brought in her bed, & she died there, never leaving it till they carried her away that Monday morning. My bedroom was over the drawing room – a huge square room standing above the rest of the house, with windows on two sides. It is so large that it has sunk in the middle, & Mrs Martyn feared the floor would give way, so just at the beginning of this dreadful time she moved all the children downstairs, & left me all alone in this big desolate room, shut off from all the rest of the house except the drawing room just under me, where I could hear the murmuring voices of the watchers, & the opening & shutting of their door as they crept in & out. I used to lie and quake even then, but when it was over, & she lay still at last, & the watchers were needed no longer, it really was almost more than I could bear. We two, she in the drawing room, & I exactly over, were quite away, shut off from everyone else, & as I lay awake half the night I can never describe the noises I heard & the various forms my dread took.

And even then my woes were not over, for when the coffin came, & she needed the bed no more, they actually put it up in the corner of my room, exactly the same as when she lay on it, & a clean white counterpane – I never looked at that bed even in the broad daylight without a sort of horror as to what I might see there, & at night – don't think me very stupid, they were real

agony to me – I could hear her laboured breathing coming from it quite plainly. The only one reason that I was glad to leave Charmouth was that room; I pray I may never have to go through such nights of misery again. And I had no one to tell my grievance to, for Mrs Martyn doesn't understand <u>that</u> kind of nerves, & besides I couldn't complain of such a thing to her own daughters. I dared not write about it for fear it should make me feel worse.

Saturday morning. What I wrote last night seeme dreadful nonsense, now in the bright sunshine of these beautiful gardens. But I shall send it to you, for I think you will understand, & it will be a relief to pass it on to someone else.

From your ever loving sister Ella

Two years later Ella was living with her mother in Catford. Her letters are so fascinating and descriptive that I feel bound to repeat another one, to her sister Millie, dated 10th July 1889:

Do you ever cast a thought towards this abode of horror? Do you, sitting in the Lap of Luxury & lying on the Bosom of Bliss and Beauty ever remember the poor soul in torment here? I am writing in difficulty for our only sitting room, the study, is many feet deep in furniture – it is not unlike the inside of a furniture van when loaded, & we cannot sit upright at meals, being so near the ceiling – which, combined with the difficulty & discomfort of holding our plates in our laps, or balancing them on umbrella stands or Chairs (upside down), or stacks of pictures or books, is gradually unhinging our minds & ruining our digestion. They have torn down the dining room ceiling & the rafters stand out like the ribs of a skeleton. Mother has taken up her bedroom carpet, & the man can see through quite plainly into her room, & she is obliged to dress with an umbrella up, for decency. The only one who enjoys the present state of affairs is Nellie, & she is beaming with contentment. Peter wanders about disconsolate & thinks us unutterable fools. The kittens are scared by the men, but rather enjoy the excite-ment, & the encampment at the top of the furniture van. I spoke seriously to Job on his bad behaviour and now Gilbert has to go out into the garden at night to prevent his running away. [Nellie and Peter were the cats, and Job the dog.]

We are frightfully gay now. There was a garden party at the Russells yesterday & is to be one at the Collins on Thursday, the Gebharts on Friday. On Saturday the Swimming Fête at Norwood, on Tuesday Gilbert and I are going to the Cornwells at Streatham. But the greatest spree of all was last Saturday. Mind you thank Florence and Geraldine heaps & heaps for that ticket, for it really was one of the nicest days I have ever had, Mr & Mrs Trist took me, you know; I had luncheon there, & started soon after. We walked up through the grounds to the marquee where the rose show was held first, but as there were three and a half millions of people there, all squashed together into a struggling & steaming & perspiring mass – as the atmosphere was dim with the smoke of them, & the odour of them was excessive, & as we could only see the roses over the shoulders of, & between the elbows of the said hot & sticky people, I cannot tell you much about the Rose Show. Indeed we ignominiously backed out of it at the first opportunity.

But – !!! Ah!!!! The Shah!!!!!! Never has the Palace looked better. A long red carpet lay from the north door to the Orchestra, all down the middle, with seats on each side (costing their weight in gold) & crowds of people all along the barriers on each side waiting to see the Procession. We soon saw the only way to see this Imperial Blaziness was to have a seat, so we expended 1/- in a seat in the Orchestra just opposite the Royal Box. All the chairs where the people sit to watch the

His Glorious Blaziness the Shah-in-Shah of Persia. From Life. By EHD, R.A.

Pantomine were cleared away, & the space arranged like the arena of a circus. The front seats were awfully expensive of course, but we could see well enough from where we were. Not only was every seat in the Orchestra taken, but rows of people were standing at the back. After having waited about three days as patiently as we could His High Mightiness arrived, causing great enthusiasm. The Princess of Wales was on the Shah's arm (her hand, I mean, not her person), the Prince of Wales & all the Royal Family followed, together with numbers of Persians.

They all went into the Royal Box, & then the fun began. First a lot of acrobats did marvellous things; then some sweet Japanese in native dress came in & did some more marvellous things; then, oh Mildred!! then came on the performing elephants, sweetest of all sweet things! They are beyond words.

As you have seen them I will not enter into details, except to say that

during the performance of the baby elephant the two senior sat side by side on a form, with their backs to us (facing the Royal Party) & the effect was most beautiful. It reminded me strongly of the Prayer meetings at Hertford in bygone days. Do you remember?

After the performance we descended as quickly as we could & obtained refreshment just in time to save us from death. We had an early lunch as we wished to get there in good time, & we did not have tea before we took our places as we wished to have good ones. As it was nearly nine before the performance was over you may imagine our feelings. Mr Trist had to carry us in fact, one over each shoulder, to the refreshment bar, & it was not till after five rolls & butter & many bath buns that we were able to stand. Then we went out & got good seats for the fireworks. That was rather difficult as it was absolutely necessary that we should be able to see plainly into the Royal balcony as well as the set pieces & general effect of the gardens, & there being no standing room anywhere increased our difficulties. But all things come to those who can push, & we could & did, & took our seats upon some stone steps leading into the gardens, immediately in front of everything. The fireworks were the best ever known – in fact they must have been a dream, for such things could not really be. And whenever there came a burst of light everyone looked up at the Shah, & he scratched his head in salute. The newspapers say he touched his cap, but it looked as though he were scratching his head. The Shah's small boy enjoyed it immensely – such a dear little chap. We could see splendidly from where we were. All the gardens were illuminated with Chinese lanterns & thousands of variegated lamps. They were beautiful. We left after the fireworks & I had supper at the Trists, getting home about half past eleven. I met heaps of people I knew there – we <u>kept</u> tumbling over the Russells in the Rose Show, then they came into seats just behind us in the orchestra, & then to the next table when we were having tea! Wasn't it funny? I am getting to love them dearly. We had a very jolly garden party there yesterday, Gilbert & I went with the Matthews. All the world was there. I had a long talk with Eustace Russell, & like him awfully. We got into very deep subjects, which amused those scoffers round, but he was so kind in explaining what I did not understand that I did not get out of my depth, & enjoyed it so much. He is going to lend me a book called 'Other worlds than ours', & I am going to lend him 'The science of Religion', which I have just finished. The stores people are going to send me another estimate, & we are standing still at present. Mother wants to know what money you will want. Mother has been rather seedy, but seems better now. Excuse a short note, but I am in rather a hurry. Give my love to Aunt Harriet & the girls.

Ever your loving sister, Ella H. Dicker

For some years Millie and Ella spent much of their time together, and looked after their mother, who died in 1903, before which Charlie had returned from Australia with his infant son, who was christened Charles George Hamilton, but was always known as Tam. Millie looked after Tam as a mother, and cared for him even more when his father was killed in an accident with his motor cycle.

A few months before his fatal accident Charlie wrote to his son at Exeter School, which he attended after a preparatory school at Uffculme, Devon:

Piddeltrenthide Vicarage, Dorchester, Dorset. 3 Feb.1912

My dear Tam,

I began a letter to you a day or two ago, but was obliged to turn to some important business connected with getting more teachers for our school – you know the Haywards are giving up – and I've had over 30 letters to write. It fairly knocked me up, as I was as weak as a sucked orange.

I am thankful to say that there's not much the matter with me now, though I must be very careful for a while. I am to take the morning service tomorrow, and Mr Collard is kindly coming for the evening one.

We all thought a good deal about you yesterday, and prayed that your 16th year may be a great step towards the fitness you are seeking for the highest service a man can do in this world.

The quickest progress is not always the best – oak grows slower than poplar or elm, but it's more useful. But an oak never wastes time – its wood shows some solid progress for every year of its life, and that's what we want you to do.

I am glad you have begun Greek; it is the best possible foundation for learning to think. It is a wonderful thing that, in God's providence, Greek was the language of the whole civilized world in the Apostles' time, for it is more complete in expressing meanings, and clearer in teaching, than any other language the world has ever known. You will find the alphabet interesting, as made up of older letters found in Phoenician & Hebrew, and then in its turn giving shapes & patterns for the newer language of the Romans.

There are several important points in Greek, you'll soon find out, which help to understand the New Testament – the tenses of verbs, such as the Aorists and participles, and the use of the Article. These were not understood when the Authorised Version was made in 1611, but a great deal of the Church's teaching depends upon our knowing them – a man who knows a text in the Greek Testament has a better grip.

And a fresh language may give you a new start in speaking plainly – a thing you've got to learn. Try and tackle the vowels and consonants strong and loud.

Mr Bridge was here yesterday, and was very interested in your shooting. He has a rifle like yours, and says he can generally hit a rabbit in the head at 25 yards with it. I think you will have to take out a licence in the holidays and shoot us a dinner.

Our new Bishop has ordered a Conference to be held in every Deanery, to consider the 'Report of the Archbishop's Committee on Church Finance'. It is suggested that every parish shall raise a certain amount of money yearly, for the Church's work – I am sending you a copy of the scheme, as I think you ought to know something about it – (put it in your pipe and smoke it.)

It is really disgraceful that the <u>richest</u> Church in Christendom should be the stingiest, which we English really are. With all our merchant princes and wealthy gentry, our Church has to struggle along chiefly on our ancient endowments, whilst every other religious body taxes itself heavily to carry on the work, and I am glad our bishops are beginning to speak up about it.

Our conference was last Tuesday, and as I couldn't go the Archdeacon presided. The Cerne Deanery met at Minterne House, & Lord Digby gave a luncheon – you may be sure they all turned up!

The Field Club has its 2nd winter meeting next week – a paper by Mr Toms on 'Piddletrenthide Valley Enclosures' is going to be read – he is giving particulars of some Sussex ones of the same character, which he thinks are of the Bronze Age.

I think I must stop now, as the study is very cold. With best love, Daddy.

It is clear that at this early age of sixteen Tam was being brought up with a view to entering the Church, but in the event this did not happen for many years. After leaving Exeter he took various clerical jobs in London during the First World War, when he held pacifist views and did not serve in the forces. In London he experienced a number of air raids, and described one:

I did not think I was so soon to really see an attack by zeppelins on London – it was a most wonderful sight. I was woken up about eleven o'clock tonight with the noise of anti-aircraft. I jumped out of bed with a horrible feeling – why I don't know – I put on my dressing-gown and ran down the passage. Hearing everyone already rushing up to the roof was reassuring as you may guess I was longing to see something of it. Absolutely everyone I should think was on the roof.

There was a bright thing in the sky where the searchlights were shining and all around it shells were bursting. It was in a north west direction from Ingram House – over in the direction of Westminster I should say. A minute or so before I arrived they say that the zeppelin could be seen very clearly, but it was not so distinct while I was there though I could see exactly where it was. The shells looked more like fireworks than anything else I have seen, and exploded all over the place, some near the zeppelin and others some way short of it. The noise, as of ordinary firing, continued of course all the time. There is a bright light in the horizon somewhere north west of here which people seem to think is a fairly large fire – to me it did not seem very much. The minutes in which we all stood watching the shells bursting were intensely exciting, everyone longing that bombs would be dropped in Stockwell Road! [where he lived]. I hear another fire engine go rushing by as I write. How everyone will look forward to future air-raids! It seemed as we stood on the roof a little while ago that the only feeling we felt was a <u>longing</u> to see – the feeling that was furthest from our minds was that it was a dangerous game to those in the thick of it and death to some who little expected it. I am enthusiastic because it is new to me, and that it is a rare or uncommon sight now.

This was a curious reaction to what must have been a terrible occasion. Tam's words were written the same night, a few minutes after the raid.

After the war he went to Keble College, Oxford for three years, where he had some difficulty with his exams, but encouraged by his Aunt Millie, who was then living in Bournemouth, he persevered, and finally emerged with a degree. On leaving Oxford he visited Tasmania to meet his mother's family, the Swans. For a short time he took a job teaching at The Hutchins School, Hobart, returning to England at the end of 1923. Then he taught at a school in Gillingham, Kent, teaching French, Latin, English and Scripture.

But all this time his heart was set on two subjects – Art and Religion. He chose the former, and took a course at the Slade School of Fine Art, University College, London, where he struck up a close relationship with William (later Sir William) Coldstream, and studied under Henry Tonks, universally known as 'Tonks', who was Slade Professor of fine art at the University. On one occasion Tam's work received the highest praise from Tonks – 'very good!' – whereas they were all quite pleased if he used the expression 'not bad'.

Rev. Charles George
Hamilton Dicker
(1896–1977)

After the Slade, Tam tried to make a career of painting, but was not greatly successful, and after a few years in Bloomsbury he joined his aunts Millie and Ella, now living in Salisbury. Shortly after finishing her book – *Some of the Fore-bears of the Hamilton Dickers*, reproduced as Chapter II, in September 1931, sadly Ella died in April 1932. Then, in 1935, Millie and Tam moved to Lewes, where they bought The Red House, Southover. Tam continued his painting, but began to take a part in local government, and was elected to Lewes Town Council as a representative of Lewes Ratepayers' Association, of which he was secretary. He soon became a very active member of the Council, and when it was proposed that Southover High Street should be classified as a business street he organized a petition opposing this on the following grounds:

(1) Southover High Street is not and never has been a business street. It contains only four small shops – a dairy, a grocery, a cobbler and a bakery, and these shops are of the village type dating from the time when Southover was a village. The remaining houses are residential, including a manor house, a rectory, Elizabethan or Jacobean as well as Georgian dwellings – some large residences and other ancient cottages.

(2) It is generally recognised that Southover High Street is of considerable antiquarian and aesthetic interest and the safeguarding of such a street both from the demolition of old houses and the erection of incongruous shop buildings was undoubtedly among the objects which Parliament had in mind when the Town Planning Act was passed.

In view of these facts we earnestly ask that the decision of the Lewes Borough Council may be revised. We do this, both as owners of property, whose interests would, we believe, be affected, and as residents, anxious to conserve this well-known street which has given pleasure to generations of Lewes people and to many visitors to the town.

This document bears the signatures of ninety-seven residents, and appears to have been signed in 1938.

Millie died at the Red House in 1939, aged eighty-six, and shortly afterwards Tam went to Cheshunt College, being ordained in 1942. After becoming a priest he was at Knighton for two years, then Leicester and Brighton, following which he was appointed Vicar of South Stoke, near Bath, in 1948, where he remained until his retirement in 1966. He then retired to Wells, Somerset, where he lived until his death in 1977.

Chapter VI

Seymour's Family

My grandparents, Seymour and Ethel, had seven children, all but the last two, Richard and Dorothy, being born in Australia. The eldest, Mildred, married Eric Biden, at Dulwich just before the end of the War, in October 1918. At that time Millie was a Second Lieutenant in the Women's Volunteer Reserve, and Eric was a Lieutenant in the Australian Imperial Forces. After the War they lived in Australia, where Eric was a land surveyor, and they had two sons, Peter and Paul. Peter was in the Australian Air Force and was killed, missing in Borneo during the Second World War. Millie died on a visit to England in 1961. Paul and his family still live in Australia.

Gilbert was born in Brisbane in 1894, and came to England with Seymour and his family in 1889. He served in the Royal Sussex Regiment during the First World War, and was appointed MBE. He married Eleanor Chapman in 1918, the officiating clergyman being Gilbert's uncle Assheton. He made a career in the cinema industry, and for some time was manager of the Old Palace Cinema, Banbury. He died in 1974, nine days after Ella. Gilbert and Ella had one daughter, June, who married Walter Griffiths, and they had three daughters and seven grandchildren.

Nancy was the fourth of the family to be born in Brisbane. She told me that she remembered her early life in Australia, but this may have been largely imagination, as she must have been very small, two or three, when they all came to England. She never married, but loved children, and when she was in her forties she founded a school at Burgess Hill, Sussex, having previously, with her younger sister Dorothy, taught in a small way at her parents' house in Brighton. Dicker House School began in Burgess Hill in 1939, at first taking boarders and day children in the house at Junction Road where Nancy and Dorothy lived with their mother Ethel, but later only day children were taught. Ethel died in 1950, and Dorothy in 1964, and eventually Nancy had to close the school in 1977, when she was eighty-two. At that time she was short of money, the school never having been very profitable, but fortunately the Freemasons came to her aid. As the unmarried daughter of a Freemason, she qualified for help from the Royal Masonic Benevolent Institution, and was wonderfully looked after for the last fourteen years of her life in Harewood Court, one of the Institution's Homes in Hove, Sussex. Nancy died in 1992, aged ninety-six.

Violet was also born in Brisbane, and came to England as a baby. In 1923 she met Alexander David Morrison (Alec) on a ship bound for Australia, and after a whirlwind romance they were married in Sydney. Alec was the engineer on the ship, and when returning to England on the same ship, SS *Hobson's Bay*, Vi had to wear her wedding ring on a piece of string round her neck, as the Ship's Officers were not allowed to have their wives on board. Alec later joined Lloyd's Register of Shipping as an Engineer Surveyor, and they spent four years near Kobe in Japan, until their home was demolished by a tidal wave, after which they returned to England. Alec died in 1972, and Violet in 1988. They had one son, Stuart, a civil engineer, who has three children and seven grandchildren.

The third son of Seymour and Ethel was Richard Maitland Hamilton Dicker, always known as Bobs. He was born in 1900, shortly after the family returned to England, and after school at Ardingly College he served in the Royal Flying Corps in the First World War. He then entered the field of journalism, serving first in Brighton, and then in London, where he was a reporter with the Westminster Press.

He then spent thirty years as a freelance reporter in Southampton, where he earned the title 'The Gentleman Reporter'.

> He belonged to a rare class who never suffer from the creeping disease of self-importance as they become well known. He was a free lance as much in the way he lived as in the way he worked. When he left his flat in the mornings, the waterfront – and the pockets of his overcoat – were his only office. He scorned the buying of information. His contacts were repaid by sitting with him, and enjoying his enthusiasm as they watched his huge pencil, thick as a cigar, breathe life into their stories of the sea for the pages of the 'News Chronicle', the 'Star', the 'Daily Mail', and, latterly, the 'Evening News'.

Late in his life Bobs made an unsuccessful marriage, which only lasted a short time. Bobs died in Southampton in December 1965.

The youngest of the family was Dorothy, who was largely responsible for the domestic side of Dicker House School at Burgess Hill. During the Second World War, when a number of children who had been privately evacuated from London were boarded, that was a particularly difficult task. She was a source of tremendous support for her sister Nancy, and for her mother in her declining years, and her death in 1964 was a great loss to the school.

Arthur Seymour Hamilton Dicker

My father was born at Hamilton Road, Brisbane, on 4 September 1892, the eldest son of Seymour and Ethel. When he was four his parents returned to England, and lived for some years at Dulwich.

He was educated at Ardingly College, where he became Head Boy, and excelled at games, winning the coveted title of Victor Ludorum. At school acting was one of his main interests, and earned him some good reviews. He secured the Oxford Local Junior in 1907, and was in the VIth Form at the age of fifteen. By 1910 he was classed above the VIth as a School Exhibitioner, and there he stayed in a rather lonely solo state some of the time. He won the Maths prize in his last year. Music brought him into the OTC as a bandsman and he rose to the rank of sergeant. He played the euphonium, and was second in the Band race in the sports of 1911. He conducted the South School Choral Society, and sang in many concerts. He sang as a soloist in *The Crucifixion* in 1912. Sport was the great area of his achievements, especially in Athletics, where he regularly won the sprint races or was second. He was Captain of Football, and gained his First XI colours at Cricket. He became a school prefect, head prefect, and Captain of School, before leaving in July 1912, not far short of his twentieth birthday. That is the official record from the school archives, but I remember him telling me that, presumably in his early days at school, some of his activities were more unruly. On one occasion he and a few others stole out of the school during the night armed with picks and shovels, and turned a signpost round. He also carved his initials on a pew in the chapel, which he showed me with pride many years later.

At home, with his two brothers and four sisters they formed a jolly family, enjoying music and theatre, and they often sang together at home in the evenings, encouraged by their father Seymour who was a Professor of Music.

After leaving school Arthur went to University College, London, but his career was cut short by the First World War. Having been a member of his school and university OTCs he was commissioned in August 1914, joining the 3rd (Special Reserve) Battalion, Royal Sussex Regiment. Early in 1915 he was posted to the 2nd Battalion in France.

Here are some extracts from his diary:

Sunday 3.1.1915. (Dover) Today, the first Sunday of the New Year, I was warned for the Front. The Adjutant told me the good news after mess in the evening. After I had visited the outposts I saw Audrey at Mangillis and had a long talk with her. We both discovered that we had been rather foolish and soon made things all right again. Having said goodbye to Mrs B. and Gladys I went to the Front with Audrey where we remained for an hour or more. Arriving back at the Fort I set to work and started packing. Au revoir, Audrey, or is it 'Goodbye'? I wonder!!

Monday 4.1.1915. The draft left at 5.45 a.m. I left by the 8 a.m. train. Audrey and Gladys came to see me off. Au revoir Audrey!

He travelled to Southampton via London, joined SS *Hantonia* and arrived at Le Havre the next afternoon. After nearly two weeks in No. 1 Infantry Base Unit at Harfleur he travelled through Boulogne and arrived at Cunchy 'right in the firing line'.

Friday 15.1.1915. First Impressions. Heavy guns in action nearly all the time. Very little infantry fire during the day, but at night the snipers are busy. All the houses nearby are in ruins. Our headquarters, once a country mansion, is now one room!

Saturday 16.1.1915. After breakfast I joined my company (A Coy) in the trenches. Reggie Shaw is also with us. He and I are the only subs in the Coy. I found a lot of my old friends in the Coy, who were very pleased to see me. The guns today are very busy again and there is little firing from the trenches. As far as I can see there is very little damage being done, tho I expect the shells are effective somewhere. Just in front of our trench there is a group of dead Germans – a rather gruesome sight! Still it is all in the day's work. We were relieved this afternoon by the North Lancs.

Sunday 17.1.1915. I had a ripping night – the best since I have been in France! I find that we are just in the line of guns. There is a battery about 100 yds to our left and it is making a devil of a noise. After breakfast I wrote to Mother and Audrey (I have not heard from A. since I left Dover – I hope all is well).

Tuesday 19.1.1915. This morning the Germans began attacking us with bombs. They kept it up all the morning but I don't think they have done any damage. Our men have made a fine job of the trench and are still working away like fury. Our guns are very busy all day and plenty of shells are bursting close to where we are.

Friday 22.1.1915. My letters today have made me feel quite homesick. Why was war invented? Why must men be killed and wounded in this murderous way? I only hope that if I must suffer it will be short and quick. Life out here seems so impossible. What will be the end of it – for me?

Monday 25.1.1915. The Germans made an attack on the trenches early this morning and captured the greater part of our line and many prisoners (Scots Guards). Sussex are going to try and retake the trenches. The attack fails and our leading Coys are compelled to dig a new trench about 100 yds. in rear of the old one. Grimshaw is hit severely in the stomach. It is fearfully cold and my feet are senseless all through the night. No chance of sleep.

Wednesday 27.1.1915. The Kaiser's birthday! Poor old Grimshaw died this morning, R.I.P. Today is a day of casualties – in our trench there are about 20. Blakeney was hit by a sniper and is in a very critical condition. Things are very busy again and we are expecting an attack any minute. The N. Lancs made a feeble attack and are hopelessly driven back. A large number of them refused to attack and ran out of the trenches! Well Lancs. you have made a bad name for yourselves tonight. Insubordinate cowards.

Thursday 28.1.1915. It is very cold and half our men are done up. We are having a terrible time of it and are suffering very painfully. Just our luck! Owing to the treachery of the North Lancs, who refuse to stay in the trenches, the Sussex are called up again this evening and we occupy our former positions in the firing trenches. The Germans are up to something and our men are feeling 'done'. Heaven help us if we are attacked! Most of us can hardly move, owing to our feet. Several casualties take place during the night. Hut is killed.

Friday 29.1.1915. It snowed hard last night and we are in an exhausted state. The Germans make a great attack in the Keep but are driven back by D Coy, who defend their positions very bravely. The Northants also do great things on our right – the amount of German casualties are colossal. A Coy is prepared for an attack but nothing happens. Banthorpe is killed during the Keep attack. Telegrams of congratulations arrived this afternoon from Gen Westmacott and Gen French – 'Well done, Sussex'. French's message promises us relief tomorrow and a long rest to follow. Thank goodness, but I doubt if we can all stand another day. This is the fifth night in the trenches and sleep is impossible.

Saturday 30.1.1915. We are relieved at last at 7.30 p.m. by the Coldstreamers. As my platoon is leaving the trench a couple of shells burst within fifty yards of us. Nobody is hurt, but I thank God for a miraculous escape, since I was leading the men and I was right in front. After a very difficult and weary struggle we eventually arrived at Bethune at midnight. 30 men dropped out on the road but arrived here later in safety. Shaw and I share a 'bed'. What a luxury, and <u>what a relief!</u>

Saturday 8.5.1915, (Trenches at Richebourg L'Avoué). We are going to attack tomorrow morning, and we spend the night lookng over the ground etc. The men are in the very best of spirits, but everybody is anxious, & will be glad when tomorrow is over. Villiers & St Croix wounded. Today I heard that I had got my second star!

Sunday 9.5.1915. '<u>Der TAG</u>.' Sussex & Northants attacked at 5.30 a.m. At the end of the bombardment (which was heavier than Neuve Chapelle) we advanced to our positions in front of the German trench. And there we stopped all day subject to heavy shell and machine gun fire. The wire was <u>NOT</u> cut! I was hit in the arm about 6 a.m., & managed to crawl back at 1.30 p.m. At midnight I was on the way to Boulogne. Our total casualties were 16 officers & about 600 men. Shaw, Austin, Finke, Lucher & Childs were killed.

Arthur soon recovered from his wound, and rejoined his battalion ten days later, receiving much sympathy for having rejoined without even one day's leave to England.

There are some interesting points which arise from his diaries. First, he mentions places and movements in detail, indicating that the level of security in those days was very much less than that which arose in the Second World War, some 25 years later.

Secondly, the conditions in the trenches were such that sleep was almost impossible, and men were only there for a few days at a time, having billets a short distance back, where they could rest on being relieved. Also, leave to England was fairly regular, Arthur returning home for eight days in July, having been in France for six months. It seems that although men were keen to go to France, it was accepted that life expectancy was not great.

Saturday 18.9.1915. Appointed A.D.C., G.S.O., Bde Major, Staff Capt., & Bottlewasher to Col. Green, DSO, commanding Green's Force.

Saturday 25.9.1915. Another 'TAG'. 1st & IVth Corps attacked at 5.50 a.m. with gas. 2nd Bde on right, 1st Bde on left. Green's Force in Centre. Triumph of Green's Force. Capture of 400 prisoners. 15th Div. captured Loos. 1st Bde held up at Hulluch.

Sunday 26.9.1915 Relieved by the 21st Div. Back again to Lone Tree Trenches for the day.

Sussex Casualties   11 Officers Killed
Orme, Lewin, Ward, Wainright, West, Richards, Banted, Bright, Harden, Ireland, Dugnell

8 Wounded
Owen, Bright, Goring, Somers, Hardy, Bromley, Barnes, Cook

Lieut. Dicker to be Capt. (Temp.)

He took part in the Battle of Loos, and later was mentioned in despatches before being wounded again in August 1916 during the German attack on Mametz Wood near Albert. He was invalided home to England.

During his convalescence he met a masseuse, Margaret Kathleen Walley, to whom he proposed and eventually married on 4 February 1918. At that time he was Adjutant of 19 Officer Cadet Battalion, at Pirbright, where he and Margaret lived until the end of the War. For war service he was appointed an MBE.

Margaret Kathleen Walley

My mother was the youngest daughter of Rev. Stephen Cawley Walley and

Margaret Kathleen (Walley) Dicker (1895–1971)

his wife Mercy Mary. Stephen had been born in 1856 in Shropshire, but his father died when Stephen was four, leaving a widow of thirty-four and six children, with very little money, and a small farm. Stephen worked very hard, and saved enough money from farming to gain entrance to Clare College, Cambridge, where he took up rowing, and just missed getting a place in the University Eight. After Cambridge he was ordained into the Church of England. During his time at Cambridge he met Mercy Mary May, who had been educated at a Dame School. She was very artistic and painted under a drawing master. She was so good at fifteen that the President of the Royal Academy wanted her to be trained at the Slade, but she was not allowed to do this as ladies must not enter the wicked world of Art! Her own mother had died at age thirty-nine of her thirteenth child due to a drunken and dirty midwife. Mercy's father was a wealthy timber merchant who lived in Dulwich, from where Stephen and Mercy were married. In

Stephen Cawley Walley (1856–1936) and Mercy Mary (May) Walley
(1854–1931)

Stephen and Mercy Walley with their children, Geoffrey (1892–1916), May
(1885–1964), Margaret (1895–1971) and Nancy (1887–1964), in 1897

1890 Stephen was appointed vicar of Kirkthorpe cum Heath, a parish in Yorkshire, where my mother, her two sisters, and her brother, were born.

All four children grew up to love Kirkthorpe, and were scarcely conscious of the grime and discomforts of an industrial and colliery district. They had many good friends in the district, and Stephen recorded that the mental atmosphere was very stimulating, and good local schools made education cheap, easy and thoroughly efficient.

Stephen played cricket with the local team, and took up golf when the course was first laid out on Heath Common. Years later my mother became a 4 handicap golfer, and attributed her success largely to her father, who used to say, 'The secret of good golf is not to play good shots, but to eliminate the bad ones!' Stephen was a Freemason, and a Past Master of Lodge of Unanimity No. 154 in Wakefield. While at Kirkthorpe Stephen did a little farming on the glebe, and he always kept a horse to pull his little brougham and dog cart.

Stephen managed to get on well with the miners, except once when he was savagely attacked after building some cottages on the basis that the tenants would become owners after paying £50 down, and rent for twenty

Geoffrey Stephen Walley (1892–1916)

years. This caused a local row, because of mistrust by potential tenants, following some events of a similar nature which had occurrred previously. But eventually peace was made, although I don't know what happened about the cottages.

In 1911 Stephen was offered by the Patrons, Clare College, the living of Hardingham, in Norfolk. In those day the powers of a Patron were much greater than they are now, and neither the Bishop nor the Parochial Church Council could block the appointment, as they can now. Not that there would have been any objection on this occasion, and Stephen and Mercy stayed at Hardingham happily for over twenty years. Life as a country parson was also very different at the beginning of this century. The rectory at Hardingham was large, in several acres of garden, and I believe that at that time the stipend was £1,000 p.a., enabling them to maintain two or three living-in maids, and a gardener-cum-chauffeur. The village, containing some 300 parishioners, was over a mile away from the rectory and church, and altogether it was a very pleasant life for the family, after witnessing the hardships of a mining district.

The Walley family were very actively involved in the First World War. Geoffrey, after Haileybury and Clare College, Cambridge, where he gained a First Class Degree and was Senior Wrangler, having obtained the highest marks in Part II of the Mathemetical Tripos, was of course the darling of the family. He was commissioned in the King's Royal Rifle Corps, and joined the 2nd Battalion in France in January 1915. He was slightly wounded in the following April, and then more seriously a month later, when he was five months recovering in England before returning to France. He was invalided from the trenches in the spring of 1916 and was killed on the Somme shortly afterwards. His death was a shattering blow to all the family. Incidentally, I was named after him when I was born some four years later.

Stephen himself volunteered as an ambulance driver with the Church Army, going to France in August 1915. He went to France for a second time in 1917, and was based at a Church Army hut at Peronne, where the devastation was complete. Little organisation had been made for the Church Army huts, but Stephen said that everywhere he was received with great consideration by officers and men. 'The senior officers provided us with most of the things we required in ministering to the bodily comforts of the many thousands of men who passed through Peronne to and from the trenches a few miles distant.' Stephen visited Geoffrey's grave at Dernancourt, marked with a wooden cross. Subsequently this was replaced with a permanent one, the wooden cross being taken to Hardingham Church, where it was hung on the outside east wall for many years, and later moved inside the church. Stephen returned home in December 1917, and shortly afterwards he officiated at the wedding of Arthur and Margaret at Hardingham.

May, the eldest daughter of Stephen and Mercy, taught at Blackheath High School until 1915, and then joined the WRNS. After the War she joined the VADs and had an interesting time in Constantinople, which was then occupied by the British Army. Returning to England via Jerusalem and Cairo she met and married Oswell Rosser, a lecturer at Dunfermline with the Carnegie Trust.

They adopted a son, who sadly died, and much later their marriage ended in divorce. May did not have a happy time in her old age, and died in Helensburgh in May 1964.

Nancy, the second daughter, was the most academic of the three girls, and after winning several scholarships she went to Newnham College, Cambridge. Like her elder sister, she served for two years in the VAD, and later with the WRNS. Soon after the War she married her cousin Richard Abraham, a medical doctor, and they went to India for a short time, later returning to Brightwalton, Berkshire, where Richard (Dick) entered into practice as a GP. Nancy was appointed a magistrate in 1938, and in 1944 she became the first woman to preside on a bench in Berkshire. Nancy died in November 1964. They had two children, Felicity, who has died, and Richard.

So Arthur and Margaret were married at Hardingham in February 1918, and nine months to the day later my elder sister Anne was born at Hardingham. They lived at Pirbright and Worplesdon, before settling down in Norfolk.

Following demobilisation, after distinguishing himself both at school and in the Army, where he was appointed MBE, Arthur had to look for a career, and he chose accountancy. With the help of his father-in-law he acquired a small cottage in Bawburgh, a village four miles west of Norwich. He took articles with a Norwich firm of chartered accountants, cycling to and from work daily. They only stayed at Bawburgh for about a year, moving to the adjacent village of Little Melton. One of my earliest memories, in about 1924, was of my father falling off his bicycle and being brought home on the back of a hay cart. Life for Arthur and Margaret must have been hard in those days. Money was short, although he did receive a small gratuity on leaving the Army. Another of my early memories was of my mother baking bread and putting the loaves on the back stairs to cool. She had to learn cooking and housekeeping the hard way, her mother never having done any housework, and the children had always been able to rely on maids for all their requirements. At first my parents had no car, but then they acquired a small Morris Cowley, with a 'dickie', in which my sister Anne and I used to travel. Anne was frightened of cows, and if we saw even one in the road Anne would crouch down on the floor so that it could not see her.

After three hard-working years, Arthur qualified as a chartered accountant in 1923, bravely rented two rooms in the centre of Norwich, and put up a brass plate to show he was in practice. In those days, and indeed until quite recently, advertising was strictly banned in the profession, and those in practice had to pretend that they did not really want clients – very much the opposite of the truth. My father's first client was the squire of Harding-ham, who paid him £5 a year to complete his tax return. However, Arthur's personality, coupled no doubt with introductions which came through his father-in-law, meant that he soon built up a reasonable practice, with a total staff of two – a secretary and an office boy from Little Melton. Then, in 1925, an old man (as he described him) called at his office and said, 'My name is Lark, the senior partner of Lovewell Blake & Co in Yarmouth. We want to acquire an office in Norwich, and I have heard good things about you. We would like you to join us as a partner. At present your practice in Norwich does not justify a whole time partner here, and it would be necessary for you to move to the Yarmouth area, spending most of your working days in Yarmouth, but retaining control of your office here in Norwich.' The terms of the offer were quite generous, and were accepted, so later that year my parents moved to Caister-on-Sea, renting quite a large house there.

At school Arthur had become very much involved in acting, and it was no surprise therefore that he became a founder member of the Norfolk and Norwich Amateur Operatic Society, and he took one of the leading tenor roles in the Society's first performance, Dorothy, in December 1925. I clearly remember watching this show, and particularly seeing a pack of hounds on the stage of the Theatre Royal, Norwich, an event which has probably never been repeated. After removal to Caister, my father continued to support and perform in the productions of the Norfolk and Norwich Society, and in later years was elected Chairman. He also took part in the productions of the Great Yarmouth Amateur Operatic and Dramatic Society.

Bertie Lark's visit in 1925 was a landmark in my father's career. Starting from nothing, he became a partner in one of the oldest accountancy firms in the country, and was able to see the firm grow and prosper throughout his business career. At that time the Institute of Chartered Accountants, which had been formed towards the end of the last century, was governed by a Council which had no representation in East Anglia. Discussions took place among the leading firms in the area, and eventually the East Anglian Society of Chartered Accountants was formed in 1934, the President being A.E.Lark, and the Secretary A.S.H.Dicker. The Institute then had 13,000 members (the membership now being in excess of 100,000), and there was not much democracy about it, the Council being in effect a self-perpetuating body. Following the formation of the East Anglian Society, the Council invited the Society to put forward names of three members who might be suitable to join the Council. Two names were found, and, according to my father, his own name was added at the last minute because they could not find anyone else willing to be nominated. But the Council selected Dicker, and in 1939 he became a member of that august body.

Another series of events are of some interest. Some years earlier Arthur had become friendly with the agent for an estate in Norfolk, named Gerald Sacré. On one occasion Sacré came to my father and asked for his help. He said he had applied for the job of agent to the Blenheim Estates in Oxfordshire, and had been shortlisted, having told them that he knew all about income tax. Could my father please tell him a lot about taxation as applicable to landed estates? My father did his best over the next few days, and Sacré got the job. Not long after the 9th Duke of Marlborough, Gerald Sacré's employer at Blenheim, visited his accountants in London, one of the big firms. He was not treated with the respect which he considered was due to a Duke, and, returning to Blenheim he said, 'Sacré, I have sacked my accountants. Find me a good accountant!' Of course Gerald Sacré said, 'I know just the right man,' and introduced my father, who dealt with the Blenheim finances for many years, until he handed over to me.

That is not the end of the story, because shortly after the Second World War began in 1939, my father was at Blenheim on a routine visit, and he ran into the Secretary of the Institute of Chartered Accountants, Alan MacIver, whom he had got to know since joining the Council. MacIver wanted to know what he was doing at Blenheim, and having learned this he said, 'Just the man we want.' MacIver was then working with MI5, which was based at Blenheim, and he recruited my father to act as Advisor to the Financial Department of the Secret Service. Since the outbreak of war the activities had increased very considerably, and it was desired to formulate a revised bookkeeping system This was introduced under my father's super-vision within a few months. He was then invited by Colonel Charles Butler, Director of 'A' Division of MI5, to continue his association by making monthly visits for the dual purpose of presenting a summary of the month's figures and of seeing that the system was proving adequate and working satisfactorily. He was at liberty to ask any questions, and it was to be part of his duty to bring to Colonel Butler's notice any abnormal item of, or variations in, expenditure from month to month.

The neatness of this arrangement at the outset was that my father's presence at Blenheim would not attract any attention. As a result, my father continued to do this work for MI5 for many years, both during and after the War. Of course this was all secret, and although my father received a modest salary for the work, it was not to be disclosed, even to the Inspector of Taxes, and if anyone were to ask questions about it they were to be referred direct to the Prime Minister. His work in MI5 was perhaps not vitally important, but it did bring him into direct touch with many senior members of the organisation, including Sir David Petrie, Sir Dick White, Sir Roger Hollis, and Sir Percy Sillitoe, and it seems that he was always highly regarded in the organisation.

Over the years my father held a number of consultative posts with the government. Between 1948 and 1950 he sat as a member of the Brown Committee dealing with land settlement, and in 1951 was a ministerial nominee to the National Council for Domestic Food Production, serving as chairman of the Council's finance committee. He was a member of the Civil Service Commission interviewing accountants for permanent appointments, and was for some years a member of the Eastern Gas Board. He remained as a member of the Council of the Institute of Chartered Accountants until 1958, and was elected President of the Institute in 1956. For many years he was an examiner and later a moderator for the Institute's examinations.

His year as President of the Institute was most successful. When he was first approached to accept nomination for the office he was at first a bit doubtful, wondering whether he could afford either the time or the money. He consulted his family, and his partners, of which I was one by then, and he also talked to some of the past Presidents, one of whom told him that he would find the biggest expense would be laundry bills. The President was, and still is, expected to attend and speak at dinners all over the country, and in those days white tie and tails was the normal dress for such occasions.

During his year as President he attended dinners of District Societies of

*Arthur Seymour
Hamilton Dicker
(1892–1974)
President, Institute
of Chartered
Accountants,
1956–57*

the Institute in Birmingham, Bristol, Norwich, Hull, Leeds, Northampton, Liverpool, Manchester, Newcastle, Nottingham, Sheffield, Brighton, Cardiff and Newquay. At that time there was much debate about a proposal to merge the Institute with The Society of Incorporated Accountants, and meetings were held in every district, including one at the Royal Festival Hall in London. Speaking at Birmingham in March 1957 my father said:

> I can assure the members of the Institute that the members of the present Council are very conscious of the extra responsibility which will be placed on them in the event of this scheme being approved. While I am asking you to put your faith in the Council, I feel I must correct (it concerns me personally) an impression which has been made on several occasions, and it was mentioned twice at the Royal Festival Hall, that the views of the Council are often the views only of the big firms from which (I quote) 'certainly the whole of the practising

members of the Council come'. I would mention that many of my colleagues on the Council belong to 'that large majority of practising members who practise in small towns and in the suburbs of large towns and cities'. I can assure you with every confidence, not only do the conditions of this 'large majority of the practising members' receive the utmost consideration of the Council and its committees, but by none more sincerely and more objectively than those members of the Council who do in fact belong to the large firms.

Traditionally, the last of the round of District Societies was East Anglia, and when he adddressed the East Anglian Society in Norwich, just before the end of his Presidential year, he said:

It is a happy happening that the end of my journeying of the district societies finds me in my home city, and it is not inappropriate for me to conclude my visitations with a reference to the activities of these societies. At these functions I have taken every opportunity to preach and spread the gospel of the value of the district society movement, a part of the framework of the Institute which is of ever increasing importance. Through the District Societies the Council is able to feel the pulse and to assess the thoughts of a great cross-section of Chartered Accountants, a cross section covering the whole country, not only geographically, but also in terms of occupation, age and experience, a gathering of opinion of invaluable benefit to the Institute and through the Institute to our profession generally.

Of course, attending dinners was by no means the main occupation of Arthur Dicker as President. He was required to chair the monthly meeting of the Council, he was an ex-officio member of all committees, and he represented the Institute at many functions both in the City of London and elsewhere. Addressing the Women's Chartered Accountants Dining Society he said that in this enlightened era it was universally accepted that the ranks of the professions included an increasing element of women, many of whom had reached the highest eminence in their spheres. Lady barristers, doctors and architects were taken for granted, and quite rightly so, because they had earned recognition. In the realms of politics and the Civil Service they were found in the highest positions, all doing a splendid job. He referred to the fact that there were then over 200 women chartered accountants, and he acknowledged the valuable contribution they were making to the general welfare of the Institute.

But in spite of all these achievements, my father never quite recovered from the effects of the First World War, and the terrible experiences of the trenches. It is not surprising that they had left marks. Whereas he had charm, and ability to mix at all levels of society, there was a neurotic side to his character which only arose occasionally, and was noticed by very few. Of course my mother knew about this, and it made life difficult for her at times. However, she understood, and was philosophic. Curiously enough, although he reached the top of his profession, and was highly regarded in every organisation in which he became involved, he was often jealous of others who, to his mind, had been more successful. Envy is one of the seven deadly sins, and I don't know why it should have affected my father, but it did, although again this was not obvious to those who did not know him intimately.

He found time for a number of other interests. Shortly after moving to Caister-on-Sea in 1925 he and my mother took up golf, which he played with pleasure but badly. My mother, on the other hand, improved rapidly, and acquired a handicap of 4, playing for Norfolk County on many occasions.

Arthur was a lover of music, especially church music, and he acted as choirmaster both at Little Melton and at Ormesby, where they moved after eight years at Caister-on-Sea.

Having an office in The Close, in Norwich, he became quite friendly with the Bishop, Rt. Rev. Percy Mark Herbert. During the War there were periods when he was able to help the Bishop by arranging for documents to be typed for him. On one such occasion some minutes were sent round to the office when my father was away, and a few days later he met the Bishop and asked if they had been typed satisfactorily. The Bishop said 'Yes, but did you see them?' My father then was shown a copy of the minutes, which, when typed, recorded 'The Bishop ended the meeting with a Benedictine.' The Bishop commented 'I wish I had!'

My mother was a loyal supporter of her husband, in a marriage which lasted over fifty-three years. As I have already mentioned, they started in a hard way, in a little cottage and with not much money. She loved painting, an interest inherited from her mother, and she produced many pictures in watercolours and oils over many years. She was an active member of the Great Yarmouth Art Circle, and had the distinction, once, of being rejected for an exhibition of the Royal Academy. Some of her pictures she sold, for between one and eight guineas. I have already mentioned her success at golf, which she played consistently, driving straight down the middle of the fairway, rarely going into bunkers, and always taking two putts – never three and only occasionally one. She was a magistrate, and served on the local bench, which took up one day a week. She was also actively involved with the British Red Cross, being a local President for many years.

Perhaps because of the tight financial situation when they first married, my mother always kept strict and meticulous household and personal accounts, which balanced to the penny. If there was a discrepancy she would 'cook' the accounts to make them balance. Her understanding of economics was limited. She would go to London during the annual sales period, staying at her club – The Lady Golfers' Club. Then each time she bought anything she would record how much she had saved at the sale, and would go on buying until she calculated she had saved enough to cover the costs of travel and the club, and then convinced herself that she had had a free trip to London.

My parents moved house several times. After Caister-on-Sea they went to Ormesby, a short distance away, and then in 1939 they bought a house in Acle, where they stayed until my mother died in 1971 and my father in 1974. After his death I received a letter from the President of the Institute of Chartered Accountants:

> His long years of involvement in Institute affairs culminated in his Presidency of 1956-57. He combined leadership and dignity with an utter lack of pomposity, and I personally remember with gratitude the friendship and encouragement he gave to me and to other junior members of the profession.

I think these words sum up his life.

Geoffrey Seymour Hamilton Dicker and Margaret Anne Hamilton Dicker, Little Melton, 1924

Chapter VII

The Family of Arthur and Margaret

Margaret Anne Hamilton Dicker

My sister Anne was born at Hardingham on 4 November 1918, just a week before the Armistice. The next big event in her life was to be a bridesmaid, at the age of two, to her Aunt Nancy, her mother's sister. We grew up together at Little Melton, Caister and Ormesby, and were aged less than two years apart, so were able to share the same interests to a considerable extent. Anne was always thought to be artistic, and painted a lot. We both went to dancing classes in Norwich, and later she attended a dancing class in Yarmouth. Anne went to Norwich High School, then to St Felix School, Southwold, and just before the War she joined the VADs (Voluntary Aid Detachments). For most of the War she was nursing, and then in 1945 she married John Charles Carisbooke Murison, always known as Pete. They had two children, Mary Anne and Robert, but sadly Pete died while visiting their son, a Professor of Psychology, in Norway in 1986. Pete had previously owned and managed a laundry in Llandrindod Wells for many years.

Susan Alice Hamilton Dicker

My younger sister was born in 1925. She went to several schools before and during the War, and then to the Royal College of Music, where she became an ARCM, after which she taught piano, having a number of very successful students. In 1946 she married William (Bill) Apsey, who had served in the Rifle Brigade in the War, being awarded the MC. They had two sons, James and Francis. James qualified as a chartered accountant in the family firm of Lovewell Blake & Co, and then joined Cooper Bros in London, but his career was spoilt when he developed epilepsy, and he died at home in tragic circumstances in 1994. Francis made an unsuccessful marriage in 1976, which only lasted a few years, and his son Peter spent most of his early life with his mother in Dublin. Sue and Bill lived for many years with my parents at Acle, Norfolk, and looked after them both until they died in 1971 and 1974 respectively. After that, and Bill's retirement as secretary of a laundry in Yarmouth, they continued to live in Acle. Sue died on 5 May 1998.

Geoffrey Seymour Hamilton Dicker

My life began at Bawburgh on 20 July 1920, but my earliest recollections are of Hill House, Little Melton, about a mile away, where my parents lived from 1922 to 1925. At Hill House my father and the gardener, Ottaway, constructed a tennis court in the garden. I don't know how they could afford it, but in addition to the gardener my parents had two daily maids, whose wages were probably very low, as was usual in those days. We had a dog, a cairn called Ready, who must have started life at Hardingham with my grandfather, because we always had to make sure that Ready was shut in at

Margaret Anne Hamilton (Dicker) Murison (b.1918) and Robert Murison (b.1951)

*Susan Alice
Hamilton (Dicker)
Apsey (1925–1998)*

night; if he got out he would turn up first thing the next morning at Hardingham Rectory, eleven miles away – this happenened on several occasions.

Anne and I did not go to school then. Instead we had lessons from a Miss Denny, who taught us many of the basics, so that by the time I was five I could read and write quite well.

The year 1925 was a busy one. My sister Susan was born in August, and very shortly afterwards several of the family caught scarlet fever, but I escaped it. Then came the move to Caister, following Mr Lark's visit to my father, and the family fortunes improved considerably. We had two living-in maids, and the gardener Ottaway moved with us. In addition to the Morris Cowley my mother acquired a Baby Austin, and she and my father started playing golf, which became their main recreation for the rest of their lives. I started playing golf at about eight; I always enjoyed this but was never much good.

Caister House, which was rented, was quite a large house in the middle of the village, with a wall along the main street. There was a good-sized garden, with a tennis lawn in the front, and a vegetable garden with greenhouses which produced some excellent peaches and grapes. I was a bit of a horror in those days. On one occasion I discovered how to get out of a skylight onto the roof, and when my parents arrived home I was waving to them from my perch on the top ridge of the roof. And I remember taking one of my father's watches to pieces to see how it worked! We had a schoolroom at the back of the house, and one day what appeared to be a large cloud appeared at the window; looking up I saw an immense object in the sky labelled 'Graf Zeppelin'. I think this must have been one of its last trips.

From my mother's family I had inherited a model boat with a number of oars – about sixteen I think – which had belonged to my Uncle Geoffrey, who had been killed in the War, and I used to play with this on the beach. One day a man approached me on the beach and wanted to know where I lived. Later he called to see my parents and said that his name was Laird Clowes, and he was a curator of the South Kensington Science Museum. My boat was apparently a valuable model which they needed in the Museum, so there it went, and as far as I know it is still there, although it is no longer on display.

We had governesses at Caister, but I became too much for them, and when I was eight I was sent to Duncan House School in Great Yarmouth. The school was about three miles from my home, and I went daily by tram, using 'scholars tickets', which I think cost two pence each. The tickets were issued in a book, and one day I lost my complete book, so I walked home. I was quite happy, but there was much consternation when I was missing for an hour or so. My mother was about to phone the police when I arrived home. I quite enjoyed Duncan House, and won my first prize in the Lower School in 1928 – *Uncle Tom's Cabin*, which of course I still have.

But in spite of this early success I was becoming a problem at home, and one day my parents saw this advertisement in the *Guardian*.

Five sons of clergymen or other professional men will be accepted at 15 guineas inclusive per term at First-Class Preparatory School opening under Mr W.R. Seagrove M.A., Clare College, Cambridge, ex-President C.U.A.C. Prospectus from Normansal, Blatchington Down, Seaford.

The reference to Clare College interested them, both my grandfather and my uncle having been there, and so I went to Normansal in May 1929. I do not know what the basic fees of a school were, but fifteen guineas must have been a bargain, even before those days when there was no inflation.

I had never lived away from home before, and at first I was very homesick, but I soon settled down, and have some very happy memories of Normansal. Bill Seagrove had been an Olympic runner, and was very keen on games and sports. He fancied himself as a psychologist, and I remember that he once wrote to my parents: 'I am getting to the bottom of his case.' My father showed me this letter and said, 'I didn't know that you had a case.' But Seagrove was a fair man and a good headmaster, and we all respected him.

So far as I was concerned Normansal made one major mistake: I was considered to be reasonably intelligent, so I was made to specialize in Classics – Latin and Greek. I was quite good at Latin, but never learned much Greek, and this let me down badly when, at the age of thirteen, I tried for a scholarship to Haileybury. In fact I had always had a leaning towards Mathematics, but this was not appreciated until after I got to Haileybury, without having gained a scholarship.

At Normansal I made several friends. Joseph Cochran was an American, whose father was the Pastor of the American Church in Paris. During holidays I went to stay with the Cochrans on several occasions, in their house on the Quai d'Orsay in Paris, and their charming villa at Barbizon, near Fontainebleau. Once, when we were at Barbizon, it was discovered that Leon Trotsky was living in the village.

Trotsky had worked with Lenin in the revolutionary years in Russia, but on Lenin's death in 1924 he had been ousted by Stalin and exiled. He continued to agitate in Russian affairs, and his discovery in Barbizon attracted the world's media. Joe Cochran and I were very young then and didn't really understand what all the fuss was about, but we certainly joined in the general excitement. I think that Trotsky subsequently disappeared from France, and was assassinated in Mexico a few years later.

Another of my friends at Normansal was Francis Noel-Baker. He was the son of Philip Noel-Baker, who was friendly with Bill Seagrove, having also been an Olympic runner and silver medallist. I used to stay with the Noel-Baker family in the holidays, and I remember being taken by them to Bertram Mills Circus at Olympia. Philip Noel-Baker, having already made a name for himself in the world of athletics, was at that time very much involved with the League of Nations, which had been founded in 1920 following the Armistice at the end of the First World War. At Normansal we were allowed to have pets, and one term Francis brought a rabbit, a chinchilla called Priscilla, which he had borrowed from his cousin, on condition that she did not have babies. But she did, and Francis, rather than take them home and face the wrath of his cousin, gave me the babies, which I took home to Caister. I don't remember the ultimate fate of the babies, but I don't think they survived very long. The point of this story is that many years later I met, and married, Priscilla's owner.

Another excitement while I was at Normansal arose in connection with my mother's golf. She achieved a handicap of 4, and played for Norfolk County. Then in 1933 she entered, with a Swedish friend, Karen Timberg, for the English Ladies' Foursomes. They won round after round, and were only beaten in the final match. There were many press reports and photographs in all the papers, so at school I basked in some reflected glory.

I went to Haileybury in 1934, after five years at Normansal. It was quite an experience to have been a senior boy at prep school, and then to start at the bottom at public school. But the new boys did not have too bad a time, and it was good for us. Fagging was practised at most public schools in those days – just running errands for the house prefects and not very onerous. The next stage after being a general fag was to be appointed a 'special', which meant that you were allocated to one prefect, and were not at the general beck and call of them all.

Although I did not get an entrance scholarship to Haileybury, after just over a year I sat for and obtained a senior scholarship, having specialized in mathematics. By early 1936 I was in the Sixth Form, having done well in the School Certificate, the equivalent of O Levels now, and later in the Higher Certificate.

In 1936 I went with a party from school, twenty-eight boys and two masters, on a visit to Germany. We started from Southampton, where we boarded the German ship *Europa*, which had held the Atlantic record in 1929, before her sister ship the *Bremen* recaptured it. There were three classes on the ship – first, tourist and third; we were travelling third class, and our small cabins were immediately over the propellers. It was a great experience to be shown over the ship, and we were all much impressed at the luxury of the first class, including a swimming pool, dance hall, cinema, dining room and tea room. We docked the next day at Bremerhaven, and were greeted by two flags, the German swastika, and the Olympic flag with five coloured rings. Many of the passengers on the *Europa* had come from America and were heading for the Olympic Games in Berlin. Our party was welcomed at Bremen and then at Hamburg, where we stayed on the *Hein*

Godewind, a large sailing ship which had been converted into a youth hostel. After Hamburg we moved to Swinemunde, on the Baltic coast, and then went on a ship along the coast to Zoppot, which was the port of Danzig.

After the First World War the Polish Corridor had been created by the Treaty of Versailles, providing Poland with access to the Baltic, thus separating East Prussia from the rest of Germany, and Danzig had become a free city. During our visit we encountered much propaganda from the Germans, who bitterly resented the loss of Danzig, and it was clear to us that they were aiming to recover the city, which they did, for a short time, in 1939. We spent ten days in East Prussia, our hosts being members of the Hitler Youth Organisation, and visited the Masurian Lakes, in lovely countryside. The Nazi propaganda continued throughout our visit, from the German boys themselves, and from officials who lectured us on many occasions. This was three years before war began, but even then it was obvious that trouble was brewing, and the Germans, particularly the young ones we were with, tried their best to impress us with the unfair provisions of the Treaty of Versailles, and the determination of Germany to recover what had been taken from them as a result of the First World War. We did not like the Hitler Youth, who were obsessed with their political aims. '*Deutschland Uber Alles!*' Leaving East Prussia, we went to Berlin for a short visit to the Olympic Games, where unfortunately I suffered from tummy trouble, and hardly saw any of the events. Then home via Ostend and Dover.

Music was one of my main interests at Haileybury. While at Normansal I had learned to play the cello, and continued this at Haileybury, playing in the school orchestra for several years. I was also a member of the school choir, and with a few others formed the Madrigal Society, which gave a performance almost every term. I joined the OTC, and learned to play a fife in the band, ending up by playing the big bass drum, which gave me a feeling of power and tremendous pleasure.

Mathematics and Science were my favourite subjects, and while at Haileybury I delivered a paper on relativity, of which this is an abridged version:

The greatest of ancient philosophers and scientists were the Greeks, who arrived at conclusions which, although perhaps shattered by modern theories, were yet brilliant as arising from entirely original assumptions, justified by the fact that there were no important theories then holding. It was not until the sixteenth century that what is now known as Modern Science began to form, and so for nearly two thousand years this movement to discover the reason why was carried on. The progress was slow, being suppressed by wars, revolutions, and religious strife, but it was progress, and we are indebted to such men as Aristotle and Archimedes for starting off this new line of thought.

The Greek genius was lucid, philosophical and logical. The men of that day based everything on clear, bold ideas, and their arguments were clear and simple, but unfortunately we are now beginning to understand that clarity is not the fundamental solution of every problem of nature. Newton, one of the middle men between old and new, wrote a set of 'Rules of Reasoning in Philosophy', in which he stated:

'We are to admit no more causes of natural things than such as are both true and sufficient to explain their appearances. To this purpose the philosophers say that Nature does nothing in vain when less will serve; for Nature is pleased with simplicity, and affects not the pomp of superfluous causes. Therefore to the same material effects we must, as far as possible, assign the same causes – as to respiration in a man and in a beast; the descent of stones in Europe and America; the heat of our fires and of the sun; the reflection of light in the earth and in the planets.'

This is typical Newtonian, in that he refused to base his theories on anything but facts, except for the most essential of assumptions.

But to return to the Greek reasoning, of which Newton was one of the important pupils – the Greeks loved drama, and this had great bearing on their views of Nature. They had a centre of the universe as the end of motion for material things, and celestial spheres for the things which, on account of their purity, were rendered weightless and so were drawn upwards away from the influence of worldly wickedness. Nature was a drama in which each thing played its part. These were not actually the original views founded by Aristotle and his contemporaries, but they are the outcome of them which found their way into European philosophy.

Newton and Galileo, the heroes of the seventeenth century, found great difficulty in explaining some phenomena without starting all over again. Newton liked to explain everything on a mechanical basis. He proved that the attraction between two bodies in the universe always obeyed a universal law of gravitation, but he said 'Would that the rest of the phenomena of nature could be deduced by a like kind of reasoning from mechanical principles.' It was at about this time that the mystery of space became evident. It had always been assumed that literally nothing existed in the millions of miles between us and the sun, but then arose the question: 'If there is nothing there, how is it that light and heat can penetrate through the nothingness from the sun?' The obvious solution came to Newton – a strange medium which filled the gaps between all material substances and through which a wave motion could pass. Newton, however, was a cautious man, and did not state that this medium actually existed, but that it would be very convenient if it did exist. This medium was called the ether, and brings me to the subject of relativity.

The main property of ether is that it is capable of conveying electro-magnetic waves, a system of transmission, including light waves, heat waves, wireless waves, x rays, and many other forms of wave motion. They all travel at the same speed of about 186,000 miles per second, and consist not of an actual bodily movement of the medium through which they pass, but of the particles of the medium vibrating, just as on the surface of a pond into which a stone has been dropped.

If now we take a simple example of the difficulties with which we shall meet, consider a ship at sea. If we drop a succession of stones into the water, each stone will set up a succession of rings, at equal intervals apart, with the point of entry of the stone as centre. The next stone, however, will not land in exactly the same place, and so the next set of rings will be slightly displaced. So we shall see a series of ring systems, each with a different centre, and from a study of these rings it may be possible to find the speed of the ship in the water. A very similar experiment has been tried in the case of the earth, but although instruments would have measured a hundredth part of the expected result, there was not the slightest detection of any relative motion between the earth and the ether. Further experiments were carried out by Michaelson, using an interferometer, and there seemed to be no getting away from the fact that that there was no relative motion between the earth and the ether, or, if this motion existed, it was eluding all known methods of detecting it. This was a bitter blow to scientists. It was still necessary to try to discover whether there was such a thing as a standard rest in the universe. To a man in a motor car the passenger beside him may seem to be at rest; to a man in an armchair the chair is at rest, and yet we say that neither are in fact at rest, for the earth is moving round the sun. We are inclined to end here, and look upon the sun as stationary, but there is no reason why the sun should not be moving around in space.

In 1905 Einstein propounded his new theory of relativity, which crushed all original ideas. The principle is contained in this law – 'Nature is such that it is impossible to determine absolute motion by any experiment whatever'. In other words, there is no reason for supposing that the earth moves round the sun, any more than that the sun moves round the earth. Motion, as we know it, is purely relative, in that it depends on the mutual connection between two bodies. We are perfectly justified in considering ourselves at rest while the earth, and all the planets rotate round us. The second hand of a clock may be imagined to be at rest while the clock, and the whole earth with it, rotates round it. However, there is still one great problem. What about this ether? Einstein produced an explanation of this which, though difficult to grasp, has apparently satisfied the great minds of modern scientists. This was the theory of the fourth dimension, begun by Einstein and developed by Minkowski. With this new theory it was shown that all electrical phenomena (and it has been proved that all physical phenomena are electrical) could only be explained under the consideration of space and time so welded together that it was impossible to detect any traces of the join. Just as in geometry we may look upon a line as of one dimension, but give it breadth and it becomes two, so we may consider a combination of one dimension of length and one of time. For instance – a train travelling on a line. On our timetable we are only concerned with distance and time, and one without the other has no meaning at all. Relativity extends this to four dimensions, and states that all electromagnetic phenomena occur in a continuum – hitherto known as the ether, which differs from our ordinary theories in that it has four dimensions, three of space and one of time. Minkowski, Einstein's contemporary, puts it this way – 'Space and time separately have vanished into the merest shadows, and only a combination of the two preserve any reality.'

The important question is this – 'Do all these new four-dimensional theories explain more fully and more extensively the physical phenonema which have already found logical justification in other lines of thought?' It has been found that perfectly satisfactory explanations follow logically, and that in many cases the new explanations are far more acceptable than the old ones. Newton's famous law of gravitation seemed satisfactory, but did not apparently account for some special irregularities of the orbit of the planet Mercury. The new formula of Einstein differed from that of Newton, and did explain these irregularities. Under the law of relativity gravitational forces have disappeared as a separate entity, and it is likely that electromagnetic forces will go the same way.

I have tried to sketch out a brief outline of one of the main thoughts in modern science, to show the line which the scientists of today are taking. We are still far from an end of our search for a final answer to the universe question, but we have every reason for believing that such men as Einstein have set us thinking in the right direction, and that Mathematics, Science, Religion and Philosophy will eventually arrive hand in hand at an ultimate conclusion.

Of course that paper was written some sixty years ago, and is no doubt now quite out of date, but it does show that I was intensely interested in modern scientific developments at that time.

I enjoyed my schooldays, particularly the last few years as a senior prefect at Haileybury. The seven or eight seniors were treated with great respect, even by the masters. We had our own dining room, called Elysium, and had comfortable studies. Qualification for studies depended on academic progress, the first stage being studies for four, then for two, and finally singles, which were reserved for the very senior, and were much sought after.

Early in my last year at school I obtained a major mathematics scholarship at King's College, Cambridge. This was my ultimate academic achievement, and I was due to go to Cambridge in September 1939. As there was no particular point in remaining at school until the last minute I chose to leave Haileybury in the spring, and obtained a job teaching at a preparatory school, Boxgrove, in Guildford, for the summer term. This was a good experience, and I earned the princely sum of £25 for the term's work. At that time I was beginning to fall in love, but no girl took my fancy for more than a week or two.

During the summer of 1939 the war clouds were beginning to roll, but having met a party of young Americans in England who were about to go on a cycling tour of France, I arranged to join them, and was caught in Britanny shortly before war was declared on 3 September. Actually the few British in the party just got back to England before war began, and I well remember arriving in Southampton on one of the first nights of the blackout. The whole country was alive with activity, reserve troops being called up, and one of my first jobs on arrival home was to drive my sister Anne to a hospital at Shenley, in Hertfordshire, where she was to join the nursing staff. I volunteered for the Army and was accepted for the Royal Artillery, but was told that I was too young to be called up immediately, so went up to Cambridge as planned.

Life at Cambridge appeared to be almost normal during the first nine months of the War. Of course there was the blackout, to which we quickly became accustomed, and at first we had to carry gas masks, but they didn't last long. There was quite a lot of social life at Cambridge, and work, which I quite enjoyed, particularly as I found that astronomy was one of the subjects included in the maths tripos.

On almost my first day at King's I met my old friend from preparatory school days, Francis Noel-Baker. We found that we each knew hardly anyone at Cambridge, but Francis asked me to his rooms to meet a cousin of his, who turned out to be a blonde called Fifi (I found out later that her real name was Josephine). We soon discovered that she had been the owner of the rabbit Priscilla, so we were almost related. That started off a romance which I pursued during and after my short time at Cambridge, and it was hard work. Fifi delighted in keeping me waiting and tantalizing me with stories of her various boyfriends. She even claimed to be engaged to a handsome Hungarian youth, who was now serving in the German Army – she was knitting a pullover for him but had only got halfway. By the time she had finished it (she was not a fast knitter) she had had second thoughts and I got the pullover.

Josephine Helen Penman

Fifi was a member of a family who lived in Bushey. She was one of three daughters of Frank Garfield Penman, having been born in 1920, and was a few months older than me. She went to a Quaker school, Sidcot in Somerset, and then to Downe House, in Berkshire. Fifi's family were dedicated to improving international relations, so she had travelled often in Europe and helped to entertain overseas visitors in the family home. On 30 September

1938 an agreement was reached in Munich between Germany, France and Great Britain 'to resolve' the crisis over the Czech Sudetenland in the hope of avoiding war. It resulted in thousands of Sudeten inhabitants leaving their homes under the threat of Nazi occupation. The opportunity arose for Mrs Penman and her stepdaughter Fifi to fly at once to Prague to give immediate help in the form of distributing aid from the *News Chronicle* and the Lord Mayor's Funds. Shortly they were joined by two other Quakers and by members of other relief organisations. Mrs Penman gave invaluable service; she spoke fluent German, and a Slav language (Serbo Croat). Fifi acted as driver of an aged car, left in Prague before the Munich crisis. She wrote the following letter to her father (her own mother had died in her infancy):

Alcron Hotel, Praha
Sunday, 16th October 1938

We have now been here nearly a week, during which time we have seen and done a great many very interesting things.

We had a wonderful journey, very comfortable indeed. I was very slightly ill before Rotterdam, but after that I felt very well. I went to sleep during a storm, which was rather disappointing. We arrived at 5.15 instead of 5.45 which was rather good. I liked going down better than going up.

When we arrived on Monday evening we drove and walked a little through the town. The impression I had then was that life in Prague was perfectly normal, and I began to wonder why we had come to help with the refugees who I had imagined would be swarming about the streets. The people on the whole looked particularly well dressed, and the shops were bright with attractive goods. We saw several little groups of people who were mournfully studying the new maps of Czechoslovakia, in book-shop windows.

The next morning as we drove round the town seeing people, we realised what a beautiful city it is. On the one side of the Vltava lies the old town, and on the other side lies the new town. In the old town there are no new buildings. There are beautiful old churches and one or two old palaces, but for the most part there are small houses in narrow cobbled streets – all these houses are very old, and nearly all of them are painted or have figures carved in stone on them.

On the hill right above the old town stands the castle, of which Prague is so proud. It has a wonderful view over the whole city. New Prague is very much like any other city of one million inhabitants. The state buildings are very fine, but the streets are on the whole very narrow. It has been a great help staying at this hotel as several of the others working for the relief funds are here. Also all the cheaper hotels are full of German refugees. You can hardly move in the restaurant of the Steiner for them. The ones who have somehow got hold of our names are asking for help with visas etc. If there was anything we could do we wouldn't mind but really there is about nothing. We have only

*Frank Garfield
Penman
(1884–1963)*

been to bed before 12 once as everyone chooses about 10.30 in the evening to call or ring up.

On the whole the car is not going too badly, but it takes an absolute age to warm up in the morning. The garage is below the hotel and I have an awful time getting it up the steep slope to the road. It simply won't take it.

The problem of the refugees in this country is a very complicated one. On October 1st there were said to be 300,000 refugees in Czechoslovakia, most of them were people who had fled because they thought the wars were going to rage over the Sudeten areas. Most of them returned as soon as possible and were treated correctly while the German troops were in occupation. There were, however, about 30,000 people

Elizabeth Grace
(Baker) Penman
(1886–1921)

Elizabeth Grace (Baker) Penman with Josephine Helen Penman, aged 6 months, and Elizabeth Penman, aged 4

who did not want to, or who could not return. They consisted of German social democrats, German and Czech Jews, refugees from Austria, and other Czechs who did not want to be under the Nazi regime.

A great many of these people have since been forced to go back. On

Josephine Helen (Penman) Dicker (b.1920) (right) with her sisters Clare Frances Grace (Penman) Campion (b.1923) and Elizabeth (Penman) Craib (b.1916)

several occasions Nazi officials have been sent in German trains across the frontier to fetch them back. When they got back into the new German territory they were liable to be put into concentration camps at once, and it is believed that some have been shot. There are now about 10,000 refugees still in Prague. As soon as camps can be organised, they are being sent out to them, as Prague finds it very difficult to provide for such a large number.

On Wednesday and Thursday we spent the time visiting the places in Prague where they are living.

We went first to the Deutsches House where there are only German refugees. They were having lunch at the time, in a vast room. There were refugees of every class, doctors, lawyers, engineers and peasants all eating here, because they had not enough money to pay for their meals. The News Chronicle Fund is helping a great deal in the feeding

Josephine Helen
(Penman) Dicker
(Fifi) (b.1920)

of these German refugees, and is making it possible for 1,500 of them to be given good simple meals three times a day.

These German refugees are the worst off. There were a great many Jews among them, who have no hope at all of ever returning to their land. If they go back they will be persecuted, and life would be impossible for them. There are at the moment Jewish refugees wandering between the Czech and German frontiers. The Czechs don't want them here, and the Germans refuse to let them in, so it is a ghastly state of affairs for them.

We then went on to a place where there were only Czech refugees. They are in a very depressed state too but there is hope that in their case they will eventually be exchanged for Germans still in Czech areas.

They are living under very bad conditions. We went and saw a big gymnasium where 130 men, women and children were all sleeping on palliasses of straw on the floor, with only one dirty rug as a covering. We spoke to some of the women who were rather bitter, and said that they had lost what money could not buy, the homes they loved and their friends. Another woman from Eger told us how her small girl of nine had been tormented in the school, because she spoke Czech.

There are a great many cases where the families have got separated, and they are frantically searching for each other. At the Deutsches House they still have children of eight and nine without parents, but most of them have been taken in by families in Prague. We went round to the stations in the evening, where the Czech Red Cross have been helping the refugees. They give them soup and medical treatment free of charge. They had some very sad stories to tell of how the people who did not want to go back were forced into the trains weeping. They also told how some of these refugees had thrown themselves onto the line in front of the train, rather than go back.

The great problem is where these refugees can eventually settle. There are very few countries who will take them because (a) they have already unemployed and (b) they would have to be supported for some time. The problem at the moment is how to get them out of this country before they are sent back. After a long time of anxiety it has now been settled that 100 shall go to England, 100 to Sweden, 30 to Finland and I think 100 to France, only temporarily of course. Those most in danger have already gone, but there are still a great number who <u>must</u> be got out within the next few days. If anyone could offer hospitality in the form of a written invitation with a blank space for the name, at once, it would be a great help, as without these they are not admitted into England. About 70 have already been received and many more are needed.

So by the time I met her at Cambridge Fifi had had a unique experience of some of the problems which were steadily and inexorably leading Europe into war.

That short period while I was up at Cambridge was sometimes described by Winston Churchill as The Twilight War, but much was happening in the world. The British Expeditionary Force of five Divisions was in France, but nothing much seemed to happen at first. The Allies, mainly Britain and

France, were busy building up their forces on land, sea and air, but to us in Cambridge the War seemed a bit remote. I joined the University OTC, but contrary to what we had earlier thought, found that I was not eligible for a commission without further training, so I awaited a call-up, which I rightly expected would come the following year. I worked quite hard, and being a scholar was expected to take Part I of the mathematics tripos at the end of my first year, instead of the second year which was normal. I obtained a 2.2, which seemed reasonable in all the circumstances. I played rugger and squash, and managed a fairly active social life, which was largely centred round Fifi, who enjoyed making me jealous and keeping me waiting when we had an assignation. I had a delightful set of rooms in King's, very close to the river, and made many friends during my short time at Cambridge. I don't remember that I had financial problems. My scholarship was worth £100 a year, and I also received an exhibition from Haileybury and a small allowance from my father, making £300 in all, which enabled me to live quite comfortably. Those who had £250 went a bit short, and £350 was luxury. Of course undergraduates did not have cars in those days, but we all had bicycles, which were our main form of transport. Cambridge was littered with bicycles, but it was never necessary to lock them – I don't remember anyone ever having their bicycle stolen.

After dark, and when attending lectures, we had to wear cap and gown, to show that we were in *statu pupillari*, and subject to University discipline. To be caught by the Proctors (Progs) when committing an offence, such as climbing into College after hours, was to be avoided.

Then, just as the spring term finished in Cambridge, came the events leading up to Dunkirk. The German onslaught began on 10 May 1940, and went rapidly through Holland and Belgium. Suddenly we all woke up to the potentially disastrous situation. Chamberlain resigned and was replaced by Churchill. Vast numbers of our troops were evacuated from France, and invasion seemed imminent. At home in Norfolk I joined the Local Defence Volunteers (LDV), the forerunners of the Home Guard, Dad's Army. It all happened so quickly that we had no uniforms – just armbands with 'LDV' on them, and we paraded, usually at night, to keep alert for enemy parachutists who were expected to arrive at any time. We could not have done much about them for we had no weapons, but we were inspired by Churchill – 'We shall fight on the beaches, we shall fight on the landing grounds, we shall fight in the fields and in the streets, we shall fight in the hills.'

My twentieth birthday was on 20 July 1940, and just at that time I was called up. I had been earmarked for the Royal Artillery, but, perhaps having regard to my academic qualifications, I was told that I would be posted to the Royal Corps of Signals. I was therefore ordered to report to the Royal Signals Depot at Catterick. There life was tough, but we accepted it – reveille at 5.00 a.m., shaving in cold water, parade ground ('square bashing') most of the day, rifle drill, range firing, barrack room cleanliness and so on.

After a month at the Depot, I was posted to 1st Operators Training Battalion, also in Catterick. There we were taught the basics of wireless telegraphy and telephony, the use of communication equipment, cable laying, and use of the morse code over and over again, so that we literally dreamed morse. Having been in the OTC at school much of this training was not new to me and I spent some time working in the cookhouse, where I learned to clean the dirtiest of utensils, and how to carry dozens of plates at the same time. While at the OTB I was warned to watch out for the Chief Instructor, a Major Fairweather, who was a bastard, or something similar. (Many years later Brigadier Claude Fairweather and I became close friends, serving together on the TA Council, and were Deputy Provincial Grand Masters of Yorkshire, North and East Ridings, and Norfolk Respectively). After three months in the OTB I was posted to 151 OCTU (Officer Cadet Training Unit) at Aldershot. This venue pleased me a great deal, as my courting of Fifi was going quite well, but I had had difficulty in going south to meet her, and it was equally difficult for her to get to Catterick, in the wilds of Yorkshire. I bought an old motorbike for £9, and used this to make some hazardous journeys between Aldershot and Bushey.

One of my visits to Bushey was not on the motorcycle, but by train. I remember this well, because Fifi met me at the station, where we got engaged. On the way to her house we went to the local jewellers shop and bought an engagement ring, which I couldn't possibly afford on two shillings a day, so we put the price (neither of us is quite sure of the amount, but I think it was about £11) on her father's account. Later that evening, sitting round the dinner table, one of Fifi's sisters drew attention to the ring and Fifi explained that we had just got engaged, and said sweetly to her father that she hoped he didn't mind that it had been put on his account. He did mind, not so much about the cost, but he felt that he should have been consulted, and the evening ended in many tears.

On being commissioned I was posted to 6th Armoured Divisional Signals, which to my great delight was stationed in the Cambridge area, and I found myself at Trumpington, only just over a year after I had come down from the University. I remember that when our time at the OCTU was coming to an end we were all concerned about our first posting, and an Armoured Division was considered to be the best, because the casualties would be high, and promotion quick. 6th Armoured Division was just being formed, and Lt Col Joe Childs had been appointed to command the Divisional Signals, with authority to select newly commissioned officers with the best reports from the OCTUs.

For some months we trained hard in East Anglia, and then in April 1942 the Division was moved to Ayrshire, in Scotland. Also in April 1942 Fifi and I were married, her father and family having accepted the idea. She came from a mainly Quaker family, but it was agreed that the wedding should be in Bushey Anglican Church. Even though this was wartime, a formal wedding and reception were planned, but a week before the wedding the Bishop of St Albans, in whose diocese Bushey was situated, found out that the bride had been neither baptized nor confirmed, and therefore was quite unsuitable to be married in one of his churches. Bishop Michael Furse was well known in the country for his strong views on certain matters, and he ruled that the wedding could not take place as arranged. This was a tremendous blow, and on the Sunday morning, six days before the wedding was due to take place, I telephoned the Bishop at his palace and argued the case, reminding him that he had officiated at my confirmation a few years earlier. Surprisingly the next morning we got a message to say that the wedding could go ahead after all, and so it did. Most of Fifi's family being Quakers the wedding reception was alcohol free, but the Dicker family had advance notice of this and prepared themselves over lunch.

My best man was Ian Hunter, who after the War became a distinguished impresario, directing musical festivals at Bath, Edinburgh, London and elsewhere. The organist at our wedding was an old school friend, Denis Mack Smith, who later became a noted historian and a Fellow of All Souls, Oxford. During the War the Penmans had provided a home for a Czech refugee family called Ambros, and their two children, Sisa and Puffi, were bridesmaid and page respectively. After the War the Ambros family returned to Prague, where sadly Puffi and his father died in tragic circumstances.

At the wedding reception the toast to the bride and bridegroom was proposed by Fifi's uncle, Philip Noel-Baker MP, who later was awarded the Nobel Peace Prize and was created a Life Peer.

The first few months of our married life were spent at Ayr, mostly in lodgings in the town, although Fifi, having qualified with a Social Services Diploma, was working for the Ministry of Information and had to visit various parts of the country.

Shortly after our arrival in Scotland I was posted to command the Signal Troop of the Ayrshire Yeomanry, who were equipped with 25-pounder field guns. During 1942 the War began to turn in our favour, and we soon realized that we were training to fight overseas, but although there were some suggestions of hot climates, we had little idea as to where we would be going. Then in November the Division set sail for North Africa, travelling from the Clyde. I was with my troop, and a battery of the Ayrshire Yeomanry on the *Empress of Australia*. The journey in the convoy of about twenty-five ships, including a naval escort, was long but fairly eventful. We were warned that if a man were to go overboard he would be abandoned, as there was no question of stopping the convoy to look for him. Our course to Gibraltar took us across the Atlantic almost to America, then back to the west coast of Africa, so that we approached Gibraltar from the south. We understood that seventy German submarines were looking for us, fortunately without success. In fact the first enemy action we encountered was an air attack as we approached Algiers. I still have the menu of our last dinner on board ship, before we disembarked.

After landing at Algiers, we took part in the campaign of the First Army, which ended successfully in Tunisia at the beginning of May 1943. After a few months living in pretty rough conditions we had our first taste of a victory, and witnessed thousands of German prisoners captured in the Cap Bon peninsula, where we had joined up with the Desert Rats and others of the Eighth Army. Perhaps my main memory of the North African campaign was our almost complete lack of air cover. The casualties in my troop were all caused by enemy aircraft, and we were taught that, in the event of an aircraft coming towards us, we should assume that it was enemy, and jump into the nearest ditch. For some weeks we were located in a farm near a village called Medjez-el-Bab, and we got used to an event early each morning when two German reconnaissance planes, which we called Gert and Daisy, would come over very high, out of the range of our anti-aircraft guns. Presumably they were photographing our positions, and an hour or two later the Stuka dive-bombers would arrive. They would approach quite high, and then all dive together towards the target. The anti-aircraft guns would start up, creating a cloud of shell bursts in the air, and the bombers would go down through the cloud in a straight course towards the chosen target, which quickly became obvious. Those in the target area would dive for cover, but the rest, in other locations, could safely stand and watch.

Most of the Stukas would pull out of the dive after releasing their bombs just before reaching the ground, but often one or more would be hit during the dive, and would go straight down, exploding as they hit the ground, to the cheers of the onlookers. I remained with the Ayrshire Yeomanry throughout the North African campaign, and we were all shocked when two commanding officers, Bill Bedford and Laurie Younger, were both killed within three days.

After the end of the North African campaign I was posted from the Ayrshire Yeomanry to become Adjutant of the Divisional Signals, a post I held for over two years. The Division spent a few months near Philippeville in Algeria, and then moved to southern Italy, arriving at Naples in February and March 1944, and we were soon in action at Cassino. It was a memorable experience to be at one of the centres of operations during the whole of the Italian campaign, and I still have detailed records of the advance of 6th Armoured Division right up to the end of the war in Europe, which we celebrated in Austria. The Division had to its credit the longest continuous advance ever made by British armour in Europe. One experience towards the end of the Italian campaign remains clearly in my memory. My regiment had just received a new Commanding Officer, and I soon formed the opinion that he was unfit to command. We all knew that we were about to launch a major attack which was likely to be the final battle against the Germans in Italy. The Second in Command was on leave in the UK, and, as Adjutant, I took the unprecedented step of telling the DAA&QMG of the Division, whom I knew very personally, that I was most unhappy about my CO, and I told him why. The next day I was ordered to report to the GSO1, who delivered an enormous rocket, telling me that it was disgraceful for me to make accusations against my CO. Then, when the rocket was over he said, 'Now, Geoffrey, tell me all about it.' I did this at some length, explaining that in my view it would be most unwise for the communications of the Division to be at risk, in the great battle which was imminent, because of the weakness of this one officer. The next morning the ADMS, chief medical officer of the Division, arrived in the office which I shared with my CO, and asked me to leave for a few minutes. After he had gone the CO told me that he was being invalided home immediately, and the Second in Command was being recalled at once from his leave, to take over command. The final battle and our subsequent advance into Austria went well, and

The Commander, Officers & Ship's Company
wish you Good Luck and a Safe Return.

Menu

Consomme with Rice

Fried Fillet of Lemon Sole, Sauce Tartare

Small Steak Saute Garni

Roast Spring Chicken
Buttered Green Beans
Boiled and Chateau Potatoes

COLD BUFFET

Roast Lamb   Oxford Brawn
Salad

Vanilla Ice Cream Chocolate Sauce
Fresh Fruit
Coffee

E.A.

Saturday, November 21, 1942

OFFS

DINNER

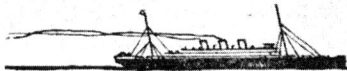

Empress of Australia, menu 21.11.42. Eve of North Africa landing

the story of the change of command never became known to any but a very few.

Later I was posted as a GSO2 to Allied Force Headquarters (AFHQ) in Caserta, near Naples, where I remained until I was demobilized in July 1946 looking, so Fifi said, like a skeleton, but actually I was very fit. For war service I was appointed an MBE, and was twice mentioned in despatches.

Fifi and I had bought a small house in Brundall, Norfolk, and in the autumn of 1946 I took articles with my father's firm, Lovewell Blake & Co., in Great Yarmouth. I did have the opportunity of returning to Cambridge to complete my degree, but by the end of the War I was aged twenty-five, and wanted to get on with earning my living. As an articled clerk I received £2 a week, and during my training the government provided £13 a month. This period of living on a small income was a good experience for us. For breakfast we could have an egg, or bacon, but never both. At first we travelled on bicycles or buses, as we had no car, until our first baby was on the way, when my father-in-law provided us with a Standard 8 which he had acquired at the beginning of the War.

Lovewell Blake & Co.

Once again I started at the bottom. My first job each morning was to light the fire in the room which I shared with two others. There was no central heating in the office, and paper, sticks, logs and coal all had to be collected and lit, in winter, before the room was fit for work. These open fires created a lot of smoke, and dust covers were laid over desks each evening to protect all working surfaces. As an articled clerk I had to take a correspondence course, which involved studying at home for several hours each week, and periodically to complete and send off test papers to my tutors. This, together with a full working week in the office, 9 to 6 Monday to Friday, and 9 to 1 on Saturday, left little time for a social life, and we lived fairly quietly at The Manor House, Brundall – not so grand as it sounds, as it was quite small, although one of the oldest houses in the village.

The traditional period of articles was five years, but this was reduced to three years after war service, and I passed my exams without difficulty, qualifying in 1950. I have always had the fortunate quality of doing my best at examinations, whereas many others whom I have met have been quite the opposite, perhaps partly through nerves at the critical moment. This means that there is a weakness in judging people purely on their success or failure in written examinations, because there is no doubt that there are some of high intelligence and ability who fall at their first, or a subsequent, fence. But for me it just happened that the system worked, although I have always felt sorry for those for whom it did not.

Shortly after qualifying as a chartered accountant in 1950 I was admitted as a partner in the firm of Lovewell Blake & Co. The existing Partners were Albert E. Lark, Bernard Walker and my father. Joining me as a new partner was R.G.R. (Bob) Sisson, who became a lifelong friend, until sadly he died many years later after we had both retired. Lark, Walker and Arthur Dicker had been the sole partners for some twenty-five years. They got on well together, but were very different in character, and hardly mixed at all socially. Indeed they never got on to Christian name terms with each other.

Bob Sisson and I saw big changes in the accountancy profession over the years. At first audit work consisted largely of checking the arithmetical accuracy of books which we knew would add up correctly, and not giving much attention to the underlying causes of the entries in the books. I remember, in connection with the audit of one of our larger clients, being given a scrap of paper with one amount on it, of about six figures, and told to include this as the value of the final stocks for the year. But that is not to say that the systems were all bad; indeed a great deal of the work was well spent. Of course there were no computers in those days, nor had electronic calculators been invented, so it was necessary to ensure that the handwritten entries were accurate. After a time Lark died, and then Walker, and as my father devoted much of his time to Institute affairs, at the 'War Office' as it was known, and Norwich office, which never really merged with the rest of the firm, Bob and I took most of the decisions to run the practice for a number of years. We got on wonderfully well together, and, as I remarked at his memorial service many years later, we never had a cross word.

Apart from Norwich, our principal offices were at Great Yarmouth and Lowestoft. We had a happy and loyal staff, adequately but not highly paid, and for a number of years, inflation not having been invented then, we took pride in arranging that any increase in profit went to the staff, the partners' share remaining more or less steady. Bob and I introduced a pension scheme in the firm, which was quite a novelty, although not as sophisticated as the schemes now in force. And we maintained a close relationship with our clients, which they, and we, appreciated.

An old friend of mine from my army service in wartime was Francis

Shearer, who was one of the senior partners in the London firm of Cooper Brothers and Co. In 1964 Francis approached me with a suggestion that our two firms might come to some working arrangement. At that time my father was friendly with two other senior partners of Coopers, John Pears and Henry Benson. We were quite happy about becoming associated with Coopers, but we did not wish to lose our identity as a separate firm, and after discussions we reached what seemed to be a satisfactory agreement, under which Bob Sisson and I became partners in Coopers, and three Coopers partners, Pears, Benson and Shearer, became partners in Lovewell Blake. A formula was agreed for an exchange of a share in the profits of each firm, calculated to be more or less equal, although this worked out slightly to our benefit. We described ourselves as 'in association with Cooper Brothers (Coopers & Lybrand)'. Lybrand was an American firm closely related to Cooper Brothers, Coopers & Lybrand being the name of the international firm. Our association worked well, and we received much technical help from Coopers, which enabled us to keep up to date with developments in the profession. I remember asking Francis Shearer what Coopers gained from the association, and he replied, somewhat to my surprise, 'respectability'.

However, eight years later, Coopers wanted to alter the arrangements between the two firms, because the name 'Coopers & Lybrand' was to be adopted on a larger scale worldwide. Accordingly a looser arrangement was agreed, and the exchange of partners ceased, but an association still continued.

Over the years various changes took place in our firm, including a merger with a Norwich firm of long standing, Bullimore and Co. In London John Pears died, and Henry Benson and Francis Shearer retired. By 1979 Lovewell Blake & Co. had sixteen partners, headed by Bob Sisson and me. Then suddenly Coopers & Lybrand, which they had become, announced that they were intending to extend their activities in East Anglia, and they wished to take over our whole firm, or, as an alternative, our Norwich practice. Neither of these proposals being acceptable to us, discussions took place over several months, and eventually five of our partners chose to leave Lovewell Blake and join the branch of Coopers which opened in Norwich. There was a certain amount of acrimony, but eventually the terms of a separation from Coopers took place on 1 April 1980, and Lovewell Blake continued to prosper as an independent firm.

So ended a period of sixteen years during which we were closely related to one of the largest firms in the country. This period was good while it lasted, but those of us who remained in the old firm never regretted the stand we had taken. Once I asked a Coopers partner what we would gain if we were taken over completely, and he replied, 'You would make more money.' I said, 'We make enough as we are, and anyway, what would happen to our small clients if we became part of Coopers?' 'Get rid of them. Small clients are no good to you,' came the reply. That convinced me that we must continue on our own. I remember another conversation a few years earlier with Henry Benson, one of the great leaders of the accountancy profession. Henry said that in the future there would only be room for big firms and little firms – no medium-sized ones. I told him that I disagreed – there would always be room for the firms in the middle. So far Henry has not been proved right.

The procedure for ending our relationship with Coopers was particularly burdensome for me, as I had to carry out most of the negotiations.

One of the biggest changes which occurred during my time in the accountancy profession was the introduction of computers, both within the firm and by our clients. I remember my father telling me that when he joined Lovewell Blake in the 1920s he asked the senior partner, Bertie Lark, on what basis he charged his clients. 'I weigh them up,' came the answer, 'and I charge what I think I can get'. By the time I retired times had changed a lot, every fifteen minutes of the working day being entered onto time sheets and transferred to a computer, which knew the charging rate of every partner and staff member, and could calculate the amount each client should be charged. This was a more efficient method than Lark's, but in many ways not so satisfactory, either for the firm or the client.

Most businesses acquired computers, and audit work consisted less of adding up columns of figures, and more of examining the accuracy of prime entries and the methods of interpreting these into meaningful accounts. Once we used to 'certify' that accounts were 'true and correct', but later we 'reported' our views of accounts, and took steps to protect ourselves from the consequences of being sued for negligence. For many years we took out an insurance policy for negligence claims, at a premium of just over £100 a year. By the time I retired we were paying many thousands yearly for the same policy. The practice of suing professionals, and others, began in the United States, and then crossed the Atlantic, and although in the accountancy profession these claims have been generally confined to the large firms, it has become necessary for all in practice to take out insurance policies as a protection.

Under the terms of our partnership agreement, a partner was required to retire at age sixty-three, and accordingly I retired on 30 September 1983, after thirty-seven years with the firm.

Norwell Offshore Services Limited

After retiring as a partner of Lovewell Blake & Co., I continued as a consultant of the firm for three years, steadily reducing my involvement with the firm and its clients, after which I fondly imagined that I might be invited to take up a few directorships, but in the event only one came my way, and this experience bordered on disaster.

Norwell Offshore Services Limited was a company based on Great Yarmouth, which had grown rapidly in recent years, and had earned a good reputation providing services to the oil industry which was expanding in the area. At the end of September 1985 I was invited to attend a meeting at which the company's bankers were pressing Norwell to tighten up their procedures in certain respects. One of the matters suggested by the bankers was that they should appoint a non-executive chairman, and I was then invited to accept this appointment. I obtained some particulars about the company, including a copy of the Memorandum and Articles, the share structure, and a copy of the audited accounts for the last financial year, ending 31 December 1984, from which it appeared that the finances of the company were sound. The auditors were Price Waterhouse, a firm of international reputation. The accounts showed a profit for the year 1984 of £1,769,145, and a net asset position at the end of the year of £2,682,510. The signed auditors' report was unqualified, and all seemed well, so I accepted the offer.

During the next few months I was involved in various discussions regarding the company's affairs, and in particular regarding an amount owing to the company in the region of £5m. The non-payment of this debt was causing cash-flow difficulties, but I was assured that a large proportion of it would be forthcoming, and even a fraction of the debt would ease the cash position. Norwell submitted an application to the Court for an interim payment from the debtor company, previously to which I had written twice to its President, suggesting that I should meet him with a view to resolving any difficulties between the two companies.

No reply was received to my first letter, and the second, a month later, was eventually acknowledged, with a suggestion that a meeting should be held a week after the court hearing, the date of which had then been fixed. A few hours before the debtor company was required to file its pleadings it did so, and the documents contained a counterclaim and a number of allegations which, if true, would amount to bribery and corruption in connection with the whole of the contract between the two companies. It was clear that whether or not these allegations were to be substantiated, no court would make an order for an interim payment. I was advised that in these changed circumstances it might take a year for the action to reach the Court.

Many discussions took place, but the outcome was that Norwell ran out of money, and the bank appointed a Receiver, following which Norwell went into liquidation, the company's creditors losing a great deal of money, and many jobs were lost. As chairman, the publicity of this disaster did me no good; I had to resign as chairman of a company which was being formed to assist development in Yarmouth, and I also resigned as vice-president of the local Chamber of Commerce.

The lesson I learnt from this experience was to be aware of the extent of corruption in the oil world. Many statements were made which were clearly untrue but could not be disproved, and I asked one person who was experienced, 'Am I right in thinking that hardly a contract is executed in the oil industry without some money passing on the side?' He replied, 'That is absolutely true.' Quite apart from this aspect, it seemed clear to me that the standards of honesty and integrity on which I had been brought up no longer existed in this area of the world of business.

Territorial Army

After my discharge from the Army in 1946, when the country was enjoying peace at last, I felt that it was a pity to throw away all that we had learned in creating what had become a very efficient military organisation. I looked around to see the chances of joining the Territorial Army, and in 1948 I was asked to form a Signal Squadron in Norwich, to be part of 61 HQ Army Signal Regiment, based in Bedford. This squadron, named 161 Infantry Brigade Signal Squadron, was quickly formed, composed at first of veterans of the Second World War – perhaps veterans did not really describe us, as we were all under thirty at the time. Then following a period of conscription, younger men joined us, and the Squadron, and indeed the Regiment, flourished.

In the early days, in addition to, but perhaps part of, our military training, we were always on the lookout to use our abilities and our equipment, to help civilian organisations when communications were needed. Two examples of this were the Royal Norfolk Agricultural Association, and Snetterton motor racing circuit, both in their early post-war years. We provided all the necessary telephones for the first two or three Norfolk Agricultural Shows, and also at Snetterton, when other facilities were not available.

Then early in 1953 the east coast of England was suddenly hit by the most devastating storm in living memory. Serious flooding occurred, particularly in Great Yarmouth, and for some miles to the north of the town. Here is a condensed version of a report about the help we were able to give.

<u>1st to 20th February 1953</u>

At the early stage of the disaster no relief organisation had been established, and almost no evacuation of flooded areas was being attempted. During the morning of Monday, 1st February it was decided to carry out a full scale evacuation of the Cobholm and Lichfield areas of Great Yarmouth, and Major Dicker approached the authorities to ask what help was required. The urgent requirement was said to be boats, as many of the houses could not be reached by vehicles. Major Dicker telephoned Sgt Peel at Norwich, and arrangements were made for five suitable boats to be loaded onto vehicles, arriving at Norwich that afternoon. Two Squadron vehicles also arrived in Yarmouth, and immediately plunged into the water to help with the evacuation. That day these vehicles evacuated 60 people from their homes, including 6 stretcher cases and 3 hysterical women. The next day, following a request for communications, radio sets were sited in Yarmouth Town Hall, at various points in the evacuation area, and on a train which carried sandbags and rubble, used to seal off areas which had been flooded and were to be pumped out. Telephone lines were laid, connecting the Town Hall with many of the key points. Telephones were also installed in the area of Sea Palling, a few miles up the coast, where the sea had broken through into the low lying areas inland. The residential areas in Yarmouth were estimated to contain about 150 million gallons of water. Members of the Squadron continued to work in aid of the civil authorities for the next two weeks.

At the end of the operation I wrote: 'The major point to be remembered is that the T.A. must always be ready to operate at short notice in an emergency, and to be flexible. When a crisis occurs, military organisation and resources can be invaluable to civil authorities. There is no doubt that work done by this Squadron had a considerable effect on the speed and efficiency with which the problems created by the floods could be tackled.'

A few years later I was appointed to command 61 Regiment, and following one of many reorganisations of the TA I commanded 54 (East Anglian) Signal Regiment from 1956 to 1959. Living 100 miles away from my Headquarters presented a few difficulties, but I had a regular Training Major and a full-time Adjutant in Bedford, and we established a system of control which worked very well. One method of keeping me in the picture was a rule that a carbon copy of every letter or other document which was typed at RHQ was posted to me each day, and I managed to visit Bedford several times a month. As time went on we recruited a number of women, a procedure quite new to me, but the girls settled in very well, and became a valuable part of the Regiment.

On relinquishing command of the Regiment early in 1959 I was promoted to Brevet Colonel, a rare and unexpected honour. A year later I was appointed Honorary Colonel of the Signal Regiment, so I was glad to continue my association with the Regiment for a further seven years, until it was absorbed into 36 Signal Regiment, as a result of yet another reorganisation. Later I became Honorary Colonel of 36 Signal Regiment.

Following my retirement from regimental command I was appointed Deputy Commander of 161 Infantry Brigade TA, an unusual post for a Royal Signals officer, and then in 1962 my TA career was further extended by being appointed Chief Signal Officer of 54th (East Anglian) Division. Both these appontments carried the rank of Colonel, and my active service ended in 1965.

Although still serving, in 1962 I was elected, on the recommendation of Sir Edmund Bacon, Lord Lieutenant of Norfolk, to the office of chairman of Norfolk TA Association. This was largely responsible for the administration of TA units in the county, particularly in regard to accommodation and relationship with employers and other civilian organisations. In those days there was a TA Association in every county, but in 1968 a number of mergers took place, and I became chairman of the newly formed East Anglian TA Association (full title: 'The Territorial Auxiliary & Volunteer Reserve Association of East Anglia), covering six counties – Norfolk, Suffolk, Essex, Cambridgeshire, Bedfordshire and Hertfordshire. The President of the

Association was normally the senior Lord Lieutenant of the six counties, and the remaining five were Vice-Presidents, and my new office, which I held for eight years, involved frequent and sometimes delicate communication and dealings with these as well as commanding officers and other senior officers and civilians over this wide area.

When I was appointed chairman of the Norfolk Association I became a member of the TA Council, under the chairmanship of the Duke of Norfolk. I was Vice-Chairman of the Council from 1975 to 1980.

In 1963, shortly after taking over as chairman of Norfolk TA Association, Sir Edmund Bacon appointed me a Deputy Lieutenant for the County.

Sir Edmund Castell Bacon of Raveningham Hall in the County of Norfolk, Baronet, Her Majesty's Lieutenant and Custos Rotulorum of the County of Norfolk

To *Colonel Geoffrey Seymour Hamilton Dicker, M.B.E., T.D., of Springfield, Brundall, Norfolk*

By virtue *of the Power and Authority in me vested, and by and with Her Majesty's approbation I do hereby constitute and appoint you, the said Colonel Geoffrey Seymour Hamilton Dicker, M.B.E,.T.D., to be a* **Deputy Lieutenant** *of and for the said County of Norfolk and you are hereby required to do and execute within the said County all and every the Powers and Authorities in that behalf and in all things to conform yourself to the duties thereof.*

Given *under my hand this twenty seventh day of March One thousand nine hundred and sixty three*

Edmund Bacon

I was proud to hold this appointment for thirty-two years, until shortly after my seventy-fifth birthday, when following my retirement I was authorized by the Secretary of State to continue to use the letters 'DL' after my name, and, if I so wished, to wear the prescribed uniform.

In 1964 I was invited by Major General Sir William Scott, Master of Signals, whom I had met during the War, to become a member of the Royal Signals Corps Committee, representing the Territorial Army on that Committee. I served on the Committee for sixteen years, became Chairman of the Corps Finance Committee, and served from 1970 to 1980 as an Honorary Colonel Commandant of the Corps. This was an unexpected honour, and I was the first non-regular of Royal Signals to be appointed a Colonel Commandant.

In 1965 I was honoured twice, first by the appointment as CBE, and then as an ADC to Her Majesty the Queen for a period of five years. This latter appointment did not involve much by the way of duties (although I was notified in writing that if I were to perform mounted duty in attendance on Her Majesty, arrangements would be made to mount me on a public horse – it never happened!), but during that period my wife and I were invited each year to a Garden Party at Buckingham Palace. These were most enjoyable occasions, though rather tiring, as there were usually several thousand other guests present. I remember once pushing my way through a crowd of people to speak to an old friend, Major General Sir Allan Adair, who I knew was a member of the Yeomen of the Guard, and I asked him what duty he was performing there. He replied 'I'm looking after the Duchess of Gloucester, and that was the Duchess whom you pushed out of the way to speak to me.'

In 1970 I was fortunate to be included in a group of twenty representing the TA Council to visit the United States at the invitation of the National Guard Association. This was a unique event which will probably never be repeated. Our Group was headed by the Council President, the Duke of Norfolk, and the Chairman, Lord Clydesmuir, and the rest of our party were drawn mainly from Chairmen of TA Associations. The National Guard sent over one of their Super-Constellations, which had been luxuriously fitted inside, and we flew from Northolt via the Azores to Washington DC, where we were received by our hosts in great style. We attended various receptions, including one at the British Embassy, and were shown round the White House, where President Nixon was not able to meet us as he was engaged in receiving some foreign dignatory. The Duke of Norfolk stood quietly at the back of our party, and it seemed that the hierarchy of the United States did not realize that the Earl Marshal of England was among their visitors that day. After Washington the same aircraft which had brought us across the Atlantic took us to visit National Guard units in training at Colorado Springs, and flew us inside the Grand Canyon en route for Houston, Texas, where we were shown round the US Space Centre. Then we were flown to New York where we visited the United Nations Headquarters, and finally home via Canada. During the ten-day trip the same aircraft was our permanent transport, the crew consisting entirely of members of the National Guard – two pilots, three navigators, two stewards, a doctor, two nurses (female), and a priest, so we were well prepared for all emergencies. The Americans were superb hosts, but they were a bit surprised that the Duke had to leave us and fly home on 11 August, as it was essential that he should be back by the 12th!

In 1973 I had a most interesting experience. The TA Council invited two of its members, Colonel Donald Shearer (from Northern Ireland) and me, to go to Rome to attend the Congress of the CIOR (Confederation Interallié des Officiers de Reserve), and to report to the Council about this organisation which was supported by most NATO countries. The delegation from the United Kingdom consisted of nine members of the British Reserve Forces Association, led by its President, Rear Admiral Philip Sharp. There were also nine young officers of the Reserve Forces, who took part in military competitions which were organized during the period of the conference.

We spent five days in Rome observing the activities of CIOR, and reported favourably on our return to UK. Subsequently the TA Council agreed to support the Reserve Forces Association, and through it CIOR, and the Ministry of Defence approved this and provided a small amount of financial support in future years.

For ten years I was actively involved with the Reserve Forces Association

Colonel Geoffrey Dicker and Rear Admiral Philip Sharp with HRH The Prince of Wales, 1977

and CIOR, becoming Chairman of RFA and a Vice-President of CIOR in 1976. Each year a Congress, consisting of about 1,000 members, took place in one of the member countries, and this enabled my wife and me to attend these interesting and enjoyable events in Oslo, Athens, Copenhagen, Bonn, Avignon, Montreal, The Hague, and Washington DC. A series of business meetings took place each year in Brussels, which enabled us to maintain a direct relationship with NATO. In 1977 our Ministry of Defence approved the holding of the Congress in London, and supported this generously, so that we were able to stage some excellent events which were intended to impress, and did, our guests from so many of our friends in NATO. The Congress was formally opened by His Royal Highness The Prince of Wales, and there was a magnificent reception at the Mansion House by the Lord Mayor of London. The Duke of Edinburgh attended another of the receptions. At that time Admiral Sharp had been elected President of CIOR, and I had succeeded him as Chairman of RFA, so I was very much involved in hosting the London Congress. There is no doubt that, quite apart from the military aspect, these meetings were a valuable contribution to international relations.

During my period as Chairman of TA Associations I became involved with the Army Cadet Force, which was represented in each county. I used to visit TA units and Cadet Units during their annual camps, and for some years was Honorary Colonel, first of the 2nd Battalion, and later of the Norfolk County Army Cadet Force. I was most impressed by the dedication of the officers and others who spent a great deal of their spare time in looking after the interests of these boys, and, later, girls. The minimum age in those days was fourteen, but many of the cadets looked much younger. On one occasion I was visiting the cadets at their annual camp in company with the County Cadet Commandant, and came to a very small boy, to whom I asked his age. He replied in a squeaky voice, 'Fourteen, sir.' I then said, 'What's your real age?' 'Thirteen, sir.' The County Commandant was most embarrassed, having previously assured me that they never recruited anyone under the age of fourteen.

So my involvement with the reserve forces lasted for over thirty years. I never doubted for one moment that this was time well spent, and that the Reserves constituted a valuable, and very inexpensive, portion of the country's defence organisation. From time to time the TA became the critical target of politicians, senior regular officers, and employers, and of course some wives and families resented the time which TA members were away from home. But the country, and indeed the whole world, was passing through dangerous times, and the insurance value of a strong reserve organisation was very often not fully appreciated.

Freemasonry

I became a Freemason in 1951. After attending the funeral of my grandmother in Sussex I mentioned to a friend in Yarmouth, Lawrence Talbot, that I had noticed how a number of Freemasons had attended and helped in the arrangements. Later, Lawrence asked me if I was interested in becoming a Mason, and I replied that I knew nothing about Freemasons, but would be glad to know a bit more. That was the start of my masonic career, and I was initiated in Lodge of United Friends in April 1951.

What I did not know at that time was that many years earlier, soon after arriving at Yarmouth, my father had been proposed for membership of that same Lodge, but then he had been asked by his proposer to withdraw his name. Apparently A.E. Lark, the senior partner of Lovewell Blake & Co., who had been a member of United Friends since 1910, had wanted to introduce his partner, Bernard Walker, into the Lodge, but Walker, having recently arrived into the town, had made himself generally unpopular and was blackballed. There was quite a row in the Lodge, Lark resigned, and it was said by some that no partner of Lovewell Blake & Co. would subsequently be admitted into the Lodge. So my father never became a mason, which was a great disappointment to him, particularly as his father Seymour had been a prominent mason in London and Brighton, and his father-in-law, Stephen Walley, had also been a keen mason, and a Provincial Grand Chaplain in Yorkshire. After this row in the 1920s I was the first partner of Lovewell Blake to become a member of the Lodge. In 1959, having passed through the necessary progressive offices, I became Master of the Lodge. One memorable event in my year of office was the visit to the Lodge of Major General Sir Allan Adair, Deputy Grand Master of the United Grand Lodge of England, as my personal guest. When I invited Sir Allan, perhaps I did not realize quite how rare it was for a VIP of that standing to visit a private Lodge, and I should not really have asked him. But he came, and it was a great evening for United Friends.

In 1968 I was greatly honoured to be nominated as Grand Treasurer of the United Grand Lodge. One Grand Treasurer is elected each year, and this must be his first appointment as a Grand Officer, a rank applying to the most senior members of the Order. Shortly after this nomination was submitted the Provincial Grand Master of Norfolk, Bishop Percy Mark Herbert, died, and was succeeded by Richard Quinton Gurney, a member of an old and distinguished Norfolk family. Dick Gurney invited me to take office as his Deputy Provincial Grand Master, and I served in that office for twelve years. At the end of that time Dick was about to retire, and I had been nominated to succeed him, but tragically he died in a riding accident just before the proposed date of his retirement.

I have always enjoyed my time in Freemasonry. It is said to be 'a peculiar system of Morality, veiled in Allegory, and illustrated by Symbols'. The Grand Principles on which the Order is founded are brotherly love, relief and truth, and it endeavours to admit into its ranks only just, upright and free men, of mature age, sound judgement and strict morals. As there are many thousands of members, not only in England but throughout the world, it is not always successful in its aims, and from time to time there has been unfortunate publicity, sometimes caused by failure of members to live up to the standards laid down, and sometimes as a result of malicious rumours which have been circulated by the media and others, often misleading and often direct lies. Freemasonry has been called a secret society, but it is not. There is very little in Masonry which is secret, and anyone who wants to find out about it can buy books on the subject. It is not a religion, but has been criticised by the General Synod of the Church of England for admitting non-Christians This is part of its strength – followers of any religion are eligible to become Freemasons, and the only requirement in this respect is that they must believe in a Supreme Being; atheists are not admitted.

Masons are taught to be good citizens, and it is sickening to hear from time to time that some are prejudiced in life solely because of their membership. I have come across cases where staff in local government have been told that they will not be promoted unless they resign from their Lodges. There is no secret about membership, but members are forbidden to use Masonry with a view to obtaining financial or professional benefits, and this is why some masons are reluctant to publicize their membership.

On one occasion Bishop Herbert was staying with us, and my wife asked him if he knew how many broken marriages there were as a result of Masonry. The Bishop chuckled, and said 'I should have thought that the wives would be very pleased that their husbands were out on such a harmless occupation as Freemasonry – just think what they might be doing.'

The following is part of a statement issued by Grand Lodge:

Everyone who enters Freemasonry is, at the outset, strictly forbidden to countenance any act which may have a tendency to subvert the peace and good order of society; he must pay due obedience to the law of any state in which he resides or which may afford him protection, and he must never be remiss in the allegiance due to the Sovereign of his native land. While English Freemasonry thus inculcates in its members the duties of loyalty and citizenship, it reserves to the individual the right to hold his own opinion with regard to public affairs. But neither in any Lodge, nor at at any time in his capacity as a Freemason, is he permitted to discuss or to advance his views on theological or political questions.

I served as Provincial Grand Master for Norfolk for fifteen years, retiring on my seventy-fifth birthday in 1995. When I was first appointed Deputy there were 44 Lodges in Norfolk and 4,612 members. In 1995 there were 69 Lodges with 4,462 members, so that over a period of 27 years the number of Lodges had increased by over 50 per cent but the membership had remained about the same. This I regarded as healthy, because it meant that Lodges were becoming smaller in size, although the actual number of masons was not clear from the figures, which are slightly distorted through dual membership – several masons belonging to more than one Lodge. I greatly enjoyed my time as Head of the Province (a Province in Freemasonry covers roughly the same area as a county), making many friends, and I hope not too many enemies; I did cross swords with a few non-masons who were critical of the organisation, usually without any grounds. There have been a few accusations in connection with the police, and on two occasions I had correspondence with ladies who suggested that the Police Force in Norfolk was corrupted by masons, who, among other things, controlled promotion in the Force. On each occasion I asked for evidence, which I would investigate and pass on my findings to the Chief Constable, but needless to say not a scrap of evidence was forthcoming.

A Provincial Grand Master has very few powers, each Lodge being autonomous to a great degree, and able to run its own affairs, although there are some matters, particularly in the sphere of discipline, when the Provincial Grand Master may become involved. He may have few powers, but he has many responsibilities, principally by setting an example within his Province, and keeping in close touch with all ranks, high and low. During my twenty-seven years as Deputy and Provincial Grand Master I made 737 visits to

Geoffrey Seymour Hamilton Dicker (b.1920) Provincial Grand Master, Norfolk, 1980–1995

Lodges in Norfolk, and was able to know, and be known by, almost every mason in the Province.

Basic masonry is known as 'Craft' masonry. In addition to this, I became involved in many other masonic orders. I was Grand Superintendent in charge of Royal Arch Masonry in Norfolk, and became Provincial Grand Master for East Anglia in another branch – Mark Masonry. Later I became Assistant Grand Master, and then Deputy Grand Master in Mark Masonry, the Grand Master of which was first the Earl of Stradbroke, and later Prince Michael of Kent. I was also Grand Supreme Ruler of the Order of Secret Monitor, a worldwide body with representation in Europe, India, South Africa, the Caribbean, the Far East, and elsewhere.

One of the pleasures of being involved in these various orders was that I was able to make visits overseas, and on many of these trips my wife accompanied me. Among places where Fifi and I were able to make new friends were St Lucia, Barbados, Bombay, Madras, Singapore, Hong Kong,

Cape Town, Port Elizabeth and Johannesburg. It was interesting to find that in all these places, and others, Freemasonry continues to thrive, incorporating men of all colours, races and religions. Indeed I have never experienced the slightest sign of racial prejudice within Freemasonry, and I have heard it said that if everyone in the world was a mason there would be no more wars. This is perhaps too sweeping a statement, but it does indicate the feeling of brotherly love and friendship which is universal.

This raises the question of women. I have often been asked why women can't become Freemasons. The first reply to this is that Freemasonry, as practised by the United Grand Lodge of England, is a man's organisation, and that I am not, and have no desire to be, a member of the Women's Institute, or any other body which consists solely of women. The second is that there are women Freemasons (I believe there are two women's Lodges in Norfolk) who run their own affairs but are not part of, or recognized by, the United Grand Lodge. Also there are, throughout the world, a number of so-called Grand Lodges which are not recognized by us for various reasons, usually because they do not adhere to the high principles which are laid down within our United Grand Lodge.

In the past Freemasonry has been regarded as a secret society, and some of its members have done much to encourage this reputation. But in the free world in which we now live, people want to know more and more about what others are doing, and Freemasonry has been moving with the times. Recently in Norfolk we have held a number of 'open meetings' on masonic premises, to which members of the public have been invited. We have explained to our visitors what we are up to, and have answered questions which have been put. I do not think there has been an occasion when a questioner has not been completely satisfied with the answer he or she has received. The Home Affairs Select Committee reported recently on Freemasonry in the police and the judiciary, and concluded that (a) there is nothing sinister about Freemasonry if its principles are properly followed, (b) Freemasonry does not encourage malpractice, (c) the number of Freemasons within the criminal justice system (i.e. judges, magistrates, officials, policemen) gives no general cause for concern.

I retired as Provincial Grand Master of Norfolk in 1995, and just before my retirement I presided at the Annual Festival of the Masonic Trust for Girls and Boys. This took place at St Andrews Hall and Blackfriars Hall, Norwich, and we were honoured by the presence of the Pro Grand Master, Lord Farnham, and Lady Farnham, together with many other distinguished visitors. The main object of these annual festivals is to raise money for the various masonic charities, and on this occasion the contribution of Norfolk Freemasons to the MTGB was quite remarkable. The grand total announced at the Festival was £2,082,677, of which Norfolk contributed £1,921,677, an average of £29,116 per Lodge, breaking all previous records.

Sailing

Throughout almost my entire life I have enjoyed boats. In about 1930 my parents bought a small cabin cruiser, Sunset, on the Broads, but we did not keep it for long because it never appealed to my father, who threatened to have a heart attack every time he put a foot on board. Just before the War my mother and my sister Anne bought a Yare and Bure one-design, Camberwell Beauty, and we joined the Norfolk Broads Yacht Club at Wroxham, but of course the War meant that we could hardly use the boat for several years. After the War, when we settled down in Norfolk, my mother gave me her share in Camberwell Beauty, and Fifi bought my sister's share, and we retained the boat for nearly fifty years. This gave us much pleasure; we

'Leomina'

Mark Seymour Hamilton Dicker (b.1979) receiving Optimist trophy from HRH The Princess Royal, 1988

won a number of trophies, perhaps the biggest triumph for the boat coming in 1980, when our son Chris won the Gold Cup at Wroxham. On another occasion, while racing at Barton Broad, Fifi, who was crewing me, fell overboard, and she said that I pulled her out of the water by her hair. This was a slight exaggeration, but she should have been grateful to me, since at least I saved her from drowning.

Because of their colour, the Yare and Bures were, and still are, known as White Boats, and the main other class of similar size on the Broads are Broads one-designs, the Brown Boats. I always hankered after a Brown Boat, and eventually acquired Tern, which I kept at Oulton Broad, frequently taking her to sea, although as the years went by she leaked more and more. There was one occasion when I was racing off Lowestoft with two elderly crew members, one of whom was pumping continuously and the other baling with a bucket; the combined ages of the three on board exceeded 200.

A story of our sailing experiences would not be complete without reference to other members of the family. Our son Chris has had a most successful career. While at Haileybury in 1967 he won the Public Schools Championship at Itchenor, and a few years later he took his Flying Fifteen to Cowes week, where to our, and probably his, surprise, he won the points cup for the week. I bought a wooden Dragon, Skal III, which I shared with Chris until he took it over when age prevented me from getting onto the foredeck, and eventually he changed this for a new fibreglass Dragon, Scorpio. Chris has been successively Secretary of the British Dragon Association, and the International Dragon Association, eventually becoming Chairman of the International Dragon Association in 1995. His two children have also excelled in boats, Selina becoming Captain of Ladies' sailing at Southampton University and Ladies Captain of British Universities Sailing Association, while Mark was Captain of sailing at Uppingham, and represented Britain in the 420 World Championship in 1997, finishing 20th.

Although basically a sailor, as age began to preclude me from the more active sport, I took to power, and owned a Freeman 24-ft, Golden Arrow, and later a Broom Crown 37-ft, Leomina, the latter being a comfortable sea-going boat which we were able to take to France, Belgium and Holland, and we also cruised from Lowestoft round the south coast to Torquay. In nine years Leomina travelled 8,408 nautical miles, and we were very sad to have to part with her in 1994. On one occasion The Princess Royal visited Lowestoft, and we took her out to sea on Leomina, to watch the National Flying Fifteen Championships.

I have taken an active part in yacht racing and club adminstration. For three years I was Commodore of the Norfolk Broads Yacht Club at Wroxham, and later for two years Commodore of the Royal Norfolk and Suffolk Yacht Club at Lowestoft. I found these appointments very rewarding. Sailing, and especially dinghy racing, is a rapidly growing sport in this country, and all over the world, and it is good to see young people taking it up.

I have never been interested in the so-called field sports of hunting, shooting and fishing, and this gave rise to a comment from a friend: 'Of course, you are not a sportsman,' but I have always preferred what I regard as a cleaner sport on the water.

Education

I have said that I enjoyed my schooldays. Probably many young people on leaving school consider taking up teaching as a career, and my short time as a schoolmaster at Boxgrove, Surrey, for one term just before the War was a valuable experience. After this I only completed one year at Cambridge, and by the end of the War I was aged twenty-five with a wife as a responsibility, and I resisted the temptation to return to university. So I did not acquire a degree, and embarked on an accountancy career. Some years later I served on the governing body of Great Yarmouth Grammar School and Girls' High School. This was interesting, but rather too much related to politics. About one third of the governors were Conservative councillors, one third Labour concillors, and the rest independent, and too often I found that the two political parties voted against each other, so that the independents, of which I was one, were inclined to hold the balance.

I was invited to serve as a Governor of Runton Hill, a delightful boarding school for girls in North Norfolk, and after a few years I became chairman of the Governors. We went through the period of high inflation, so that we were forced to increase fees rapidly, and this caused some difficulties. At the same time boys' public schools started to take girls, first into their sixth forms, and later throughout the schools, and the practice grew of girls leaving their schools to enter sixth forms of boys' public schools. This became very popular, and a state was reached when many boys' schools were saved financially by taking girls. But the effect on girls' schools was disastrous, and many had to close. This development may have been very good for independent education generally, but it has been sad to see the demise of a number of excellent girls' schools. Runton Hill got through the early stages of these problems, but eventually, some years after I had retired from the Board, the school was forced to close.

I also joined the governing body of Thorpe House School at Norwich. This was a most successful day school for girls, which managed to charge relatively low fees and achieve good results. My experience of various schools has taught me that success or failure depends to a very large extent on the qualities of the headmaster or headmistress. The governors, premises, staff and other factors all play their part, but the Head can make or break a school. I always took the view that the principal responsibility of the governors was to appoint the Head, back him or her up, and sack him or her if necessary. I remember asking a member of the board of another school, 'Who runs the school?' The reply was 'We do, the governors.' I thought and said that this was quite wrong. It is essential to give the Head a free hand, within certain limits.

In 1970 I was invited by the Vice-Chancellor of the University of East Anglia, Professor Frank Thistlethwaite, to join the Council of the University.

I spent twenty years on the Council, and after some time as Treasurer I was elected Pro-Chancellor and Chairman of the Council. This was a most rewarding period, during which I served under two Chancellors, Lord Franks, and Rev. Professor Owen Chadwick, and two Chairmen, Sir Edmund Bacon and Mr (later Sir) Timothy Colman. The University had been founded in 1966, and it was intensely interesting to take part in its development during the first twenty-four years. When I retired from the Council there were about 4,500 students; the University has continued to expand, and I believe has doubled in size since 1990.

In 1985 I was honoured by the award of the Degree of Doctor of Civil Law, Honoris Causa, at the University of East Anglia.

Other Interests

For some time I served on Brundall Parish Council, of which I was chairman for ten years. I became Chairman of Brundall Conservatives, and for seventeen years was President of Yarmouth Conservative Association. In 1957 I joined the Rotary Club of Great Yarmouth, of which I was President in 1975. Since 1955 I have taken an interest in the world of insurance, and I served on the local Board of the Eagle Star Insurance Company, being Chairman of the Eastern Region Board from 1969 until its dissolution in 1986. I became an underwriting member of Lloyds in 1979, and having dispensed with the services of my original agents and appointed new ones with whom I was able to establish a personal relationship, I escaped the disasters which hit many names in the early 1990s. For a few years I was Treasurer of the Scientific Exploration Society, which organized Operation Raleigh, providing immense opportunities for young people to take part in expeditions by sea and land all over the world. It was a great opportunity to see at first hand the contribution which this organisation, headed by Colonel John Blashford-Snell, is making to the young generation.

I became a founder member of The Broads Society, founded in 1956 by Len Ramuz – 'to foster and further the appreciation and usage of Broadland by all Broads lovers'. I was Chairman in 1961, and President from 1968 to 1994.

Other bodies of which I am, or have been, President, are: The Great Yarmouth Amateur Operatic and Dramatic Society (I invented a tradition that the President is allowed into any dressing room at any time, without knocking, which I do!), The Norfolk and Suffolk Animal Trust, and The Royal Norfolk Veterans' Association.

Our Family

In May 1947 our first child, Sally, arrived. She was born in Queen Charlotte's Hospital, London, for the price, inclusive of ante-natal and post-natal treatment, of £25. She was christened Sara Elizabeth Hamilton, and was a great joy to us. Christopher followed, also in Queen Charlotte's, in February 1950, and both children enjoyed their early days at The Manor House, which had a small but attractive garden. Sally started school, but at the end of 1953, when she was six, she developed a brain tumour, and after a distressing time involving two operations at Great Ormond Street she died in June 1955.

Sara Elizabeth Hamilton Dicker (1947–1955) with 'Nettie'

Sara Elizabeth Hamilton Dicker (1947–1955) and Christopher Hamilton Dicker (b.1950)

This gave rise to much sadness for us all, and we provided a screen in memory of her in the children's corner of Blofield Church, in the next village, where she had attended Sunday School.

I well remember an old friend, Rev. Frank Bracecamp, who took the funeral service for Sally, saying to me afterwards, 'You must have another.' We did, and Elizabeth (Lib or Libby), arrived in November 1957.

Christopher started school in Norwich, but never got on very well there. His report for the autumn term 1958 included: 'Number in Form 12. Science/Nature Study 13'. Then in 1959 the school introduced a system of intelligence tests, showing levels from '180 Excellent' downwards. In the category '90-100, Poor, examination success of any sort seems unlikely', Christopher scored 92, with no explanation. That removed any confidence which we might have had in the system of IQ Tests. We removed him from that school, and he went to Boxgrove, the preparatory school in Guildford where I had taught briefly just before the War. There he got on splendidly, and moreover was happy. Indeed he once confided in a friend that he was looking forward to going back to school at the end of the holidays, ' . . . but

Christopher Hamilton Dicker (b.1950)

Christopher, Gail, Selina and Mark

Joseph William Brown (b.1988) and Sarah Elizabeth Brown (b.1990)

Elizabeth Anne Hamilton (Dicker) (Manion) Brown (b.1957)

don't tell my parents!' In his first term at Boxgrove the Headmaster wrote to me: 'Christopher is obviously enjoying life here, he gets on very well with the other boys and with all the members of the staff, and we all like the look of him.' Later he went to Haileybury, became a chartered accountant, and joined me as a partner in Lovewell Blake & Co, of which he was elected senior partner in 1998. Chris married Gail Nicholson and they have two children.

Lib went to Norwich High School, and later to Runton Hill. Then she was at a sixth form college, which included a year in Canada, tried nursing for a very short time, had two failed marriages, and now lives happily with her three children in Lowestoft.

As our children grew up, The Manor House became too small for us, and Fifi and I moved to Springfield, also in Brundall. This was a lovely house with a large garden of about three acres where we built a hard tennis court. We had many happy parties in the house and garden, and kept various

Sophie Phillips Brown (b.1993)

animals – dogs, cats and up to three donkeys. Much of our summers were spent sailing, and we all enjoyed skiing in winter. For several years we spent Christmas at Arosa in Switzerland. Then after our children had left to raise their own families, we moved to The Hollies, Strumpshaw, the next village to Brundall.

It is a joy to us to have our two children and five grandchildren living near to us, so that we see them all frequently, but I am not proposing to extend this family record beyond my own generation any further, except to say that our grandson Mark is now the only surviving Dicker descendant of his generation of my great grandfather Hamilton Eustace. I hope that Christopher and Mark between them will maintain the family archives for future generations.

Chapter VIII

The Family Face

It is now some 500 years since John Dicker lived in Buxted, and he was followed there by six generations, all of whom were respected members of the local community in Sussex. It has given me great pleasure to study the family archives, and to place some, but by no means all, on record. My great-aunt Ella did a wonderful job, not only in writing the story of our Barkway ancestors, but in preserving for posterity many documents and articles which have been in the family for a long time, most of which have survived until the end of the twentieth century.

Now, as the symptons of old age become apparent, it is appropriate for me to reflect on what has been, and what might have been.

Recently I asked a friend whether, if he had his life over again, he would do anything differently. He replied no, implying that he was quite satisfied with everything he had done. To most of us, this is not so. 'We have left undone those things which we ought to have done, and we have done those things which we ought not to have done.' At least eleven generations of Dickers before me, and their families, have made their own contributions to the community, both in this country and abroad, and as far as I can tell there is not a lot of which we need be ashamed. I think it is fair to say that we have all done our best, although no doubt each of us could have done better. Now, as did our predecessors, we live in a changing world, and the future is in the hands of the youth of future generations. May they all understand the responsibilities which they will inherit, learning from the mistakes, and benefiting from the experiences, of their predecessors.

One of my cousins calculated that in the last 600 years we had each had 262,144 ancestors, basing his figures on three generations each century. Actually I think his sums were wrong, but we have certainly had many forefathers. Probably, during the period which I have covered since the early eighteenth century, we have each had over 500 ancestors, of which half were alive 250 years ago. It would be a mistake to claim that we inherit all the characteristics of our predecessors, through genes transmitted from generation to generation, but few of us fail to recognize in ourselves some of the strengths or weaknesses of our parents and earlier ancestors.

For a hundred years from the mid-eighteenth century the three Thomas Dickers were inspired by deep religious beliefs, and their lives were dedicated to serving their God and their fellow men. Writing about the second Thomas after his death, a critic said: 'Great Britain now reckons in every rank of society its pious and enlightened laymen. Such men are the hope, and will be the safety of the Church in England. Mr Dicker was one of these faithful servants of God.' The successors of the Thomases have all been different, and yet the same, continuing in their various ways the desire to be useful members of society, and to unite in the grand design of being happy, and communicating happiness.

What might have been? If the faithful Sarah Cootes had not wrapped up an apparently dead baby in her petticoat, while the young Dr Balding poured brandy down its throat, none of us would be here today, and if Hamilton Eustace had lived beyond the age of thirty-eight we should all have been descended from a bishop. It is easy to imagine all sorts of things which could have changed our lives, decisions we have made or not made which have altered the course of the lives of ourselves and others. We cannot foretell the future, but it is important that we should look back and consider whether we are living up to the standards which have been set us in the past.

One of my regrets is that I have had to leave out so much. I have hundreds of letters and other documents which throw light on how people lived and thought in the past, and it has just not been possible to refer to every detail, but I hope that what I have put together will be of value to future generations, and of interest to a wider number of readers.